THE HUMAN ORGANIZATION:
Its Management and Value

THE HUMAN ORGANIZATION: Its Management and Value

RENSIS LIKERT
Director, Institute for Social Research
and Professor of Psychology and Sociology
The University of Michigan

McGRAW-HILL BOOK COMPANY
New York St. Louis San Francisco
Toronto London Sydney

THE HUMAN ORGANIZATION: Its Management and Value

Library of Congress Catalog Card Number: 67-16931

37851

1234567890 MP 7432106987

TO THE STAFF OF THE INSTITUTE FOR SOCIAL RESEARCH

PREFACE

This volume is intended for all those who are interested in applying the results of quantitative research to improve the management of the human resources of their enterprises. The nature of science-based management is described and evidence presented concerning the need for more adequate and accurate data than are now ordinarily available to guide policy and operating decisions.

The material in this volume draws heavily on research done in all three centers of the Institute for Social Research: the Survey Research Center, the Research Center for Group Dynamics, and the Center for Research on the Utilization of Scientific Knowledge. It also has been greatly influenced by the writing, suggestions, and criticisms of many members of the senior staff of the institute, including particularly: Angus Campbell, Dorwin P. Cartwright, Sidney Cobb, John R. P. French, Jr., Basil S. Georgopoulos, Thomas F. Hagerty, Robert L. Kahn, George Katona, Daniel Katz, Floyd C. Mann, Robert M. Norman, Martin Patchen, Donald C. Pelz, Stanley E. Seashore, Arnold S. Tannenbaum, and Alvin F. Zander. It has drawn extensively on the work of several other members of the institute staff and has benefited from their suggestions. These include. Frank M. Andrews, Jerald G. Bachman, David G. Bowers, D. Anthony Butterfield, George F. Farris, Stephen C. Iman, Glenn D. Jones, Philip M. Marcus, Paul E. Mott, Franklin W. Neff, Kurt R. Student, and George F. Wieland.

Several persons, in addition to the staff of the institute, have read drafts of chapters and made most helpful criticisms and suggestions: Everett H. Bellows, Thomas Burns, William M. Day, Donald Grant, Mason Haire, John J. Hayes, Edwin R. Henry, John Paul Jones, Laflin C. Jones, Dwight Meader, Herbert H. Meyer, Raymond E. Miles, W. C. Patterson, Dan F. Smith, William Swartley, William J. Underwood, Claire Vough, William F. Wrightnour, and John D. Young. Others have provided highly useful comments and observations. R. Lee Brummet's counsel on accounting matters was especially helpful. I am indebted also to J. Stacy Adams, William Blackie, Herbert D. Doan, Richard A. Dunnington, L. L. Ferguson, Charles W. L. Foreman, P. E. Haggerty, John M. Henske, Vern H. Holmes, Mason E. Horton, John W. Joanis, Stuart M. Klein, Donald G. Marquis, Alfred J. Marrow, Allan H. Mogensen, M. Scott Myers, Floyd C. Peterson, L. Chase Ritts, Jr., David Sirota, Charles A. Waters, and R. A. Whitehorne.

Jane Gibson Likert, my wife, has worked with me on this volume and has contributed to the insights and interpretations presented. She has also edited the manuscript.

Margaret M. Johnson has given indispensable help. She coordinated the preparation of the manuscript, made valuable suggestions on style and content, prepared the bibliography and index, and drafted figures and charts for the artist.

The data-processing staff of the institute under the direction of Ralph Bisco and Carl Bixby carried out the major computations reported. Ofelia Rodriguez performed essential statistical analyses and prepared several of the charts.

Pamela Uchman and duplicating machine operator David Forner have conscientiously reproduced copies of the chapters through what seemed to them—and to me—countless revisions. Mrs. Dorothy Hargis typed the final manuscript. Their assistance is deeply appreciated.

For permission to quote from their publications and to use some of the material published previously, I am grateful to the following: Accounting Studies Press, Ltd.; Doubleday & Co., Inc.; *Harvard Business Review;* McGraw-Hill Book Company; Society for the Psychological Study of Social Issues; and The University of Michigan Bureau of Business Research.

Rensis Likert

CONTENTS

THE HUMAN ORGANIZATION: Its Management and Value

Chapter I

NEW FOUNDATIONS FOR THE ART OF MANAGEMENT

All the activities of any enterprise are initiated and determined by the persons who make up that institution. Plants, offices, computers, automated equipment, and all else that a modern firm uses are unproductive except for human effort and direction. Human beings design or order the equipment; they decide where and how to use computers; they modernize or fail to modernize the technology employed; they secure the capital needed and decide on the accounting and fiscal procedures to be used. Every aspect of a firm's activities is determined by the competence, motivation, and general effectiveness of its human organization. Of all the tasks of management, managing the human component is the central and most important task, because all else depends upon how well it is done.

Most organizations today base their standard operating procedures and practices on classical organizational theories. These theories rely on key assumptions made by well-known practitioners of management and reflect the general principles they expound. Practitioners' points of view vary one from the other and through time as new schools of practice become fashionable. The more prestigious the practitioner, the more weight his judgment carries. As his influence wanes, principles and practices based on his judgment are discarded and new ones embraced.

Until recently, the shifting sands of practitioner judgment were the major if not the only source of knowledge about how to organize and run an enterprise. Now, research on leadership, management, and organization, undertaken by social scientists, provides a more stable body of knowledge than has been available in the past. The art of management can be based on verifiable information derived from rigorous, quantitative research. Independent investigators can repeat the research and test the validity of the findings. Not only is the body of knowledge more stable and accurate, but it is likely to grow continuously as the results of additional research on management are accumulated. Quantitative research anywhere in the world can add to this body of knowledge. Its rate of growth can be accelerated by increasing the expenditures for social science research focused on organizations.

Research is beginning to be substituted for practitioner judgment in all aspects of management. It has particular relevance in this volume to the management of the human enterprise, which will be our primary orientation.

In the course of these discussions, the science-based system of management initially proposed in *New Patterns of Management* (Likert, 1961) is described more fully, and additional research findings which deal with it are reported. The focus is on the systemic nature of the enterprise and the motivational forces at work. The application of scientific procedures to relatively specific activities, such as selection and job skill training, are not discussed. These topics are covered in other volumes by social scientists specializing in these fields.

This volume was originally intended to be the first section of a single book which has now grown into three. The second volume will describe in considerable detail the science-based system of management derived from the principles and practices of the highest-producing managers. The third will examine the experiences of the Institute for Social Research and of others in aiding companies to shift to science-based management. It will report what is being learned about the strategies of organizational change and about how best to develop a mastery of the important principles and the required skills.

Many persons approach all social science research with a healthy skepticism. This is excellent and to be encouraged. It is, however, at least as important to examine traditional principles and practices with skepticism. Long acceptance does not make a matter right. Common practice does not make it the best practice. Newness does not necessarily ensure an improvement. When deciding what knowledge to accept, what principles and practices to employ, it is decidedly worth while to ask, "What is the evidence? How do you know?" Tough-minded examination of the evidence and rigorous separation of objective, quantified data from impressions, expressed judgment, or fads can significantly improve the art of management.

Chapter 2

A LOOK AT MANAGEMENT SYSTEMS

This volume will be more interesting and more readily understood if a few minutes are taken now to complete the following form in accordance with these directions:

"Please think of the *most* productive department, division, or organization you have known well. Then place the letter *h* on the line under each organizational variable in the following table to show where this organization would fall. Treat each item as a continuous variable from the left extreme of System 1 to the right extreme of System 4."

Now that you have completed the form (Table 2-1) to describe the highest-producing department or unit you know well, please think of the *least* productive department, division, or organization you know well. Preferably it should be about the same size as your most productive unit and engaged in the same general kind of work. Then put the letter *l* on the line under each organizational variable in Table 2-1 to show where, in the light of your observations, you feel this least-productive organization falls on that item. As before, treat each item as a continuous variable from the left extreme of System 1 to the right extreme of System 4.

After you have completed Table 2-1 to describe both the most and the least productive departments you know well, compare the relative position of your two answers on each item. You are very likely to discover that on all items, or virtually all, your *l*'s are to the left of your *h*'s, i.e., that your high-producing department has a management system more to the right in the table and your low-producing department is characterized by having a management system more to the left.

Many different groups of managers, totaling several hundred persons, have completed Table 2-1 describing both the highest- and lowest-producing departments which they knew well. They have varied in their descriptions of the most productive departments; some are quite far to the right, the *h*'s being largely under System 4. For others, the most productive unit was largely under System 3. The striking fact, however, is that irrespective of where the *h*'s describing the high-producing unit fall in the table, the *l*'s for the low-producing department fall to the left. Quite

TABLE 2-1

TABLE OF ORGANIZATIONAL AND PERFORMANCE CHARACTERISTICS OF DIFFERENT MANAGEMENT SYSTEMS

Organizational variable	*System 1*	*System 2*	*System 3*	*System 4*
1. Leadership processes used				
Extent to which superiors have confidence and trust in *subordinates*	Have no confidence and trust in subordinates	Have condescending confidence and trust, such as master has to servant	Substantial but not complete confidence and trust; still wishes to keep control of decisions	Complete confidence and trust in all matters
Extent to which superiors behave so that subordinates feel free to discuss important things about their jobs with their immediate superior	Subordinates do not feel at all free to discuss things about the job with their superior	Subordinates do not feel very free to discuss things about the job with their superior	Subordinates feel rather free to discuss things about the job with their superior	Subordinates feel completely free to discuss things about the job with their superior
Extent to which immediate superior in solving job problems generally tries to get subordinates' ideas and opinions and make constructive use of them	Seldom gets ideas and opinions of subordinates in solving job problems	Sometimes gets ideas and opinions of subordinates in solving job problems	Usually gets ideas and opinions and usually tries to make constructive use of them	Always gets ideas and opinions and always tries to make constructive use of them

2. Character of motivational forces				
Manner in which motives are used	Fear, threats, punishment, and occasional rewards	Rewards and some actual or potential punishment	Rewards, occasional punishment, and some involvement	Economic rewards based on compensation system developed through participation; group participation and involvement in setting goals, improving methods, appraising progress toward goals, etc.
Amount of responsibility felt by each member of organization for achieving organization's goals	High levels of management feel responsibility; lower levels feel less; rank and file feel little and often welcome opportunity to behave in ways to defeat organization's goals	Managerial personnel usually feel responsibility; rank and file usually feel relatively little responsibility for achieving organization's goals	Substantial proportion of personnel, especially at high levels, feel responsibility and generally behave in ways to achieve the organization's goals	Personnel at all levels feel real responsibility for organization's goals and behave in ways to implement them
3. Character of communication process				
Amount of interaction and communication aimed at achieving organization's objectives	Very little	Little	Quite a bit	Much with both individuals and groups

Table 2-1 (*Continued*)

Table of Organizational and Performance Characteristics of Different Management Systems

Organizational variable	*System 1*	*System 2*	*System 3*	*System 4*
Direction of information flow	Downward	Mostly downward	Down and up	Down, up, and with peers
Extent to which downward communications are accepted by subordinates	Viewed with great suspicion	May or may not be viewed with suspicion	Often accepted but at times viewed with suspicion; may or may not be openly questioned	Generally accepted, but if not, openly and candidly questioned
Accuracy of upward communication via line	Tends to be inaccurate	Information that boss wants to hear flows; other information is restricted and filtered	Information that boss wants to hear flows; other information may be limited or cautiously given	Accurate
Psychological closeness of superiors to subordinates (i.e., how well does superior know and understand problems faced by subordinates?)	Has no knowledge or understanding of problems of subordinates	Has some knowledge and understanding of problems of subordinates	Knows and understands problems of subordinates quite well	Knows and understands problems of subordinates very well

4. Character of interaction-influence process				
Amount and character of interaction	Little interaction and always with fear and distrust	Little interaction and usually with some condescension by superiors; fear and caution by subordinates	Moderate interaction, often with fair amount of confidence and trust	Extensive, friendly interaction with high degree of confidence and trust
Amount of cooperative teamwork present	None	Relatively little	A moderate amount	Very substantial amount throughout the organization
5. Character of decision-making process				
At what level in organization are decisions formally made?	Bulk of decisions at top of organization	Policy at top, many decisions within prescribed framework made at lower levels	Broad policy and general decisions at top, more specific decisions at lower levels	Decision making widely done throughout organization, although well integrated through linking process provided by overlapping groups
To what extent are decision makers aware of problems, particularly those at lower levels in the organization?	Often are unaware or only partially aware	Aware of some, unaware of others	Moderately aware of problems	Generally quite well aware of problems

TABLE 2-1 (*Continued*)

TABLE OF ORGANIZATIONAL AND PERFORMANCE CHARACTERISTICS OF DIFFERENT MANAGEMENT SYSTEMS

Organizational variable	*System 1*	*System 2*	*System 3*	*System 4*
Extent to which technical and professional knowledge is used in decision making	Used only if possessed at higher levels	Much of what is available in higher and middle levels is used	Much of what is available in higher, middle, and lower levels is used	Most of what is available anywhere within the organization is used
To what extent are subordinates involved in decisions related to their work?	Not at all	Never involved in decisions; occasionally consulted	Usually are consulted but ordinarily not involved in the decision making	Are involved fully in all decisions related to their work
Are decisions made at the best level in the organization so far as the motivational consequences (i.e., does the decision-making process help to create the necessary motivations in those persons who have to carry out the decisions?)	Decision making contributes little or nothing to the motivation to implement the decision, usually yields adverse motivation	Decision making contributes relatively little motivation	Some contribution by decision making to motivation to implement	Substantial contribution by decision-making processes to motivation to implement

Item				
6. Character of goal setting or ordering				
Manner in which usually done	Orders issued	Orders issued, opportunity to comment may or may not exist	Goals are set or orders issued after discussion with subordinate(s) of problems and planned action	Except in emergencies, goals are usually established by means of group participation
Are there forces to accept, resist, or reject goals?	Goals are overtly accepted but are covertly resisted strongly	Goals are overtly accepted but often covertly resisted to at least a moderate degree	Goals are overtly accepted but at times with some covert resistance	Goals are fully accepted both overtly and covertly
7. Character of control processes				
Extent to which the review and control functions are concentrated	Highly concentrated in top management	Relatively highly concentrated, with some delegated control to middle and lower levels	Moderate downward delegation of review and control processes; lower as well as higher levels feel responsible	Quite widespread responsibility for review and control, with lower units at times imposing more rigorous reviews and tighter controls than top management

Table 2-1 (*Continued*)

Table of Organizational and Performance Characteristics of Different Management Systems

Organizational variable	*System 1*	*System 2*	*System 3*	*System 4*
Extent to which there is an informal organization present and supporting or opposing goals of formal organization	Informal organization present and opposing goals of formal organization	Informal organization usually present and partially resisting goals	Informal organization may be present and may either support or partially resist goals of formal organization	Informal and formal organization are one and the same; hence all social forces support efforts to achieve organization's goals
Extent to which control data (e.g., accounting, productivity, cost, etc.) are used for self-guidance or group problem solving by managers and nonsupervisory employees; or used by superiors in a punitive, policing manner	Used for policing and in punitive manner	Used for policing coupled with reward and punishment, sometimes punitively; used somewhat for guidance but in accord with orders	Largely used for policing with emphasis usually on reward but with some punishment; used for guidance in accord with orders; some use also for self-guidance	Used for self-guidance and for coordinated problem solving and guidance; not used punitively

consistently, the high-producing department is seen as toward the right end of the table.

For the vast majority of managers, this has been the pattern for every item in the table irrespective of the field of experience of the manager—production, sales, financial, office, etc.—and regardless of whether he occupies a staff or a line position. In about one case in twenty, a manager will place the low-producing unit to the right of the high on one or two items. But with very few exceptions, high-producing departments are seen as using management systems more to the right (toward System 4) and low-producing units as more to the left (toward System 1).

One would expect that such extraordinary consensus would lead managers to manage in ways consistent with it. When managers or nonsupervisory employees are asked, however, to use Table 2–1 to describe their own organization as they experience it, the answers obtained show that most organizations are being managed with systems appreciably more to the left than that which managers quite generally report is used by the highest-producing departments.

Parenthetically, some low-producing managers, although they display the same pattern of answers as other managers, believe that a manager should move toward System 4 *after* he has achieved high levels of productivity (Miles, 1966). They feel that the way to move from low to high productivity is to use a management system well toward the left (e.g., System 1 or 2) and move toward System 4 only after high productivity is achieved. Their view is essentially that of the supervisor of a low-producing unit who said: "This interest-in-people approach is all right, but it is a luxury. I've got to keep pressure on for production, and when I get production up, then I can afford to take time to show an interest in my employees and their problems." Research results show that managers who hold this view are not likely to achieve high productivity in their units (Likert, 1961, Chap. 2).

The impressively consistent pattern of answers to Table 2-1 obtained from most managers poses important and perplexing questions: Why do managers use a system of management which they recognize is less productive than an alternate system which they can describe correctly and presumably could use? All these managers keenly want to achieve outstanding success. What keeps them from using the management system which they recognize yields the highest productivity, lowest costs, and best performance? We shall seek to shed light on these questions in the rest of this volume, but before doing so, there are two related questions which should be considered.

A significant finding emerges when experienced managers are asked the following: "In your experience what happens in a company when the senior officer becomes concerned about earnings and takes steps to cut costs, increase productivity, and improve profits? Does top management usually continue to use the management system it has been employing, or does it shift its operation to a management system more toward System 1 or more toward System 4?" Most managers report that, when top management seeks to reduce costs, it shifts its system more toward System 1, i.e., toward a system which they know from their own observations and experience yields poorer productivity and higher costs, on the average and over the long run, than does the existing management system of the company.

What causes the top management of a firm, when it wishes to reduce costs, to take steps which shift its management system in the direction which will actually increase costs over the long run rather than reduce them? What are the inadequacies in the accounting methods and in the financial reports which lead managers and boards of directors to believe that with the shift toward System 1 their costs and earnings are improving, when the actual facts are to the contrary? Why are not the reported increases in earnings shown for what they really are: cash income derived from what is usually an even greater liquidation of corporate human assets?

These are extremely important questions which affect the success or even the survival of companies. They will be discussed fully in the subsequent chapters.

Chapter 3

PRODUCTIVITY AND LABOR RELATIONS UNDER DIFFERENT MANAGEMENT SYSTEMS

Are managers correct in their view that companies with management systems more to the right in Table 2-1 (i.e., toward System 4) are more likely to have higher productivity, lower costs, higher earnings, and more favorable employee attitudes than are other companies? Are they on sound ground in believing that companies whose managers use management systems more toward the left are more likely to have higher costs, lower productivity, lower earnings, and less favorable employee attitudes?

Most of the items in Table 2-1 are taken from a longer table (Table 14-1) published in *New Patterns of Management* (Likert, 1961, pp. 222–234). Table 3-1 below is the same as Table 14-1 in *New Patterns of Management.* It was devised initially to show the comparative differences among management systems. The possibility of using this table to measure the nature of the management system employed by a particular organization was recognized after the publication of the book.[1] To test how well the table would work as a method of measuring the management system of an organization, an answer sheet, Form A, was prepared (Figure 3-1).

In the process of developing Form A it became evident that Table 3-1 could be used not only to discover what an individual believes are the present characteristics of his organization but also to find out what he would *like* the characteristics of his organization to be. The instructions for obtaining the latter reactions are as follows:

- Opposite each operating characteristic, please indicate on the continuum where you would *like* to have your organization fall with regard to that item, as defined in Table 3-1.

These instructions were used on Form B, which otherwise is the same as Form A.

[1] This idea was suggested by Dr. William Swartley, who at the time was in personnel training at RCA.

Table 3-1*

Organizational and Performance Characteristics of Different Management Systems Based on a Comparative Analysis

Operating characteristics	System of organization			
	Authoritative		Participative	
	Exploitive authoritative	*Benevolent authoritative*	*Consultative*	*Participative group*
1. Character of motivational forces				
a. Underlying motives tapped	Physical security, economic security, and some use of the desire for status	Economic and occasionally ego motives, e.g., the desire for status	Economic, ego, and other major motives, e.g., desire for new experience	Full use of economic, ego, and other major motives, as, for example, motivational forces arising from group processes
b. Manner in which motives are used	Fear, threats, punishment, and occasional rewards	Rewards and some actual or potential punishment	Rewards, occasional punishment, and some involvement	Economic rewards based on compensation system developed through participation. Group participation and involvement in setting goals, improving methods, appraising progress toward goals, etc.
c. Kinds of attitudes developed toward organ-	Attitudes usually are hostile and counter to	Attitudes are sometimes hostile and counter to	Attitudes may be hostile but more often	Attitudes generally are strongly favorable

* From Rensis Likert, *New Patterns of Management*. New York: McGraw-Hill Book Company, 1961. Reprinted by permission of the publisher.

ization and its goals	organization's goals	organization's goals and are sometimes favorable to the organization's goals and support the behavior necessary to achieve them	are favorable and support behavior implementing organization's goals	and provide powerful stimulation to behavior implementing organization's goals
d. Extent to which motivational forces conflict with or reinforce one another	Marked conflict of forces substantially reducing those motivational forces leading to behavior in support of the organization's goals	Conflict often exists; occasionally forces will reinforce each other, at least partially	Some conflict, but often motivational forces will reinforce each other	Motivational forces generally reinforce each other in a substantial and cumulative manner
e. Amount of responsibility felt by each member of organization for achieving organization's goals	High levels of management feel responsibility; lower levels feel less. Rank and file feel little and often welcome opportunity to behave in ways to defeat organization's goals	Managerial personnel usually feel responsibility; rank and file usually feel relatively little responsibility for achieving organization's goals	Substantial proportion of personnel feel responsibility and generally behave in ways to achieve the organization's goals	Personnel feel real responsibility for organization's goals and are motivated to behave in ways to implement them
f. Attitudes toward other members of the organization	Subservient attitudes toward superiors coupled with hostility; hostility toward peers and contempt for subordinates; distrust is widespread	Subservient attitudes toward superiors; competition for status resulting in hostility toward peers; condescension toward subordinates	Cooperative, reasonably favorable attitudes toward others in organization; may be some competition between peers with resulting hostility and some condescension toward subordinates	Favorable, cooperative attitudes throughout the organization with mutual trust and confidence

Table 3-1 (*Continued*)

Organizational and Performance Characteristics of Different Management Systems Based on a Comparative Analysis (*Continued*)

Operating characteristics	*System of organization*			
	Authoritative		*Participative*	
	Exploitive authoritative	*Benevolent authoritative*	*Consultative*	*Participative group*
g. Satisfactions derived	Usually dissatisfaction with membership in the organization, with supervision, and with one's own achievements	Dissatisfaction to moderate satisfaction with regard to membership in the organization, supervision, and one's own achievements	Some dissatisfaction to moderately high satisfaction with regard to membership in the organization, supervision, and one's own achievements	Relatively high satisfaction throughout the organization with regard to membership in the organization, supervision, and one's own achievements
2. Character of communication process				
a. Amount of interaction and communication aimed at achieving organization's objectives	Very little	Little	Quite a bit	Much with both individuals and groups
b. Direction of information flow	Downward	Mostly downward	Down and up	Down, up, and with peers
c. Downward communication				
(1) Where initiated	At top of organization or to implement top directive	Primarily at top or patterned on communication from top	Patterned on communication from top but with some initiative at lower levels	Initiated at all levels

(2) Extent to which communications are accepted by subordinates	Viewed with great suspicion	May or may not be viewed with suspicion	Often accepted but at times viewed with suspicion. May or may not be openly questioned	Generally accepted, but if not, openly and candidly questioned
d. Upward communication				
(1) Adequacy of upward communication via line organization	Very little	Limited	Some	A great deal
(2) Subordinates' feeling of responsibility for initiating accurate upward communication	None at all	Relatively little, usually communicates "filtered" information but only when requested. May "yes" the boss	Some to moderate degree of responsibility to initiate accurate upward communication	Considerable responsibility felt and much initiative. Group communicates all relevant information
(3) Forces leading to accurate or distorted information	Powerful forces to distort information and deceive superiors	Occasional forces to distort; also forces for honest communication	Some forces to distort along with many forces to communicate accurately	Virtually no forces to distort and powerful forces to communicate accurately
(4) Accuracy of upward communication via line	Tends to be inaccurate	Information that boss wants to hear flows; other information is restricted and filtered	Information that boss wants to hear flows; other information may be limited or cautiously given	Accurate
(5) Need for supplementary upward communication system	Need to supplement upward communication by spy system, suggestion system, or some similar devices	Upward communication often supplemented by suggestion system and similar devices	Slight need for supplementary system; suggestion system may be used	No need for any supplementary system

Table 3-1 (*Continued*)

Organizational and Performance Characteristics of Different Management Systems Based on a Comparative Analysis (*Continued*)

Operating characteristics	System of organization			
	Authoritative		*Participative*	
	Exploitive authoritative	*Benevolent authoritative*	*Consultative*	*Participative group*
e. Sideward communication, its adequacy and accuracy	Usually poor because of competition between peers and corresponding hostility	Fairly poor because of competition between peers	Fair to good	Good to excellent
f. Psychological closeness of superiors to subordinates (i.e., how well does superior know and understand problems faced by subordinates?)	Far apart	Can be moderately close if proper roles are kept	Fairly close	Usually very close
(1) Accuracy of perceptions by superiors and subordinates	Often in error	Often in error on some points	Moderately accurate	Usually quite accurate
3. Character of interaction-influence process				
a. Amount and character of interaction	Little interaction and always with fear and distrust	Little interaction and usually with some condescension by superiors; fear and caution by subordinates	Moderate interaction, often with fair amount of confidence and trust	Extensive, friendly interaction with high degree of confidence and trust

b. Amount of cooperative teamwork present	None	Virtually none	A moderate amount	Very substantial amount throughout the organization
c. Extent to which subordinates can influence the goals, methods, and activity of their units and departments				
(1) As seen by superiors	None	Virtually none	Moderate amount	A great deal
(2) As seen by subordinates	None except through "informal organization" or via unionization	Little except through "informal organization" or via unionization	Moderate amount both directly and via unionization	Substantial amount both directly and via unionization
d. Amount of actual influence which superiors can exercise over the goals, activity, and methods of their units and departments	Believed to be substantial but actually moderate unless capacity to exercise severe punishment is present	Moderate to somewhat more than moderate, especially for higher levels in organization	Moderate to substantial, especially for higher levels in organization	Substantial but often done indirectly, as, for example, by superior building effective interaction-influence system
e. Extent to which an adequate structure exists for the flow of information from one part of the organization to another, thereby enabling influence to be exerted	Downward only	Almost entirely downward	Largely downward but small to moderate capacity for upward and between peers	Capacity for information to flow in all directions from all levels and for influence to be exerted by all units on all units

TABLE 3-1 (*Continued*)

ORGANIZATIONAL AND PERFORMANCE CHARACTERISTICS OF DIFFERENT MANAGEMENT SYSTEMS BASED ON A COMPARATIVE ANALYSIS (*Continued*)

Operating characteristics	*System of organization*			
	Authoritative		*Participative*	
	Exploitive authoritative	*Benevolent authoritative*	*Consultative*	*Participative group*
4. Character of decision-making process				
a. At what level in organization are decisions formally made?	Bulk of decisions at top of organization	Policy at top, many decisions within prescribed framework made at lower levels	Broad policy and general decisions at top, more specific decisions at lower levels	Decision making widely done throughout organization, although well integrated through linking process provided by overlapping groups
b. How adequate and accurate is the information available for decision making at the place where the decisions are made?	Partial and often inaccurate information only is available	Moderately adequate and accurate information available	Reasonably adequate and accurate information available	Relatively complete and accurate information available based both on measurements and efficient flow of information in organization
c. To what extent are decision makers aware of problems, particularly those at lower levels in the organization?	Often are unaware or only partially aware	Aware of some, unaware of others	Moderately aware of problems	Generally quite well aware of problems

d. Extent to which technical and professional knowledge is used in decision making	Used only if possessed at higher levels	Much of what is available in higher and middle levels is used	Much of what is available in higher, middle, and lower levels is used	Most of what is available anywhere within the organization is used
e. Are decisions made at the best level in the organization so far as				
(1) Having available the most adequate and accurate information bearing on the decision?	Decisions usually made at levels appreciably higher than levels where most adequate and accurate information exists	Decisions often made at levels appreciably higher than levels where most adequate and accurate information exists	Some tendency for decisions to be made at higher levels than where most adequate and accurate information exists	Overlapping groups and group decision processes tend to push decisions to point where information is most adequate or to pass the relevant information to the decision-making point
(2) The motivational consequences (i.e., does the decision-making process help to create the necessary motivations in those persons who have to carry out the decision?)	Decision making contributes little or nothing to the motivation to implement the decision, usually yields adverse motivation	Decision making contributes relatively little motivation	Some contribution by decision making to motivation to implement	Substantial contribution by decision-making processes to motivation to implement
f. Is decision making based on man-to-man or group pattern of operation? Does it encourage or discourage teamwork?	Man-to-man only discourages teamwork	Man-to-man almost entirely, discourages teamwork	Both man-to-man and group, partially encourages teamwork	Largely based on group pattern, encourages teamwork

Table 3-1 (*Continued*)

Organizational and Performance Characteristics of Different Management Systems Based on a Comparative Analysis (*Continued*)

Operating characteristics	*System of organization*			
	Authoritative		*Participative*	
	Exploitive authoritative	*Benevolent authoritative*	*Consultative*	*Participative group*
5. Character of goal-setting or ordering				
a. Manner in which usually done	Orders issued	Orders issued, opportunity to comment may or may not exist	Goals are set or orders issued after discussion with subordinate(s) of problems and planned action	Except in emergencies, goals are usually established by means of group participation
b. To what extent do the different hierarchical levels tend to strive for high performance goals?	High goals pressed by top, resisted by subordinates	High goals sought by top and partially resisted by subordinates	High goals sought by higher levels but with some resistance by lower levels	High goals sought by all levels, with lower levels sometimes pressing for higher goals than top levels
c. Are there forces to accept, resist, or reject goals?	Goals are overtly accepted but are covertly resisted strongly	Goals are overtly accepted but often covertly resisted to at least a moderate degree	Goals are overtly accepted but at times with some covert resistance	Goals are fully accepted both overtly and covertly
6. Character of control processes				
a. At what hierarchical levels in organization	At the very top only	Primarily or largely at the top	Primarily at the top but some shared feeling	Concern for performance of control func-

does major or primary concern exist with regard to the performance of the control function?			of responsibility felt at middle and to a lesser extent at lower levels	tion likely to be felt throughout organization
b. How accurate are the measurements and information used to guide and perform the control function, and to what extent do forces exist in the organization to distort and falsify this information?	Very strong forces exist to distort and falsify; as a consequence, measurements and information are usually incomplete and often inaccurate	Fairly strong forces exist to distort and falsify; hence measurements and information are often incomplete and inaccurate	Some pressure to protect self and colleagues and hence some pressures to distort; information is only moderately complete and contains some inaccuracies	Strong pressures to obtain complete and accurate information to guide own behavior and behavior of own and related work groups, hence information and measurements tend to be complete and accurate
c. Extent to which the review and control functions are concentrated	Highly concentrated in top management	Relatively highly concentrated, with some delegated control to middle and lower levels	Moderate downward delegation of review and control processes; lower as well as higher levels feel responsible	Quite widespread responsibility for review and control, with lower units at times imposing more rigorous reviews and tighter controls than top management
d. Extent to which there is an informal organization present and supporting or opposing goals of formal organization	Informal organization present and opposing goals of formal organization	Informal organization usually present and partially resisting goals	Informal organization may be present and may either support or partially resist goals of formal organization	Informal and formal organization are one and the same; hence all social forces support efforts to achieve organization's goals

Table 3-1 (*Continued*)

Organizational and Performance Characteristics of Different Management Systems Based on a Comparative Analysis (*Continued*)

Operating characteristics	*System of organization*			
	Authoritative		*Participative*	
	Exploitive authoritative	*Benevolent authoritative*	*Consultative*	*Participative group*
7. Performance characteristics				
a. Productivity	Mediocre productivity	Fair to good productivity	Good productivity	Excellent productivity
b. Excessive absence and turnover	Tends to be high when people are free to move	Moderately high when people are free to move	Moderate	Low
c. Scrap loss and waste	Relatively high unless policed carefully	Moderately high unless policed	Moderate	Members themselves will use measurements and other steps in effort to keep losses to a minimum
d. Quality control and inspection	Necessary for policing	Useful for policing	Useful as a check	Useful to help workers guide own efforts

Instructions: Opposite each operating characteristic, please indicate on the continuum approximately where you feel your organization falls with regard to that item, as defined in Table 14-1.

Operating characteristics		Exploitive—authoritative	Benevolent—authoritative	Consultative	Participative group	Item no.
Motivations	1a					1
	b					2
	c					3
	d					4
	e					5
	f					6
	g					7
Communication	2a					8
	b					9
	c(1)					10
	(2)					11
	d(1)					12
	(2)					13
	(3)					14
	(4)					15
	(5)					16
	e					17
	f					18
	(1)					19
Interaction	3a					20
	b					21
	c(1)					22
	(2)					23
	d					24
	e					25
Decision making	4a					26
	b					27
	c					28
	d					29
	e(1)					30
	(2)					31
	f					32
Goal setting	5a					33
	b					34
	c					35
Control	6a					36
	b					37
	c					38
	d					39
Performance	7a					40
	b					41
	c					42
	d					43
Total						

Fig. 3-1. Form A answer sheet.

To test their usefulness, both forms were tried experimentally with a group of managers. These managers were all at the middle- or upper-management levels of several excellent companies, including Aluminum Company of Canada, Detroit Edison, Dow Chemical, General Electric, Genesco, Humble Oil, International Business Machines, Lever Brothers, Mountain States Telephone, Sun Oil, Thompson-Ramo-Woolridge, Union Carbide, and U.S. Rubber.

A frequency distribution was prepared consolidating the answers these managers gave on Form A concerning the management system they believed their organization used. This distribution, based on the manager's answers, appears as Figure 3-2. An examination of Figure 3-2 shows a relatively wide range on each item. The bulk of the answers for all the men, however, fall under the "benevolent authoritative" and "consultative" systems of management. (The headings "exploitive authoritative," "benevolent authoritative," "consultative," and "participative group" were used initially on Table 14-1 of *New Patterns of Management*. They have been changed, respectively, to "System 1," "System 2," "System 3," and "System 4," as shown in Table 2-1. The reason for the change is given later in this chapter. Both sets of headings are shown on Figures 3-2 through 3-10.)

Figure 3-3 shows a profile of the means of the answers to each item that these managers gave on Form B. An examination of Figure 3-3 shows that virtually every one of these managers "would like to have" his company use System 4 (the participative-group system of management).

A comparison of Figure 3-2 with Figure 3-3 shows that there is a large discrepancy between the management system these managers see their companies using and the management system they would like their companies to use.

The descriptive statements of characteristics under each system of organization for each item in Forms A and B proved to be clear. Managers in a wide variety of working situations seemed to feel that the resulting descriptions and profiles of their organizations were valid.

The Causal, Intervening, and End-result Variables

In this volume, extensive use will be made of three broad classes of variables labeled, respectively, causal, intervening, and end-result. They are discussed more fully in Chapter 8 and Appendix III. They can be defined briefly as follows:

- The "causal" variables are independent variables which determine the course of developments within an organization and the results achieved

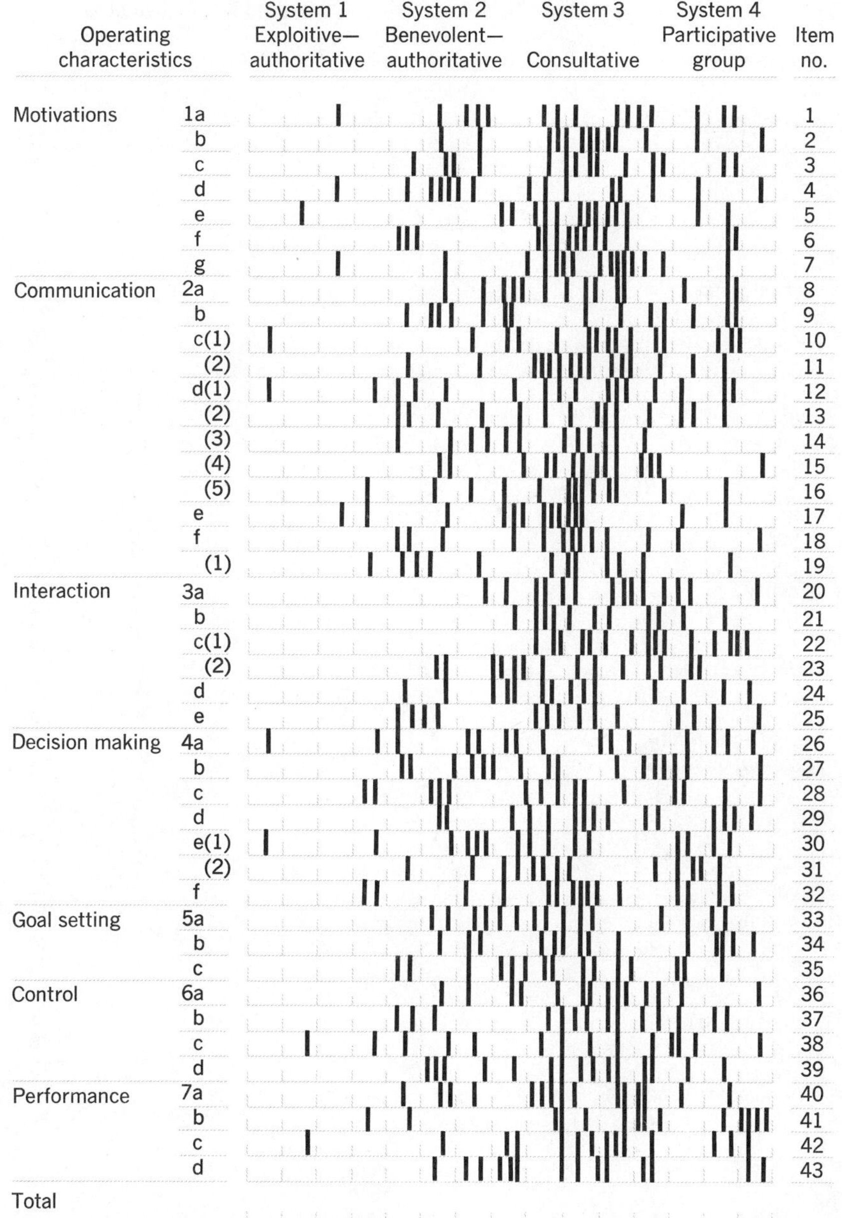

Fig. 3-2. Distribution of answers on Form A of middle- and upper-level managers in several well-managed companies.

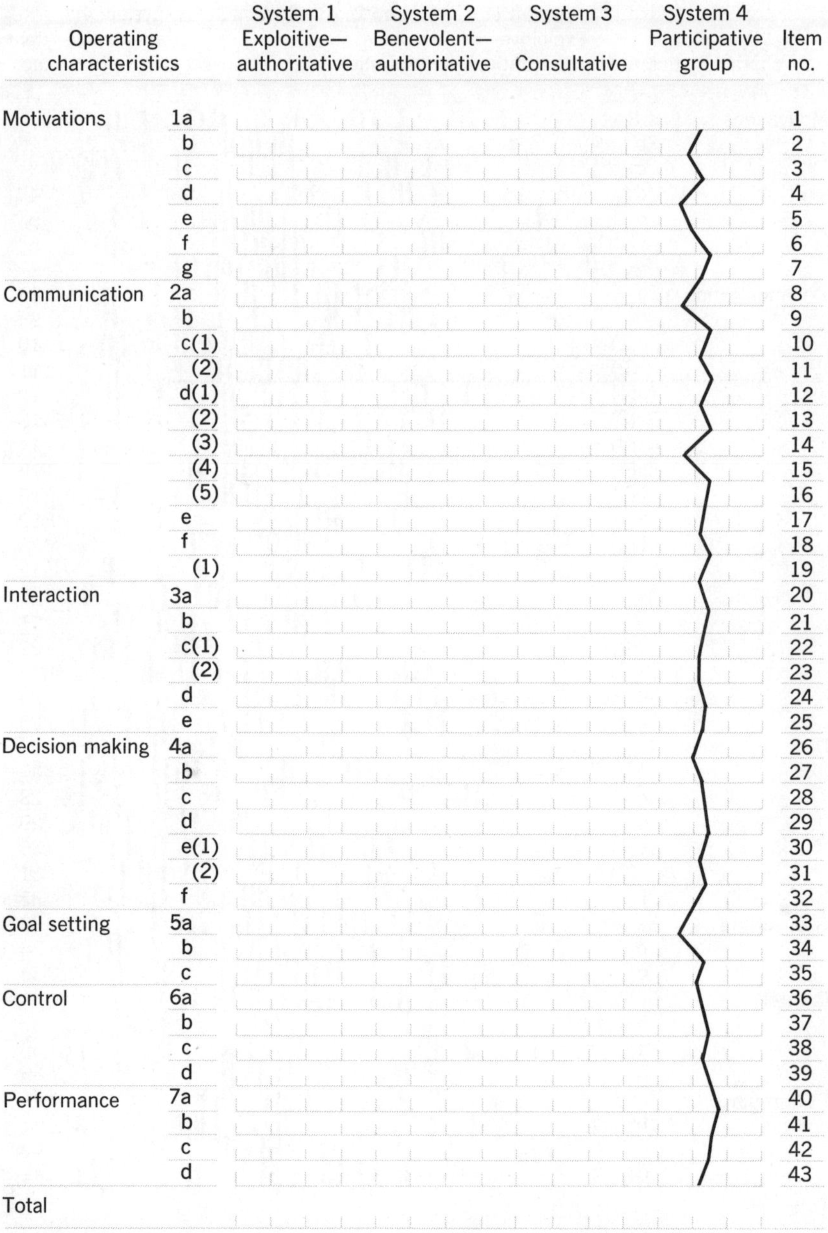

Operating characteristics		System 1 Exploitive—authoritative	System 2 Benevolent—authoritative	System 3 Consultative	System 4 Participative group	Item no.
Motivations	1a					1
	b					2
	c					3
	d					4
	e					5
	f					6
	g					7
Communication	2a					8
	b					9
	c(1)					10
	(2)					11
	d(1)					12
	(2)					13
	(3)					14
	(4)					15
	(5)					16
	e					17
	f					18
	(1)					19
Interaction	3a					20
	b					21
	c(1)					22
	(2)					23
	d					24
	e					25
Decision making	4a					26
	b					27
	c					28
	d					29
	e(1)					30
	(2)					31
	f					32
Goal setting	5a					33
	b					34
	c					35
Control	6a					36
	b					37
	c					38
	d					39
Performance	7a					40
	b					41
	c					42
	d					43
Total						

Fig. 3-3. Profile of answers on Form B of middle- and upper-level managers in several well-managed companies, i.e., the management system they would like to have.

by the organization. These causal variables include only those independent variables which can be altered or changed by the organization and its management. General business conditions, for example, although an independent variable, is not included among the causal list. Causal variables include the structure of the organization and management's policies, decisions, business and leadership strategies, skills, and behavior.

- The "intervening" variables reflect the internal state and health of the organization, e.g., the loyalties, attitudes, motivations, performance goals, and perceptions of all members and their collective capacity for effective interaction, communication, and decision making.
- The "end-result" variables are the dependent variables which reflect the achievements of the organization, such as its productivity, costs, scrap loss, and earnings.

A Large Shift in a Management System

In January, 1962, the Harwood Manufacturing Company, the leading firm in the pajama industry, purchased the Weldon Company, which was second in volume in this industry. This industry is so highly competitive that one of the nation's leading shirt manufacturers decided not to enter the field because costs had already been so greatly reduced that it would be hard to establish a profitable operation. The Weldon Company had been unprofitable for several years. These same years, however, had been profitable for the Harwood Manufacturing Company.

After its purchase, the corporate management of the Weldon Company was taken over by Harwood, but the plant manager and the managerial and supervisory staffs in the Weldon plant were retained. A few additional supervisors were appointed subsequently. The Weldon plant is located in Williamsport, Pennsylvania, and employs approximately 800 employees.

Starting in 1962, a number of changes were introduced in the management system of the Weldon plant and in the layout and organization of the work. These changes are described in a book edited by Marrow, Bowers, and Seashore (1967).

Briefly, the major changes involved extensive engineering modifications in the organization of the work, improved maintenance of machinery and equipment, an "earnings development" training program for employees, training of managers and supervisors in the principles and skills required by a system of management well toward System 4, the use of this system by the plant manager, and his encouragement of all of his subordinate managers and supervisors to do the same. All of these changes were initiated and supported by the new top management of the company.

At the request of Dr. Alfred Marrow, chairman of the board of the Harwood Manufacturing Company, Seashore and Bowers of the Institute for Social Research have been obtaining measurements each year since 1962 of the causal and intervening variables in the Weldon plant and of changes in these variables from year to year.

Results from the analysis of these data suggested the desirability of asking the managers and supervisors in the Weldon plant to fill out the Form A answer sheet to describe the management system used by the former management, i.e., the system used prior to 1962. They were also asked to complete Form A to indicate how they saw the organization at that time (as of April, 1964). The results, computed and plotted by Bowers, are shown in Figures 3-4 through 3-6. Figure 3-4 shows how upper management, supervisors, and assistant supervisors at the Weldon plant described the management system used prior to 1962; Figure 3-5 shows the management system being used in April, 1964, as seen by these three levels; Figure 3-6 shows the management system they would like to have. The mean of each item at the three different management levels is plotted.

Marked shifts in the management system as perceived by Weldon managers and supervisors are revealed for all three levels of management by comparing the exhibits for the period prior to 1962 with the exhibits for April, 1964.

The success achieved by the Harwood corporate management in introducing into the Weldon plant the management system used so profitably in the Harwood plants can be seen by comparing Figure 3-5 with Figure 3-7. The curves in Figure 3-7 show the perceptions of the line management in one of the Harwood plants concerning the management system used there in April, 1964. As a comparison of Figure 3-5 with Figures 3-4 and 3-7 reveals, the management system used in the Weldon plant after January, 1962, resembles that of the Harwood plant much more than it resembles the Weldon plant prior to 1962. It is not yet as close to the System 4 end of the continuum, however, as that of the Harwood plant. The kind of management desired by supervisors in the Weldon and Harwood plants is strikingly similar. (Compare Figure 3-6 with Figure 3-8.)

The shifts shown graphically in Figures 3-4 and 3-5 can also be computed arithmetically. Each horizontal line opposite an item on Form A is divided into 15 segments by short vertical marks. If a value of 1 is assigned to each segment, the mean total score ($\overline{M}$) on Form A and Form B can be computed for each level of management for each time period. These results are shown in Table 3-2 along with comparable data for the Harwood plant.

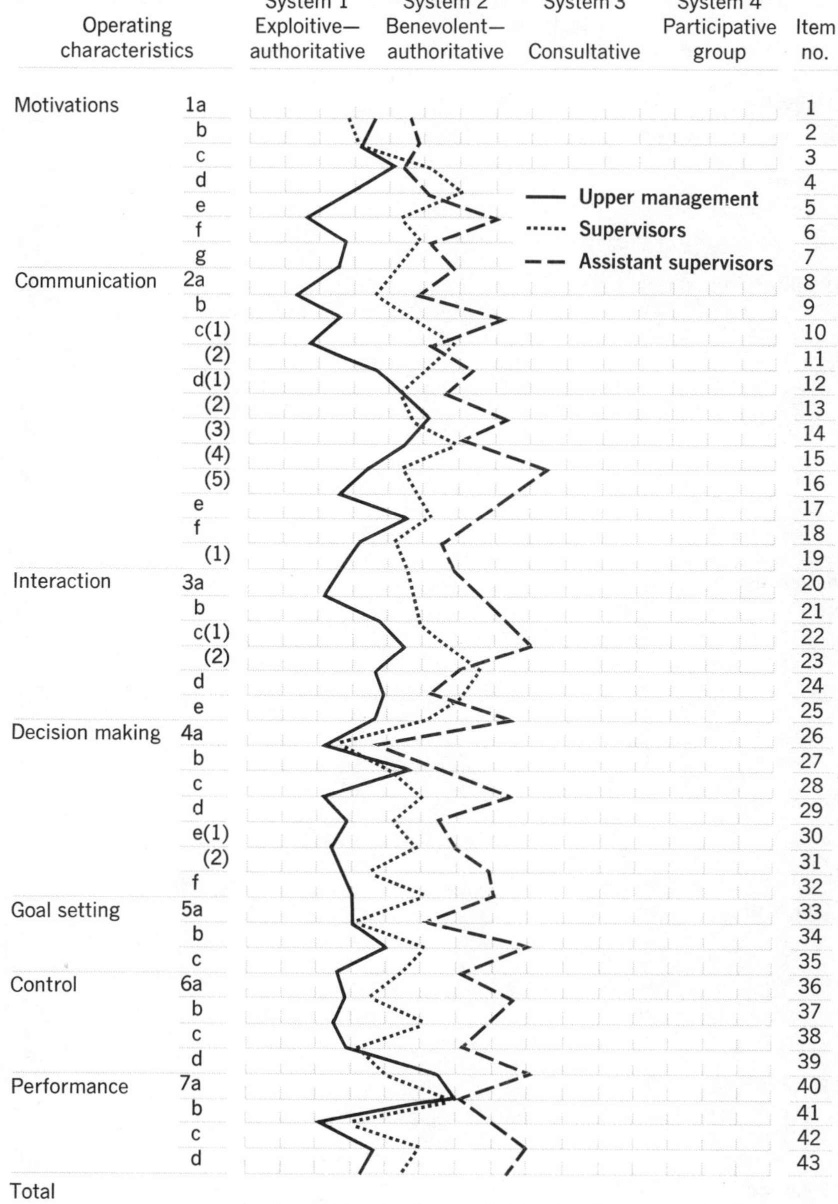

Fig. 3-4. Management system used by Weldon Plant prior to January, 1962, as seen by upper management, supervisors, and assistant supervisors.

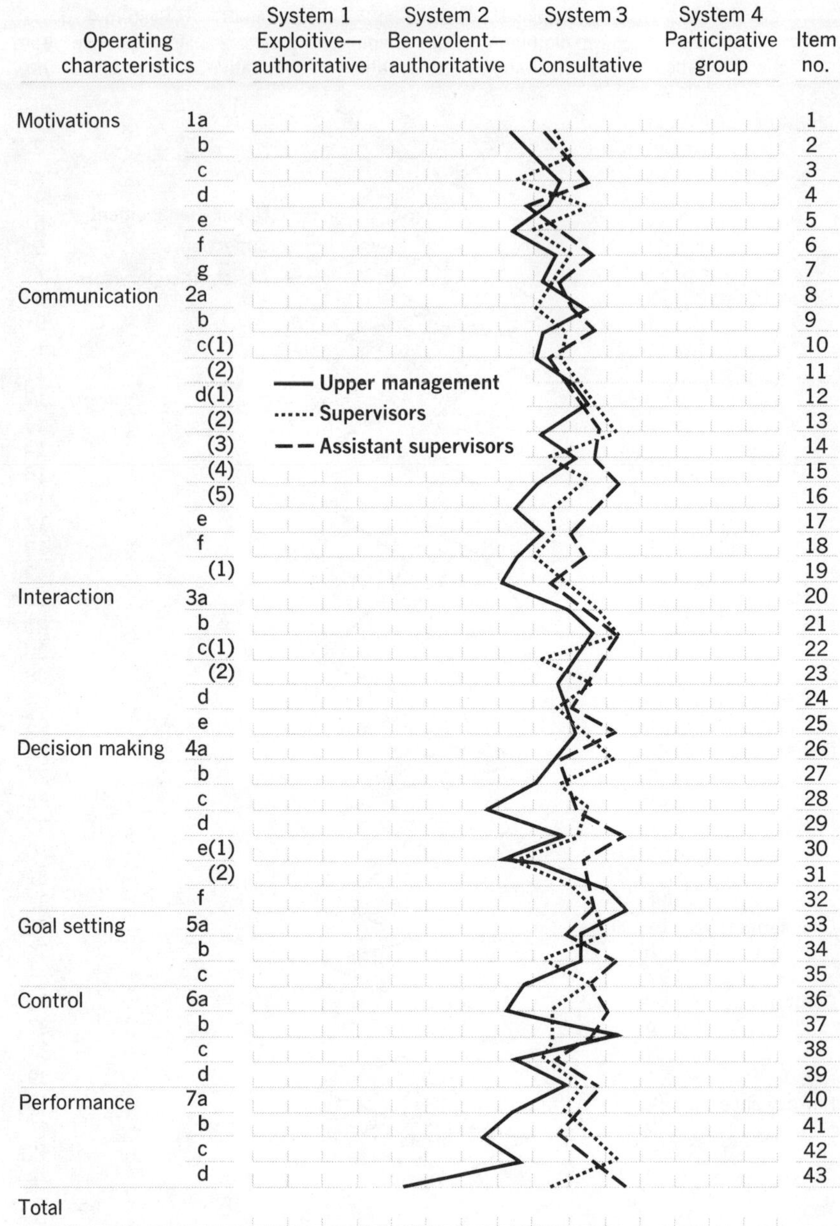

Fig. 3-5. Management system used by Weldon Plant in April, 1964, as seen by upper management, supervisors, and assistant supervisors.

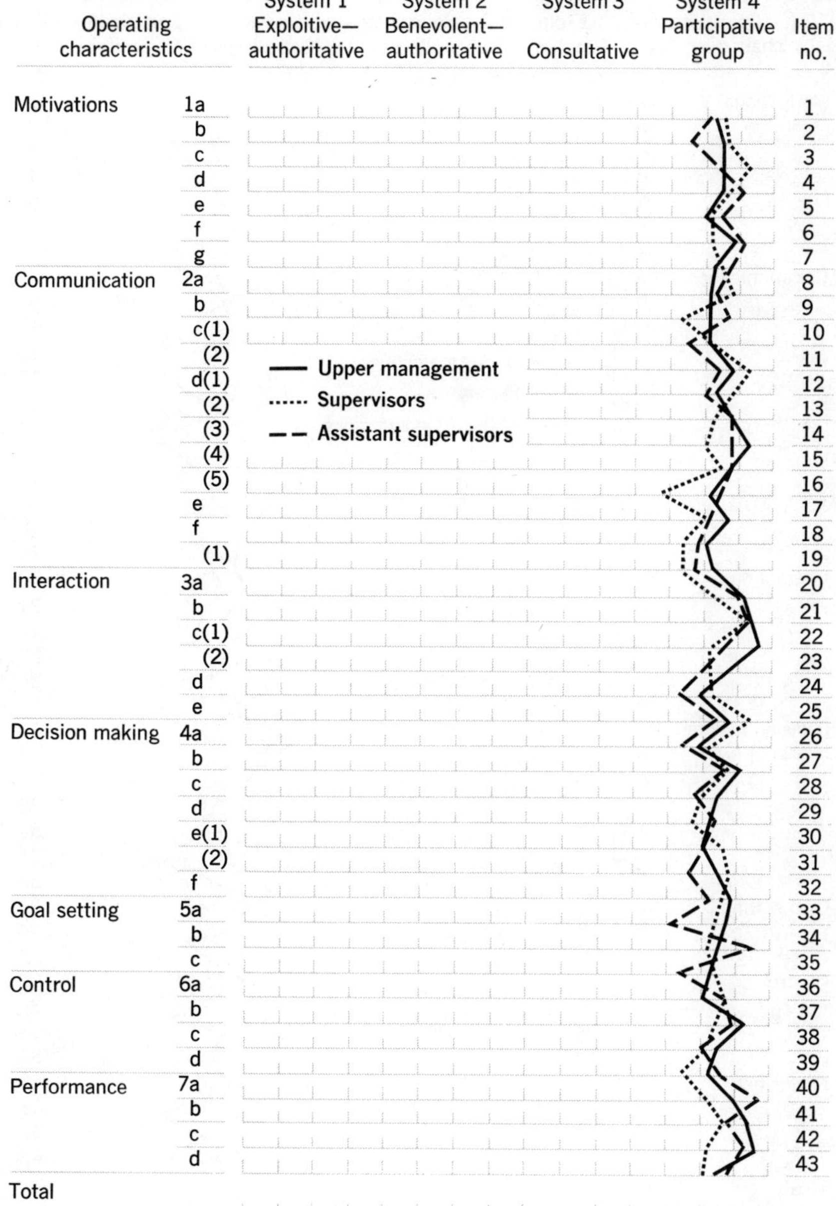

Fig. 3-6. Management system desired by Weldon managers and supervisors.

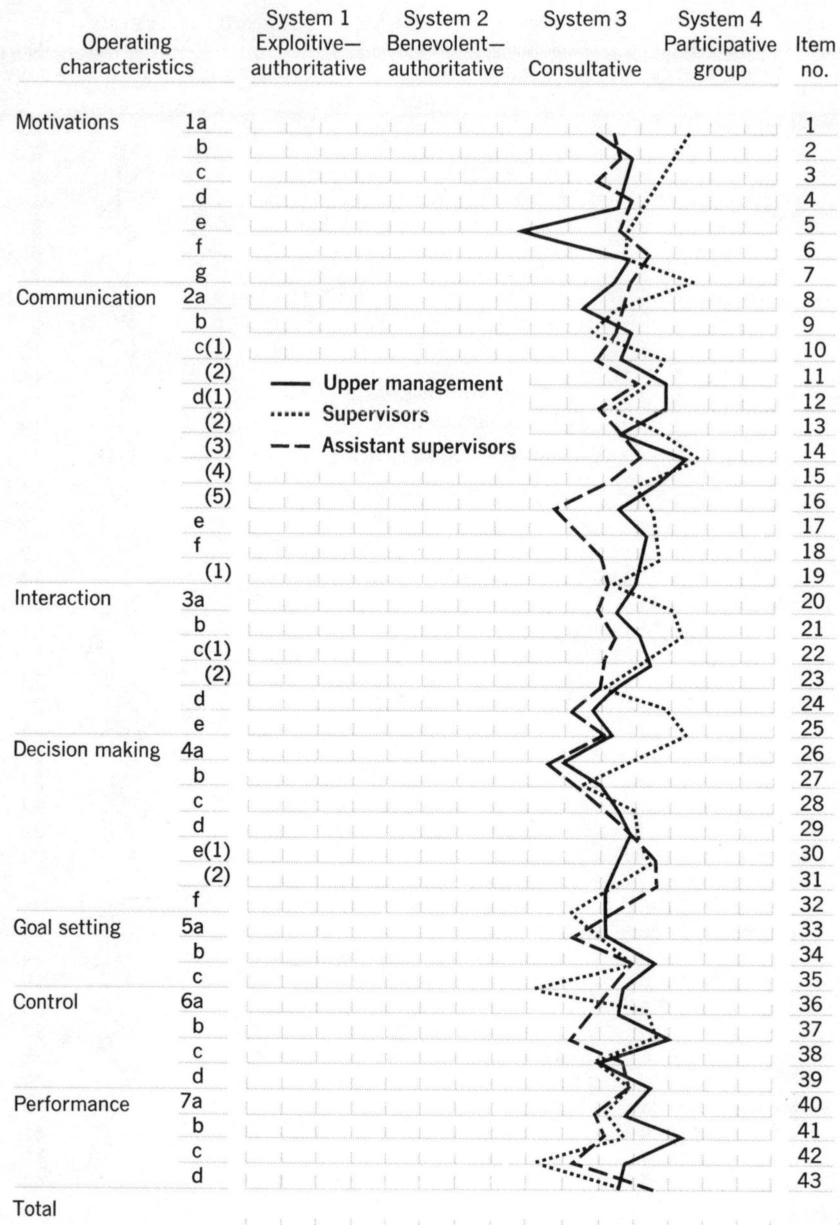

Fig. 3-7. Management system used by Harwood main plant in April, 1964, as seen by upper management, supervisors, and assistant supervisors.

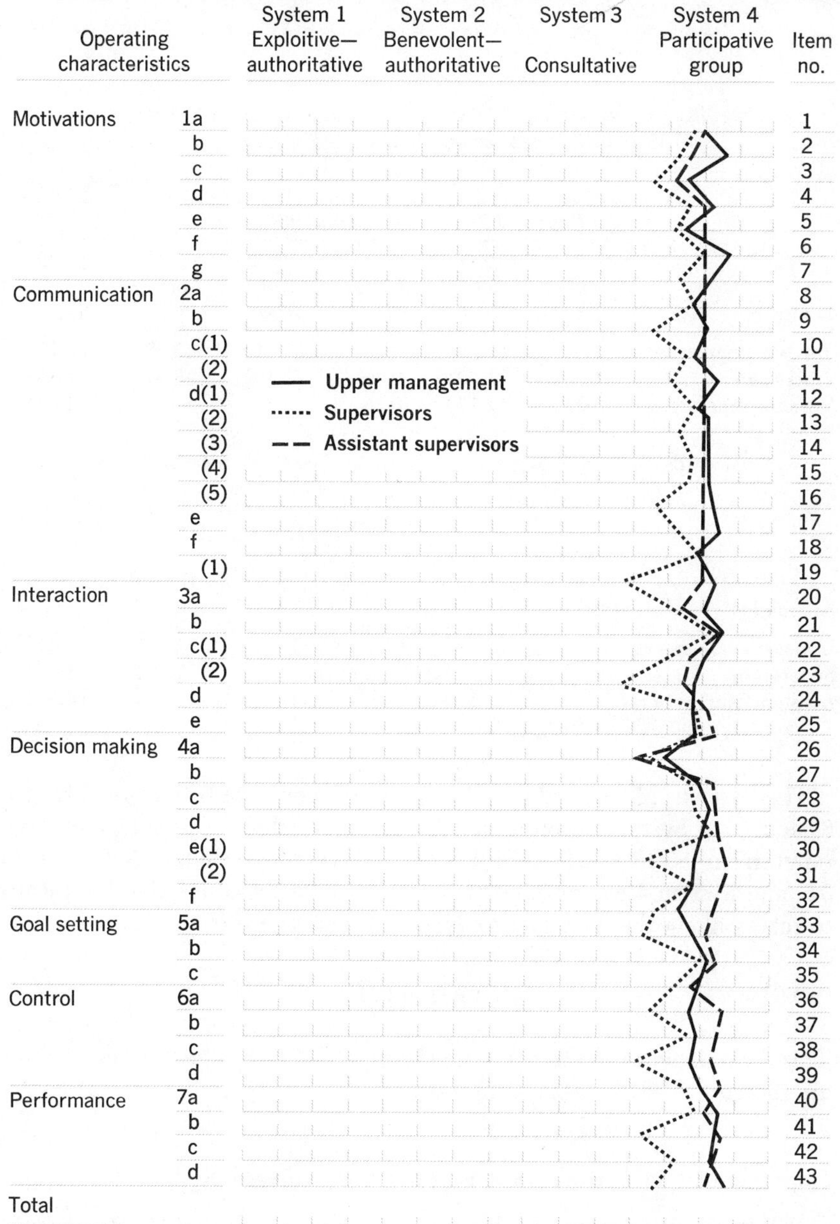

Fig. 3-8. Management system desired by Harwood managers and supervisors.

TABLE 3-2

MANAGEMENT SYSTEM USED—OR DESIRED—IN THE WELDON PLANT AS REVEALED BY MEANS FOR PERIOD SHOWN

	Used				*Desired*	
	Prior to 1962		*Early 1964*			
As seen by:	*Form A* $\overline{M}$	*Systems 1–4 Score*	*Form A* $\overline{M}$	*Systems 1–4 Score*	*Form A* $\overline{M}$	*Systems 1–4 Score*
Upper management. .	3.25	(1.37)	9.40	(3.01)	13.56	(4.12)
Supervisors	4.50	(1.70)	9.99	(3.16)	13.37	(4.06)
Assistant supervisors. .	6.27	(2.17)	10.38	(3.27)	13.36	(4.06)

MANAGEMENT SYSTEM USED—OR DESIRED—IN THE HARWOOD PLANT

	Used		*Desired*	
	Early 1964			
As seen by:	*Form A* $\overline{M}$	*Systems 1–4 Score*	*Form A* $\overline{M}$	*Systems 1–4 Score*
Upper management	11.66	(3.61)	13.92	(4.21)
Supervisors	11.77	(3.64)	13.24	(4.03)
Assistant supervisors	11.30	(3.51)	14.02	(4.24)

The means ($\overline{M}$) in Table 3-2 are readily converted to scores along a System 1 to System 4 continuum by assuming that System 1 covers the range from 0.5 to 1.5, System 2 covers 1.5 to 2.5, System 3 covers 2.5 to 3.5, and System 4 covers 3.5 to 4.5. The formula for converting the means to scores along the System 1-to-System 4 continuum is

$$\text{Score} = (\text{observed } \overline{M})\ 4/15 + .5$$

This formula was used to compute the System 1 to System 4 scores, which are shown in Table 3-2 in parentheses.

Improvement in Performance Follows Shift toward System 4

While all of the complex changes occurring in the Weldon plant make it impossible to estimate precisely the amount of the increase in productivity which can be attributed to the change in the management system, it is possible to make a reasonable estimate. This can be done by using an index based on changes in the earnings of the hourly workers. This method of measuring productivity improvement eliminates the effect of changes in technology, since the hourly earnings are based on piece-rate payments. Whenever changes occur in the work or the method, the job is retimed on the basis of the new job content, and new rates are set.

These measurements show that the changes in the management system have resulted in substantial increases in productivity. As Figure 3-9 shows, the index of productivity based on hourly earnings per month reveals that the increase from January, 1962, to March, 1964, amounts to 26 percent. (Productivity has continued to increase since that time.)

The chairman of the board of directors of Harwood has summarized the results as follows (Marrow, 1964b, pp. 19–20):

Fig. 3-9. Index of productivity based on average hourly earnings per month of employees on piece rates in the Weldon Plant, expressed as percentage of base period.

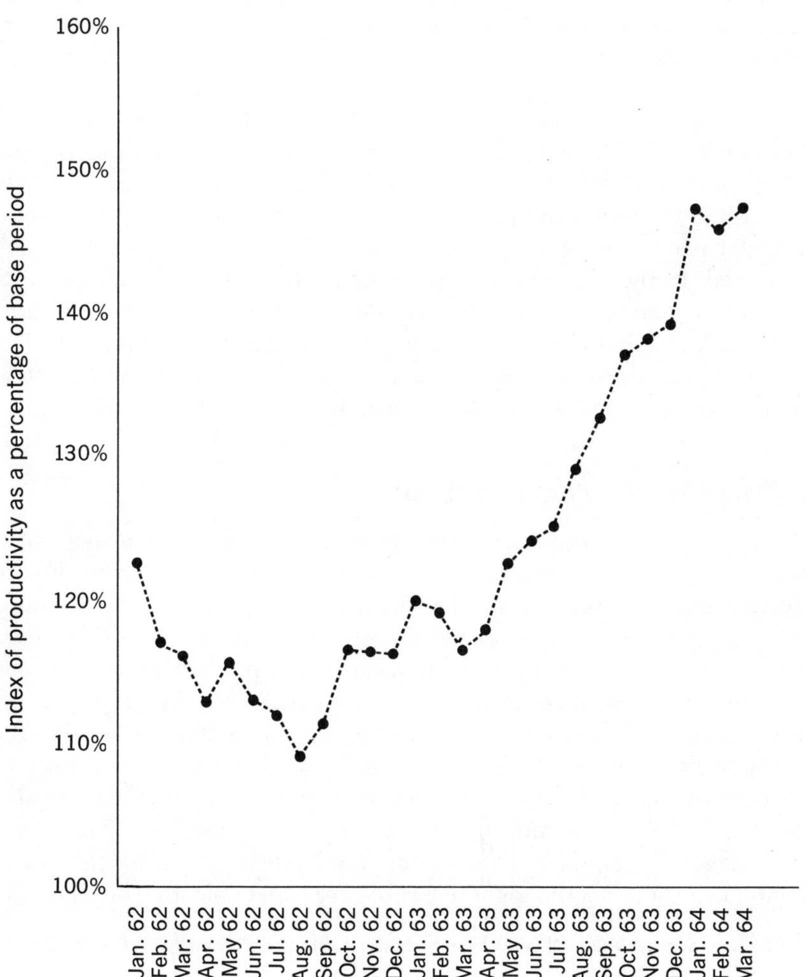

The improvements in cooperative relationships were noted by the technical consultants and production workers as well as by the Michigan researchers. The change in motivation and morale was reflected in the following ways:

Average earnings of piece-rate workers increased by nearly 30%. At the same time total manufacturing costs decreased by about 20%. Turnover dropped to half of its former level. Length of employee training was substantially reduced. Interviews by the Michigan researchers reflected vastly more friendly attitudes towards the company. The image of the company in the community changed and the organization began to show a profit.[2]

This was attained without a single replacement in managerial or supervisory personnel at the plant. All the original members of the staff continue in their same jobs.

The basic wage structure has not been changed. The increases in earnings were a result of heightened motivation and improved managerial skills. Increases due to technological changes were adjusted within the existing rate setting structure.

Large-scale field experiments by (1) Mann; (2) Katz, Kahn, Morse, and Reimer (Likert, 1961, Chap. 5; Morse & Reimer, 1956; Tannenbaum, 1966); and (3) Norman (Seashore & Bowers, 1963) have shown how difficult it is to effect substantial changes in the management system of a particular plant, department, or company and how long a period of time is required. In the light of these experiments, the magnitude of the shifts in the management system of the Weldon plant and the relatively short time it took to bring about these changes are particularly impressive. The plans and procedures used for achieving this substantial improvement in management are described by Marrow, Bowers, and Seashore (1967).

An Extraordinarily Productive Plant

Data from other studies support the conclusion that the management system of a firm is a major factor in determining its productivity. Figure 3-10 shows the distribution of answers on Form A for Plant L obtained from personnel at the middle- and upper-management levels, other than the plant manager. This plant is the most highly productive plant in one of the most successful companies in the United States. In addition to its outstanding productivity, it has a comparably excellent record for the quality of its products which have taken the lion's share of their markets.

A comparison of Figure 3-10 with Figure 3-2 reveals an impressive difference. The middle and upper levels of management in Plant L see the management of their plant resembling System 4 to a much greater extent (i.e., more to the right in Table 3-1) than do the managers in

[2] Profit as a percentage of investment changed from −17 percent to +15 percent and is still improving.

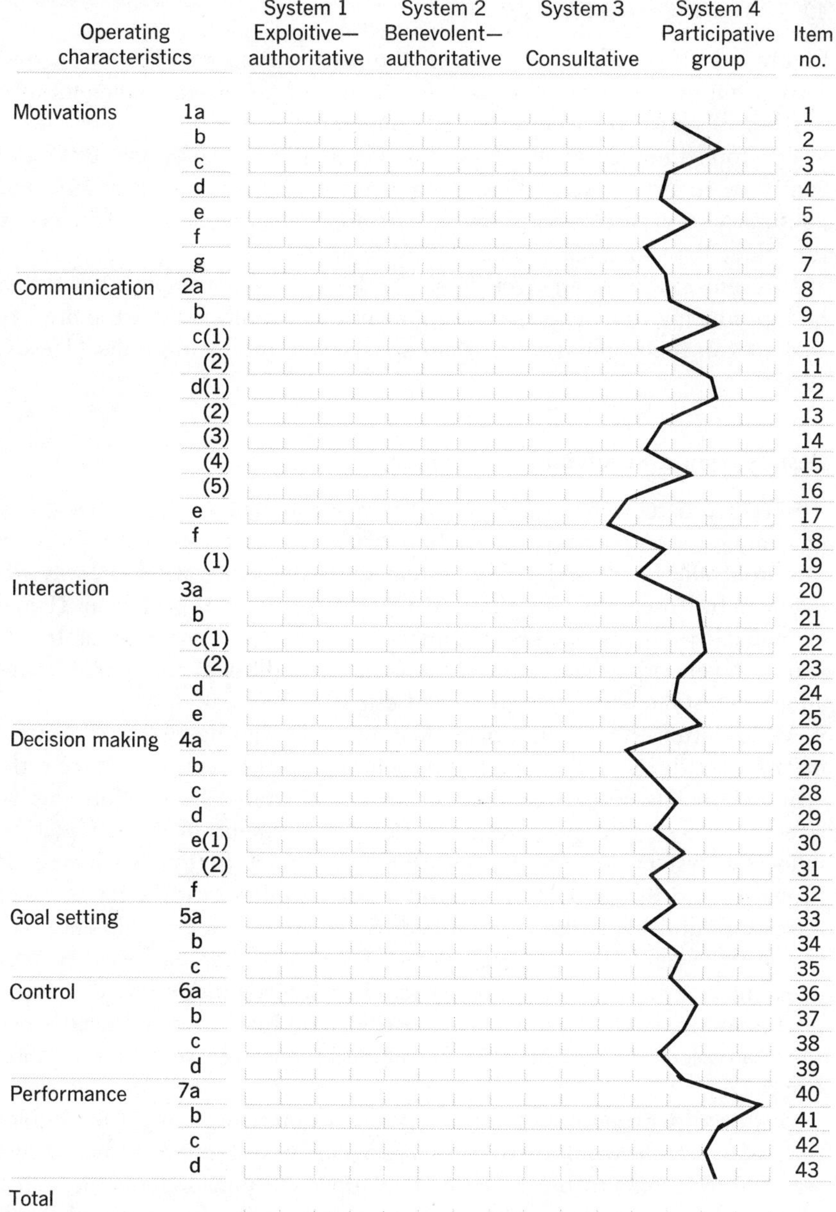

Fig. 3-10. Management system used by the most productive plant (Plant L) of a well-managed company, as seen by middle- and upper-level managers.

Figure 3-2. The difference between the distributions in Figures 3-2 and 3-10 is impressive, since the data in Figure 3-2 are from managers in a number of relatively well-managed companies.

The total number of employees in Plant L is in excess of 3,500 and continues to grow. Attitude surveys conducted among supervisory and nonsupervisory employees show appreciably more favorable attitudes in this plant than in other plants of this company.

A recent study in an agency of the Federal government shows that high-producing units engaged in automatic data processing are more like System 4 in their management than are the low-producing units (Heslin, 1966).

Results from a Scanlon-plan Company

Recently data were obtained on the management systems of a group of companies employing the Scanlon plan. This is a rather unique plan for profit sharing based on labor-management cooperation. It was developed by Joseph N. Scanlon (1948) just prior to World War II and extended by him to several companies prior to and subsequent to the war (Davenport, 1950). Since then many additional companies have adopted it, some with great success (Lesieur, 1959).

All too often the Scanlon plan—like all profit-sharing plans—is thought of only as a device for increasing the motivational forces arising from the economic needs of the members of an organization. As Scanlon emphasized, however, the plan requires the development of an interaction-influence system in which ideas for developing better products and processes and for reducing costs and waste can flow readily, be assessed, improved, and expeditiously applied. Such an interaction-influence system is appreciably more characteristic of System 4 than of the other management systems. System 4 actually requires an even more fully developed interaction-influence system than most Scanlon-plan companies now use. (For a discussion of interaction-influence systems, see Likert, 1961, Chap. 12.)

One would expect, consequently, that a company using the Scanlon plan successfully would display a management system well toward System 4. This seems to be the case. The supervisory-managerial personnel of several Scanlon-plan companies filled out a revised version of Table 3-1. (This revised version consisted of the items in Tables 3-1 and 7-1 [page 120] with the omission of items 7*c* and *d* of Table 3-1. It contains, consequently, a few more items than Table 3-1, but the profiles obtained from it can be compared directly with those obtained from using Table 3-1.) The instructions used in administering this revised version were as follows:

"Please place an *o* at the appropriate point on each line to show where, *in your experience*, you feel your organization falls on that item. Each line is continuous from the left end to the right end so place your *o* at that point above the line which best describes your organization.

"If you feel your organization is different today from what it was two or three years ago, place an *x* (either to the left or right of the *o*) indicating where your organization fell on that item previously. If you were not in your present plant or department two or three years ago, please fill in the profile with an *o* on each line and omit the *x* marks."

Figure 3-11 shows the *o* and *x* responses of the president of one of these Scanlon-plan companies. As Figure 3-11 shows, he sees the management system used today (*o*'s in Figure 3-11) as much more to the right in the table, toward System 4, than the management system used a few years ago (*x*'s). The supervisory and managerial personnel of this company have similar perceptions. This is revealed by examining Figure 3-12. The line management of this company sees its present management system (shown by the broken line in Figure 3-12) as appreciably closer to System 4 than the system used about two years ago (the solid line in Figure 3-12). This company (Company H), like Plant L (Figure 3-10), has the lion's share of the market for its product. It is also successfully selling its product in Japan and Europe in competition with products manufactured there. The company has grown steadily in recent years. In 1964, in comparison with 1963, its volume increased by 33 percent and its earnings by 84 percent. It is doing very well.

The data recently obtained from some other companies which are making successful use of the Scanlon plan display patterns like those in Figures 3-11 and 3-12. The line managements of these other successful companies see their management systems moving toward System 4 but not yet as close to System 4 as Company H and Plant L.

Science-based Management and Labor Relations

The science-based organizational theory emerging from the research findings on management and organizational performance has obvious implications for labor-management relationships. One would predict that the labor-management relations of a firm, on the average, would be better the closer to System 4 is its management system. Similarly, shifts toward System 4 should result in improvement in labor-management relationships, and shifts toward System 1 should have the opposite outcome.

The Institute for Social Research has completed three field experiments (several others are now underway) in companies where the management systems were moved toward System 4. We also have data from situations in which the management system was moved toward Systems 1 and 2.

Item no.	System 1	System 2	System 3	System 4
1		X	O	
2		X	O	
3		X	O	
4		X	O	
5		X	O	
6			X	O
7			X	O
8		X	O	
9			X	O
10		X		O
11		X	O	
12		X		O
13			X	O
14			X	O
15		X		O
16		X	O	
17				XO
18		X	O	
19		X	O	
20			X	O
21		X O		
22		X	O	
23			X	O
24		X	O	
25			X	O
26			X	O
27	X		O	
28				
29			X	O
30			X	O
31			X	O
32			X	O
33			X	O
34			X	O
35		X	O	
36		X		O
37			X	O
38			X	O
39			X	O
40		X		O
41		X		O
42			X	O
43			X	O
44		X		O
45		X	O	
46			X	O
47				X O
48			X	O
49			X	O
50			X	O

0 = Today

X = 2 or 3 years ago

Fig. 3-11. Management system of Company H, as seen by the president.

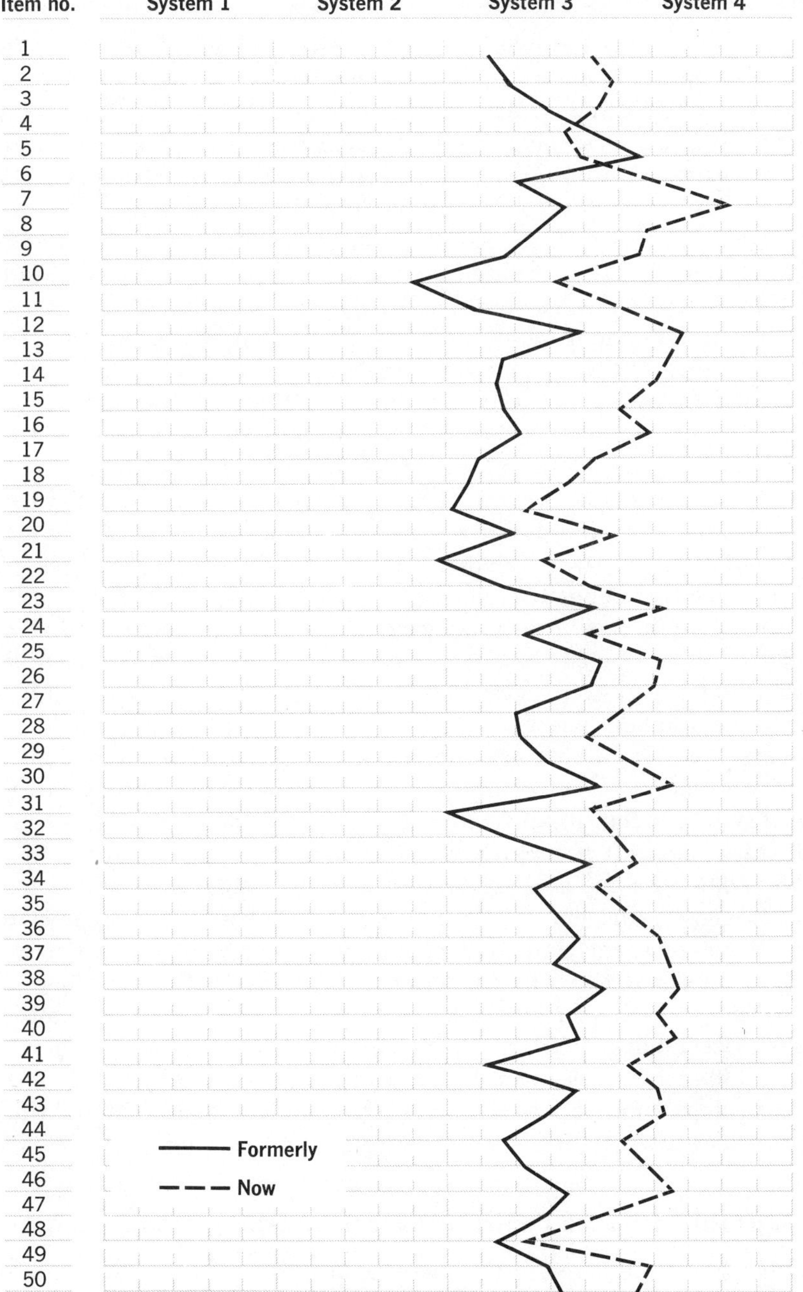

Fig. 3-12. Management system of Company H, as seen by managerial and supervisory personnel.

These studies have involved several hundred employees. Reports on two of these studies have been published (Likert, 1961, Chap. 5; Morse & Reimer, 1956; Seashore & Bowers, 1963). In addition to these field experiments, data have been obtained in situations where firms have introduced major changes in their management systems, not as an experiment, but in an effort to improve performance. Several thousand employees were involved. In some of these firms, measurements have been obtained by the institute; in others, the data were secured by the personnel research staff of the company. These results have not been published.

The evidence from these large-scale field experiments and the other studies indicates that the management system of a firm exercises an important influence on its labor relations. Typically, as they shifted their management system from System 2 to well over toward System 4, there was a marked change in union-management relationships. Real and important differences continued to exist between the union and the company, but as the shift toward System 4 progressed there was a great increase in the capacity to attain acceptable solutions to difficult problems. Effective problem solving replaced irreconcilable conflict. Differences did not become formal grievances because they were solved at the point of disagreement. New contracts were negotiated without strikes and without work stoppages. Both companies and union members have derived substantial financial benefits from the improved relationships.

These large-scale field experiments and other situations in which the top management of a company, plant, or department shifted the management system of the enterprise toward System 4 provides several instances in which this shift resulted in an improvement in labor relations. Similarly, other data are available which show that companies and departments whose management systems approach System 4 have appreciably better union-management relations than do those whose management system resembles System 1 or 2 (Fleishman & Harris, 1962).

Briefly stated, labor relations appear to be best in plants whose management system falls toward the right (System 4 end) in Table 3-1; they are poorest in plants whose management systems fall toward System 1. These relationships improve when the management system shifts toward System 4; they worsen when a shift toward System 1 occurs.

Constructive Action on Failures in Labor-management Relationships

The results presented in this chapter, and their further elaboration in Chapter 5, point to the desirability of a major change in top managment's approach to labor relations. Since both the management system itself and shifts in the system, as revealed by periodic measurements, are related to the labor relations of a plant or company, they can be used to predict trends in the character of these relationships. Measurements concerning the nature of the current management system of a plant or department can be obtained rapidly and easily. In addition, measurements can be taken at regular intervals over a period of time to show the trends in the management system. Such data would reveal whether the operation is moving more toward System 4 or toward System 1.

When these measurements and the data on current union-management relations, e.g., grievances, stoppages, turnover, and absence, show that the labor climate is such that there is likely to be irreconcilable conflict and a serious breakdown before or at the time of the next round of contract negotiations, then action to improve the management system being used should start *at once*. If the likelihood of a costly work stoppage and a collapse of negotiations can be predicted a couple of years in advance, there is no justification for failing to start taking the needed remedial steps long before the breakdown actually occurs and work stops.

Corrective steps, such as shifting toward a System 4 management, if started as soon as the data show the need for it, would prevent a large proportion of the present failures in labor-management relations. All parties adversely affected by work stoppages—the employees, the company, and the public—would benefit greatly from such positive steps.

Variations in Styles of Supervision

The results from the Weldon plant (Figures 3-4 and 3-5) point to two additional findings. The distributions of answers for the period prior to 1962 show that the profile of the supervisors is somewhat more toward System 4 than is that of upper management. The profile of the assistant supervisors is even more to the right.

Some of the managers and supervisors at each hierarchical level in the Weldon plant apparently had sufficient conviction and courage prior to January, 1962, to use a management system somewhat more toward the system which they themselves desired and believed more productive than the system their own superior used. At each lower level, successively, the management system tended to be more like the desired system (Figure 3-6) than was the level above it. This relationship is seen by comparing the relative position of the three lines shown in Figure 3-4. Some of the managers and supervisors were evidently protecting their subordinates from the kind of management system which they, themselves, did not like and probably did not feel was productive.

The second finding shown by the profiles of Weldon prior to 1962 is that most of the managers and supervisors at each level did not feel free to deviate from the System 1 management used at the top of the corporation. At each level, many apparently felt pressure to manage in the same style as their superiors. This finding, shown also in other studies (Harris, 1952; Katz, Maccoby & Morse, 1950, p. 30), reflects, no doubt, the pressure each manager feels from his own superior to behave as he feels his superior wishes him to behave in dealing with his subordinates.

Managers typically seem to believe that their subordinate managers should use the superior's style of management. They reward those subordinate managers who do and put pressure to conform on those who deviate.

The finding that managers tend to manage in accordance with the same leadership principles which their own superiors use may help to answer, in part, the questions posed at the end of Chapter 2. Because of the restraints and rewards imposed by their immediate superiors and by higher echelons, many managers at middle and lower levels do not deviate from the prevailing management style of the firm even though they, themselves, believe that better performance would be achieved if they did so.

Conclusion

This chapter started with questions about the relative productivity of Systems 1, 2, 3, and 4. Research findings support the perceptions of managers that management systems more to the right in Table 2-1 or Table 3-1, i.e., toward System 4, are more productive and have lower costs and more favorable attitudes than do those systems falling more to the left, toward System 1. Those firms or plants where System 4 is used show high productivity, low scrap loss, low costs, favorable attitudes, and excellent labor relations. The converse tends to be the case for companies or departments whose management system is well toward System 1. Corresponding relationships are also found with regard to any shifts in the management system. Shifts toward System 4 are accompanied by long-range improvement in productivity, labor relations, costs, and earnings. The long-range consequences of shifts toward System 1 are unfavorable.

A science-based management, such as System 4, is appreciably more complex than other systems. It requires greater learning and appreciably greater skill to use it well, but it yields impressively better results, which are evident whenever accurate performance measurements are obtained. The next chapter examines more fully the nature of System 4 management as well as some of the causes which contribute to its capacity to achieve outstanding results.

Chapter 4

THE INTERDEPENDENT, INTERACTING CHARACTER OF EFFECTIVE ORGANIZATIONS

In this chapter we shall examine the effect on performance of three basic concepts of System 4 management: (1) the use by the manager of the principle of supportive relationships, (2) his use of group decision making and group methods of supervision, and (3) his high performance goals for the organization.

The principle of supportive relationships is a general principle which the members of an organization can use to guide their relationships with one another. The more fully this principle is applied throughout the organization, the greater will be the extent to which (1) the motivational forces arising from the noneconomic motives of members and from their economic needs will be harmonious and compatible and (2) the motivational forces within each individual will result in cooperative behavior focused on achieving organizational goals. The principle is stated as follows:

The leadership and other processes of the organization must be such as to ensure a maximum probability that in all interactions and in all relationships within the organization, each member, in the light of his background, values, desires, and expectations, will view the experience as supportive and one which builds and maintains his sense of personal worth and importance (Likert, 1961, p. 103).

In applying this principle, the relationship between the superior and subordinate is crucial. This relationship, as the principle specifies, should be one which is supportive and ego-building. The more often the superior's behavior is ego-building rather than ego-deflating, the better will be the effect of his behavior on organizational performance. In applying this principle, it is essential to keep in mind that the interactions between

NOTE: This chapter draws heavily upon a study by David G. Bowers and Stanley E. Seashore.

the leader and the subordinates must be viewed in the light of the subordinate's background, values, and expectations. The subordinate's perception of the situation, rather than the supervisor's, determines whether or not the experience is supportive. Both the behavior of the superior and the employee's perceptions of the situation must be such that the subordinate, in the light of his background, values, and expectations, sees the experience as one which contributes to his sense of personal worth and importance, one which increases and maintains his sense of significance and human dignity.

It is possible to test readily whether the superior's (and the organization's) behavior is seen as supportive by asking such questions as the following: (If the principle of supportive relationships is being applied well, the subordinate's answer to each question will be favorable to the superior or to the organization. The following questions are equally applicable to both.)

1. How much confidence and trust do you feel your superior has in you? How much do you have in him?
2. To what extent does your boss convey to you a feeling of confidence that you can do your job successfully? Does he expect the "impossible" and fully believe you can and will do it?
3. To what extent is he interested in helping you to achieve and maintain a good income?
4. To what extent does your superior try to understand your problems and do something about them?
5. How much is your superior really interested in helping you with your personal and family problems?
6. How much help do you get from your superior in doing your work?
   a. How much is he interested in training you and helping you learn better ways of doing your work?
   b. How much does he help you solve your problems constructively—not tell you the answer but help you think through your problems?
   c. To what extent does he see that you get the supplies, budget, equipment, etc., you need to do your job well?
7. To what extent is he interested in helping you get the training which will assist you in being promoted?
8. To what extent does your superior try to keep you informed about matters related to your job?
9. How fully does your superior share information with you about the company, its financial condition, earnings, etc., or does he keep such information to himself?
10. Does your superior ask your opinion when a problem comes up which

involves your work? Does he value your ideas and seek them and endeavor to use them?

11. Is he friendly and easily approached?
12. To what extent is your superior generous in the credit and recognition given to others for the accomplishments and contributions rather than seeking to claim all the credit himself?

Group Decision Making and Supervision

The use by the superior of group decision making and supervision in the management of his work group is the second fundamental concept of System 4 whose effect on performance we shall examine in this chapter.

Fig. 4-1. Man-to-man and group patterns of organization. (*From Rensis Likert. New patterns of management. New York: McGraw-Hill Book Company, 1961. By permission of the publishers.*)

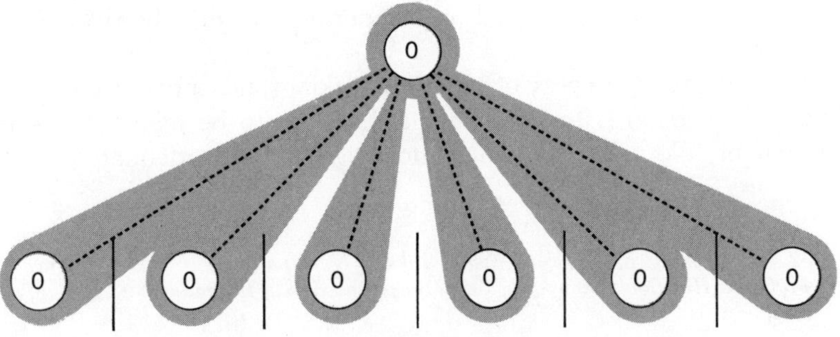

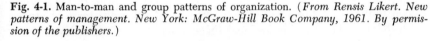

(a) Man-to-man pattern of organization

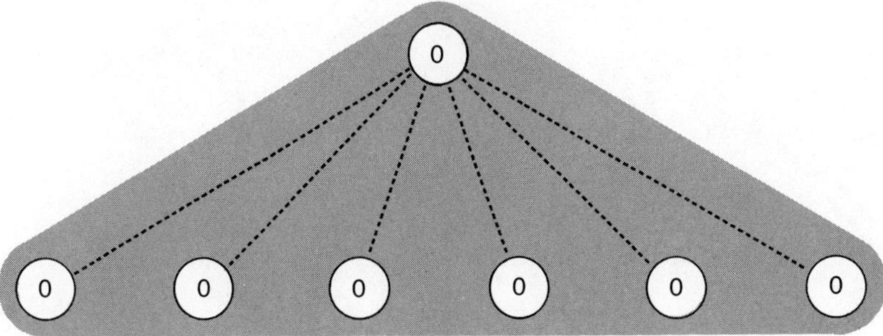

(b) Group pattern of organization

The traditional organizational structure (Systems 1 and 2) does not use a group form of organization but consists of a man-to-man model of interaction, i.e., superior-to-subordinate (Figure 4-1*a*). In this model, starting at the top of the firm, the president has full authority and responsibility. He delegates to each vice-president specific authority and responsibility and holds each accountable. Each vice-president in turn does the same with each of his subordinates, and this continues down through the organization. The entire process—stating policy, issuing orders, checking, controlling, etc.—involves man-to-man interaction at every hierarchical level.

System 4 management, in contrast, uses an overlapping group form of structure (Figure 4-1*b*) with each work group linked to the rest of the organization by means of persons who are members of more than one group. These individuals who hold overlapping group membership are called "linking pins" (Figure 4-2). The interaction and decision making relies heavily on group processes. Interaction occurs also, of course, between individuals, both between superiors and subordinates and among subordinates. At each hierarchical level, however, all subordinates in a work group who are affected by the outcome of a decision are involved in it. (A work group is defined as a superior and all subordinates who report to him.)

When the group process of decision making and supervision is used properly, discussion is focused on the decisions to be made. There is a minimum of idle talk. Communication is clear and adequately under-

Fig. 4-2. The linking pin. (*From Rensis Likert. New patterns of management. New York: McGraw-Hill Book Company, 1961. By permission of the publishers.*)

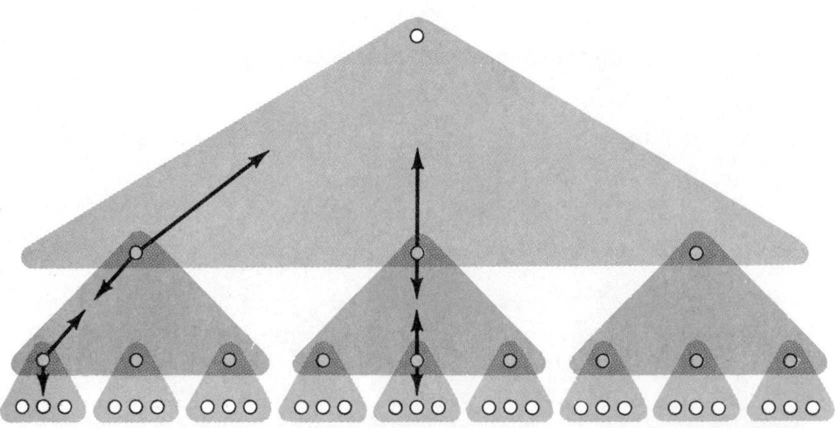

(The arrows indicate the linking-pin function)

stood. Important issues are recognized and dealt with. The atmosphere is one of "no nonsense" with emphasis on high productivity, high quality, and low costs. Decisions are reached promptly, clear-cut responsibilities are established, and tasks are performed rapidly and productively. Confidence and trust pervade all aspects of the relationship. The group's capacity for effective problem solving is maintained by examining and dealing with group processes when necessary.

It is essential that the group method of decision making and supervision not be confused with committees which never reach decisions or with "wishy-washy," "common-denominator" sort of committee about which the superior can say, "Well, the group made this decision, and I couldn't do a thing about it." Quite the contrary! The group method of supervision holds the superior fully responsible for the quality of all decisions and for their implementation. He is responsible for building his subordinates into a group which makes the best decisions and carries them out well. *The superior is accountable for all decisions, for their execution, and for the results.*

High Performance Aspirations

The third concept whose influence on organizational effectiveness will be considered deals with performance goals. Many studies (Kahn, 1958; Miller & Form, 1964) show that employees rather generally want stable employment, job security, opportunities for promotion, and satisfactory compensation. They also wish to be proud of the company they work for and of its performance and accomplishments. Since these needs and desires are important to the members of the organization, the principle of supportive relationship requires that they be met. This can be done best by an organization which is economically successful. A firm must succeed and grow to provide its employees with what they want from a job: pride in the job and company, job security, adequate pay, and opportunities for promotion. Economic success is a "situational requirement" (Likert, 1961, pp. 112, 211–220) which can be met only when the organization, its departments, and its members have high performance goals.

Superiors in System 4 organizations, consequently, should have high performance aspirations, but this is not enough. Every *member* should have high performance aspirations as well. Since these high performance goals should not be imposed on employees, there must be a mechanism through which employees can help set the high-level goals which the satisfaction of their own needs requires.

System 4 provides such a mechanism through: (1) group decision making, and (2) multiple, overlapping group structure. As a consequence, System 4 organizations set objectives which represent an optimum integration of the needs and desires of the members of the organization, the shareholders, customers, suppliers, and others who have an interest in the enterprise or are served by it. Since economic and status needs are important to the members of an enterprise, the goal-setting processes of System 4 necessarily lead to high performance goals for each unit and for the entire firm. Any time these high performance aspirations do not exist, there is a deficiency in the interaction processes of the organization and a failure to recognize the situational requirements.

A Test of the Concepts

An opportunity to collect data to test the effect upon organizational performance of these three central concepts of System 4 management occurred just as the manuscript for *New Patterns of Management* was being completed. Bowers and Seashore (Bowers, 1963; Bowers, 1964; Bowers & Seashore, 1964; Bowers & Seashore, 1966) undertook a study of the management and performance of the sales offices of a large company which operates nationally. An unusual advantage offered by the study was the excellent data on productivity, costs, and many other performance variables available for each sales office. Another advantage so far as research design was concerned was that all sales offices were doing the same job and with the same general technology.

Although the results examined in the following pages are from sales units, the general findings and the principles discussed are fully consistent with data from other kinds of work. The principles appear to be applicable to all kinds of undertakings. Managers of operations other than sales can profitably apply the principles and points discussed to their own enterprises.

The data reported here are from 40 separate sales offices of this company. Each office is independently owned and managed. These units are widely scattered throughout the nation. They vary in size from 8 salesmen to some 50 salesmen, with a supporting staff of clerical and supervisory personnel.

The 40 units consist of 20 pairs selected from a total of approximately 100 such units in the company. One unit of each pair comes from the best twenty units in the company. The top sales management of the company selected these units on the basis of such criteria as sales volume, costs, quality of business sold, and development of manpower. Each of these units was then matched by size and type of market with a unit which was not among the top 20. Some of the matching units were about average or above, some were below.

An index was constructed to measure the extent to which each manager of a sales unit was seen by his salesmen as behaving in ways consistent with the principle of supportive relationships. This index, based on answers taken from a longer questionnaire completed by each salesman anonymously, included 16 items like those mentioned at the beginning of this chapter. The 1 to 5 method of scoring was used to combine the items into a total score (Likert, 1932). This index is called the "Sales Managers' Supportive Behavior Score."

A second index was developed to measure the extent to which the manager, as seen by his salesmen, seeks high performance and also the extent to which he tries to have his salesmen use a well-organized plan of operation. Since the level of his sales goals and the extent to which a manager has a well-organized sales plan were found to be highly correlated for these sales offices, they have been combined into a single index called "Sales Managers' Performance Goals."

Supportive Behavior and High Goals Yield High Performance

In Figure 4-3, the 20 superior units, which we shall refer to as "high-performing sales offices," are indicated by a plus sign (+). The other 20 units, the poorer of each matched pair, we shall call "low-performing sales offices." They are shown by a minus sign (−).

An examination of Figure 4-3 reveals many important facts. Managers who apply the principle of supportive relationships well (shown by a high score on the vertical axis) and also have high performance goals (the horizontal axis) are much more likely to have better sales units than are the managers who display the opposite behavior. As will be observed in Figure 4-3, all of the sales units whose managers' supportive behavior scores are above 25.00 and whose managers' performance goals are above 6.60 are high-performing sales offices (shown by +). All of the sales units, except one, whose managers' supportive behavior scores are below 22.00 are low-performing units (shown by −). In the sales offices which fall in the middle range of the managers' supportive behavior scores, i.e., between 22.00 and 25.00, there is an appreciable relationship between the managers' performance goals and the success of the unit. Those which are below 6.60 on the managers' performance goals are all low-performing units. Of the nine offices where the performance goals score is above 6.60, six are high performers.

One of the forty sales offices was originally ranked by the national sales headquarters as one of their top twenty offices. By the time all the data were collected in this study and were in the process of analysis, the national sales staff recognized that this office did not really belong among the top 20. The manager is a very able salesman and sells an extraordinarily large volume of business personally. After he took over the management of this office, he maintained its volume by his own selling,

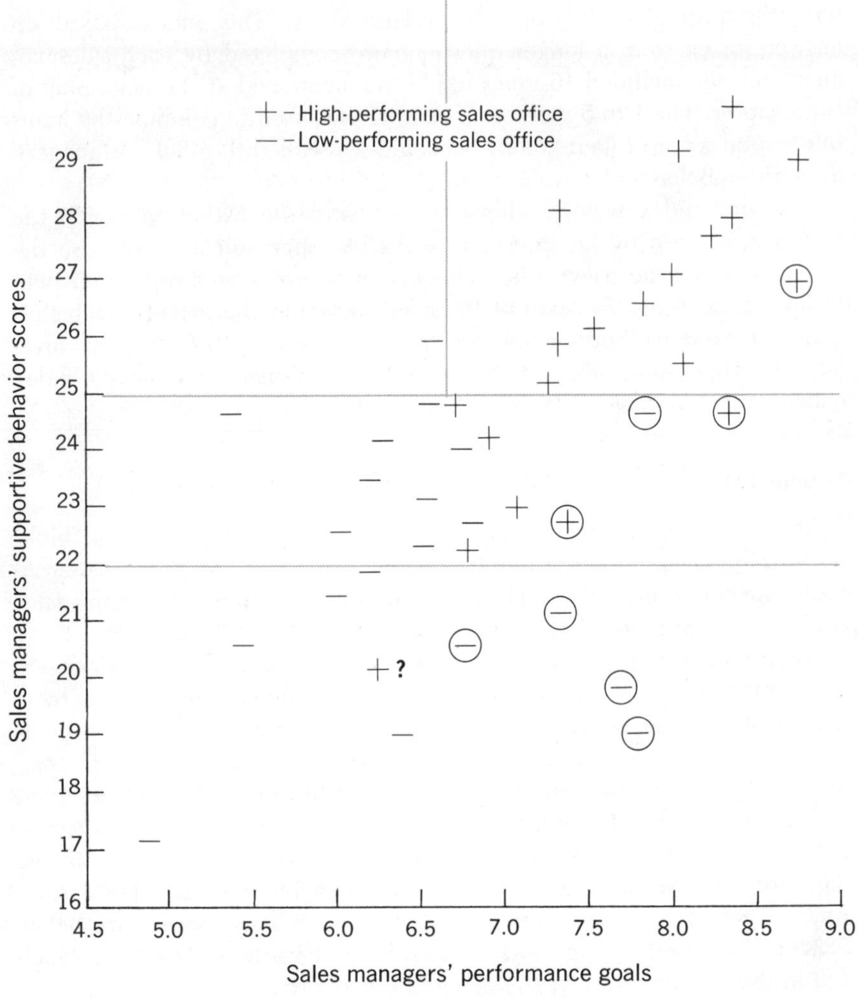

Fig. 4-3. Relation of sales office performance to sales managers' supportive behavior scores and sales managers' performance goals. (*After Rensis Likert. New patterns in sales management. In Martin R. Warshaw (Ed.), Changing perspectives in marketing management. Ann Arbor, Mich.: Univer. of Michigan Bureau of Business Research, 1962. By permission of the publishers.*)

but he did not build and maintain an effective sales organization. His managerial behavior did not put his unit in the top 20 so far as *sales management* was concerned, even though his personal selling made the volume, earnings, and cost of the office look impressive. In Figure 4-3 and in the other charts, this office is shown by a question mark to the right of the plus sign.

High Managerial Goals without Supportive Behavior Are Resented

Eight of the sales units in Figure 4-3 are circled. These units fall in the top 10 of all 40 units concerning the extent to which the men feel the manager is putting unreasonable pressure on them to produce. In relation to the other units, these tend to be below and to the right of a 45° diagonal line in Figure 4-3. They are, therefore, units whose managers have relatively high performance goals in comparison with the extent to which these managers are applying the principle of supportive relationships. In these units, the ratio of the managers' performance goals to his application of the principle of supportive relationships is above that of the other sales offices. These data demonstrate that when levels of direct, hierarchical, managerial pressure for production are high in relation to the amount of the manager's supportive behavior, a feeling of unreasonable pressure is produced in the men.

All of the managers of the 13 sales offices in the upper-right quadrant of Figure 4-3 (supportive behavior scores above 25.00 and performance goals scores above 6.60) are using group methods of supervision. In contrast, none of the managers with a supportive behavior score of less than 22.00 is using group supervision.

The Group Method of Supervision

Information on the extent to which the manager of a unit uses group decision making and group methods of supervision was supplied by persons in the national headquarters of the company. These persons are responsible for encouraging sales managers of the offices to use these and related supervisory and training procedures. It is not based, as are the other two scores, upon reports from the salesmen as to how they see the situation.

The information about each sales manager made it possible to place the offices into four categories: (1) offices in which the manager was using group methods of supervision at the time the study was made, (2) offices in which the manager was just starting to do so, (3) offices in which the manager was using group supervision irregularly or ineptly (for example, although he held group meetings, he structured the interaction in these meetings on a man-to-man basis, i.e., between himself and each of the individual salesmen), and (4) offices in which no use was made of group methods of supervision.

In those offices where the manager was starting to make some use of group methods of supervision, most of the managers were limiting this procedure primarily to new salesmen, i.e., salesmen with less than three years' experience. Only a few of the 40 managers were using group supervision with all of their salesmen.

The group method of sales supervision in these offices grew out of a coaching system originated in the organization several years ago by a member of the headquarters sales management staff. He launched the coaching system when he recognized that more had to be done to help new salesmen, who had been carefully selected and extensively trained, to become successful. In each sales unit, the manager, or a supervisor, was asked to meet regularly in group coaching sessions with the salesmen who had less than two or three years' experience. The purpose of conducting the meetings in groups was to have each new man learn not only from the manager's analysis of that individual's sales performance but also from hearing the manager's analysis of the work of each of the other new men and from the coaching he provided them. After several months' experience with these group sessions, some managers noticed that the salesmen liked to join in the analysis and coaching process and encouraged them to do so. In some of the sales units, this led to a fundamental change in the process. The manager became aware that more was accomplished when he served as a chairman and group leader rather than as the coach. The process became one of group problem solving, group coaching, and group goal setting. Each member committed himself to the group and to the manager to meet the target which the group had helped him set.

The exact process of these group sessions varies appreciably from unit to unit but is likely to be about as follows: The salesmen meet regularly in group meetings. The number of men varies depending upon the number in the territory but usually does not exceed 12 or 15. They meet at regular intervals every two weeks or every month. As a rule, the sales manager or one of his sales supervisors presides. Each salesman, in turn, presents to the group a report of his activity for the period since the last meeting of the group. He describes such things as the number and kinds of prospects he has obtained, the calls he has made, the nature of the sales presentations he has used, the closings he has attempted, the number of sales achieved, and the volume and quality of his total sales. The other men in the group analyze the salesman's efforts, methods, and results. Suggestions from their experience are offered. The outcome is a valuable coaching session. For example, if sales results can be improved through better prospecting, this is made clear, and the steps and methods to achieve this improvement are spelled out. After this analysis by the group, each man, with the advice and assistance of the group, sets goals for himself concerning the work he will do, the procedures he will use, and the results he intends to achieve before the next meeting of the group.

The manager or supervisor acts as chairman of the group, but aside from occasional discussion of complex, technical matters, the analyses and interactions are among the men. The chairman keeps the orientation of the group on a helpful, constructive, problem-solving basis. He sees that the tone is supportive, not ego-deflating. He encourages the group to set high performance goals which will help each man realize his full potential.

Each salesman, as a consequence of the group meeting, feels a commitment to the group and his manager to do the work and achieve the results which he has set for himself. His motivation is often stimulated between meetings by members of the group who remind him of his goals and commitments if they see him lagging or failing to make the needed sales calls. Moreover, because of the group loyalty created by the meetings, a salesman can, if he needs it, obtain coaching on some problem or assistance on a case not only from his supervisor but also from the other salesmen who had discussed the problem or offered relevant suggestions in the previous meeting. Each salesman has available the technical knowledge and skills of his colleagues as well as that of his supervisor or manager.

Salesmen derive four important benefits from this kind of group meetings: (1) they set higher sales goals, goals which more nearly reflect their own potentiality; (2) they are more highly motivated to achieve these goals, and they obtain greater satisfaction from their accomplishment; (3) they receive more technical assistance in selling by obtaining help from both their superior and their peers; and (4) new appeals, new markets, and new strategies of selling, when discovered by any individual salesman, are shared promptly with the group and improved and perfected by them. Often this improvement is facilitated by experimental field testing between group meetings. Important skills are not bottled up in a particular individual but are rapidly shared and cooperatively improved.

These group meetings are effective when the manager (or supervisor) does a competent job of presiding over the interactions among the men. Appreciably poorer results are achieved whenever the manager, himself, analyzes each man's performance and results and sets goals for him. Such man-to-man interactions in the meetings, dominated by the manager, do not create group loyalty and have a far less favorable impact upon the salesman's motivation than do group interaction and decision meetings. Moreover, in the man-to-man interaction little use is made of the sales knowledge and skills of the group.

The group method of supervision in this company was employed initially with only the new salesmen, men with less than three years with the company. In many sales offices, however, the advantages of the group process were recognized by the established salesmen and at their request this process was extended to include them. The most successful sales units, i.e., those with the largest volume and lowest costs, are now using group processes of supervision for both their new salesmen and their established salesmen. As a rule, each of the different groups within a sales office consists only of new salesmen or only of experienced men. This has proved desirable since many of the problems of new salesmen are different from those of established salesmen.

In most of the sales offices, the men do not have specified sales territories. Many of them compete with one another for sales in the same market. They are paid, moreover, on a commission basis. The time they devote to the meetings is taken from their income-producing sales work. But in spite of these two limitations, the salesmen in the offices using group methods of supervision sell more on the average than do men in the other offices, and they have more favorable attitudes toward their work.

The use of group methods of supervision does not mean that there is no place for leadership. The superior plays at least as crucial a leadership role as he does in any other system of management. The leader has many essential tasks in a System 4 organization. He sees that all members of the group are well trained in group decision making and in group interaction processes as well as in the technical aspects of their work. He seeks through both group and individual supervision to help each salesman set high and realistic goals for himself and strive to reach them. He is an important source of technical knowledge, is responsible for seeing that the unit is efficiently organized and that planning, scheduling, and related activities are done well. He sees that the principle of supportive relationship is applied. He links the unit to the rest of the enterprise. He is a source of restless dissatisfaction with present accomplishments and a stimulus to innovation.

Although group decision making strives for consensus, every member does not have an equal influence on every decision nor do decisions reflect the point of view of the least competent member. A recent study of 151 engineers by Farris (1966) shows that an engineer's performance affects his capacity to exert influence on the decisions dealing with his technical goals. The results show the pervasive influence of the excellence of performance. The high-performing engineer saw himself as being able to exert more influence on establishing the goals designated for him. He was more absorbed in his work, had better subordinates, and a better salary. These results make a great deal of sense. We would expect that individuals who have demonstrated greater capacity would have more influence on decisions and related activities both within their work group and in the organization generally. Effective group decision making enables every person to be heard, but the weight of each in the decision-making process is influenced appreciably by his demonstrated competence.

The results shown in Figure 4-3 provide impressive evidence that System 4 management is as effective in achieving better performance in sales organizations as it is in managing other kinds of human enterprises (Likert, 1961, Chap. 9). When sales managers apply the principle of supportive relationships effectively, use group methods of supervision, and have high performance goals, they are much more likely to have high-performing sales offices than are managers who score low on one or more of these variables. The managers who apply these principles of System 4 management are also, as we shall see, more likely to have organizations in which there is better teamwork and in which the salesmen, themselves, have higher performance goals.

Salesmen's Performance Goals and Sales-office Success

As we have seen in Figure 4-3, a sales manager's goals have a substantial effect on the success of his unit. This occurs because of the marked influence of the manager's goals on the goals of his men (Figure 4-4). The vertical axis in Figure 4-4 is the same variable (the managers' performance goals) as that used on the horizontal axis in Figure 4-3. The horizontal axis in Figure 4-4 shows measurements reflecting the extent to which the *men* in the unit have a well-organized plan of work and have high sales goals. As with the managers, these two variables are highly correlated for the men and have been combined into a single index. The mean (average) score for all of the men in a sales office is shown in Figure 4-4 and is called the "Salesmen's Performance Goals." The numbers assigned to the two axes are comparable, since identical questions were used to obtain the men's perceptions of the job organization and the sales goals of their manager and also to obtain the job organization and sales goals of their colleagues.

An examination of Figure 4-4 reveals many important facts. First, there is a marked relationship between the performance-goal scores of the managers and those of the men in their unit. The higher the performance goals of the manager of a sales unit, the higher in general are the performance goals of its men.

The second important finding revealed by Figure 4-4 is that, on the average, the performance goals of the men in a unit are appreciably lower than those of their manager. There is not a single unit in which the men on the average have higher performance goals than the manager, not a single sales office in the lower-right quadrant of Figure 4-4. The mean performance-goal score of all of the men (approximately 5.5) is about

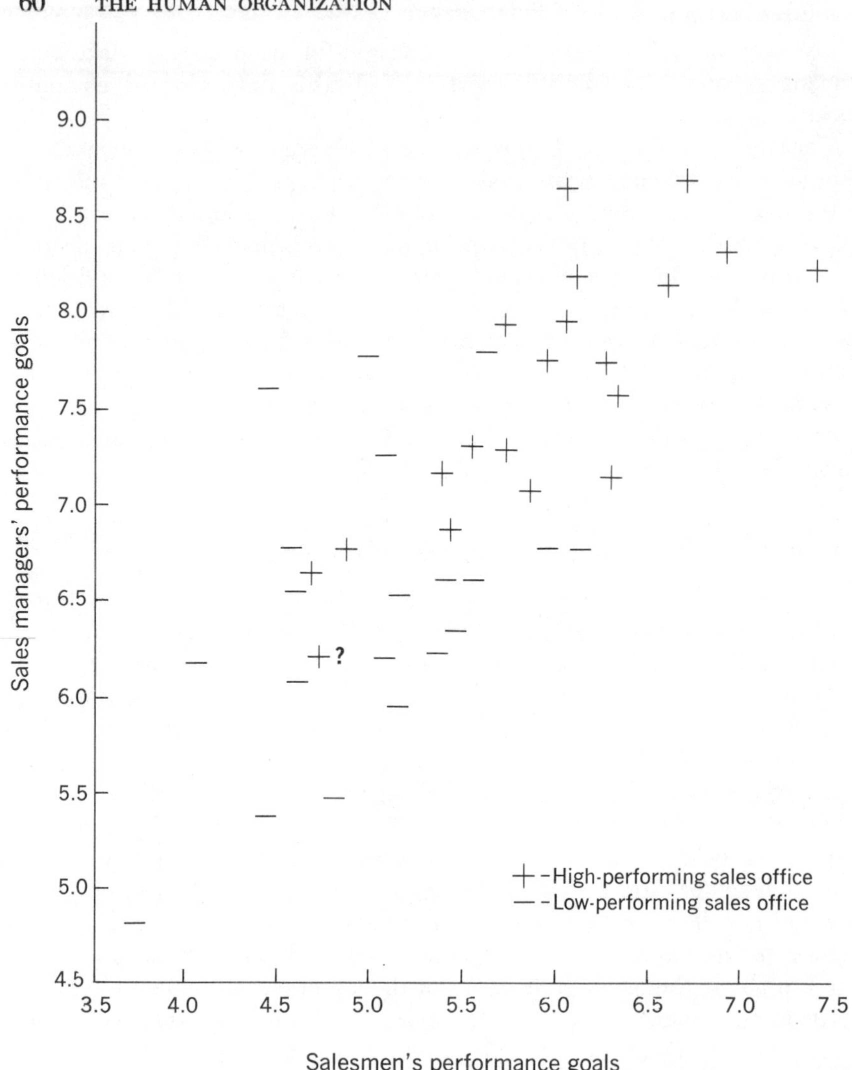

Fig. 4-4. Relation of sales office performance to sales managers' performance goals and salesmen's performance goals. (*After Rensis Likert. New patterns in sales management. In Martin R. Warshaw (Ed.), Changing perspectives in marketing management. Ann Arbor, Mich.: Univer. of Michigan Bureau of Business Research, 1962. By permission of the publishers.*)

one and one-half points lower than the performance-goal score of all of the managers (approximately 7.0).

The results in Figure 4-4 demonstrate that it is necessary for a sales manager to have high performance goals if the men in his sales office are to have high goals. Moreover, it is necessary for the manager to have higher goals and aspirations for his office and his men than he expects the men to have for themselves. The manager's performance goals for his office and the manager's organization of the job of his men exert an important influence on the goals and job organization of his men.

The third important finding revealed by Figure 4-4 is that the better units (+) are overwhelmingly in the upper right-hand part of the figure and the poorer units (−) are in the lower left-hand portion. To achieve outstanding performance, *both* the sales unit's manager and its men must have high performance goals. Both manager and men need to have a well-organized plan of operation and high sales goals. As Figure 4-4 shows, it is *not* sufficient for the manager alone to score high on job organization and performance goals.

Creating High Performance Goals among Salesmen

Three of the sales offices shown in Figure 4-4 have managers with high performance scores but men with below-average scores. All three are poorer units. These results raise the questions: What must a manager do, in addition to having high performance goals for his men and his office, to create high performance goals in his men? How does a manager assist his men to develop well-organized plans of work and to establish high sales goals in addition to having them himself?

The results in Figure 4-5 help to answer the questions. Figure 4-5 is exactly the same as Figure 4-4 except for the added dotted lines, squares, and circles. The dotted lines in Figure 4-5 mark off the upper-right quadrant of the figure. The managers in the sales offices marked off in this manner are behaving differently from the rest of the sales managers. Of the 20 sales managers in the units in this upper-right quadrant, 16 are using group methods of supervision in managing their sales organization. The other four either were not using group methods of supervision or were doing so irregularly or unskillfully. (In the figure, these four units have solid squares around them.) It is noteworthy that 17 of the 20 units in the upper-right quadrant are high-performing units.

The management practices of the other 20 offices contrast sharply with the practices used by the managers of the 20 units which we have just examined. Only one of the managers of these other offices, namely, those not in the upper-right quadrant, uses group methods of supervision. (In Figure 4-5, this office has a dotted square around it.) It is significant that in most of these other 20 units, the salesmen have lower performance goals and 17 of the 20 units are poorer offices.

In contrast to the sales offices in the upper-right quadrant, the *men* in the three sales units which are circled in Figure 4-5 have relatively low performance goals. The *managers* of these three units have high per-

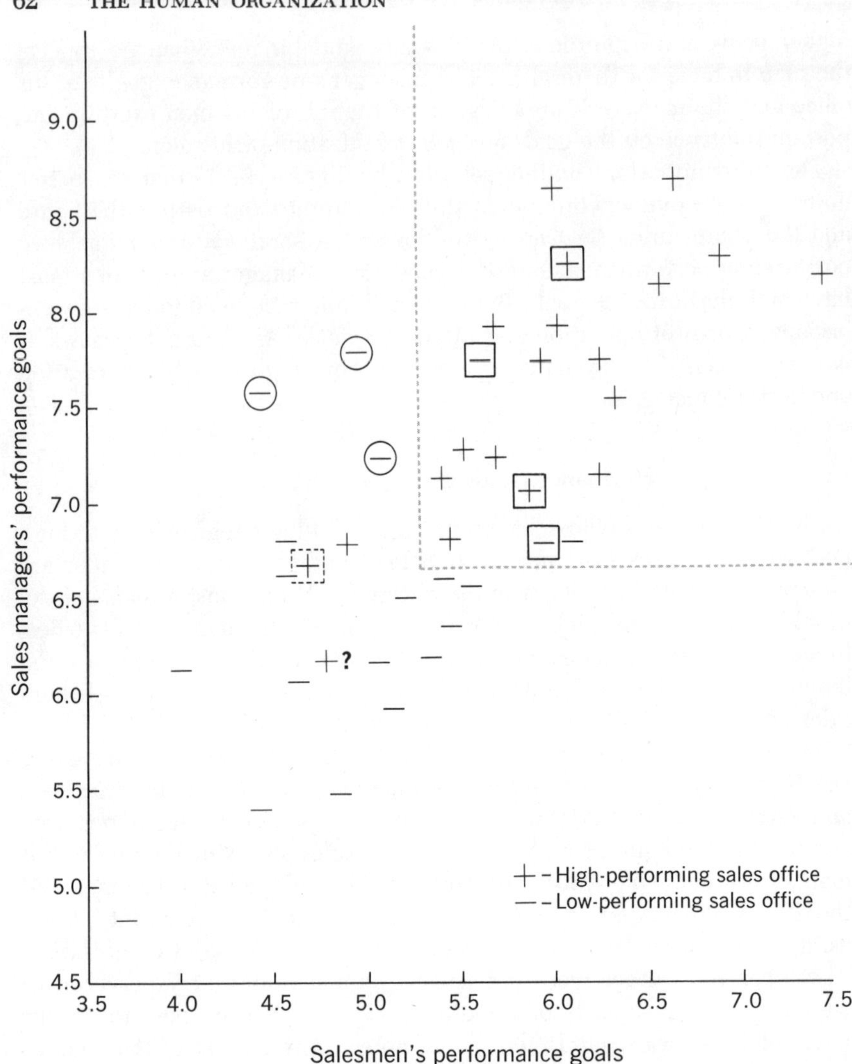

Fig. 4-5. Salesmen's performance goals as influenced by sales managers' behavior and performance goals. (*After Rensis Likert. New patterns in sales management. In Martin R. Warshaw (Ed.), Changing perspectives in marketing management. Ann Arbor, Mich.: Univer. of Michigan Bureau of Business Research, 1962. By permission of the publishers.*)

formance goals, as do the managers of units in the upper-right quadrant, but unlike the latter, these three managers have not been successful in encouraging the men in their units to set high performance goals for themselves. The men in these three units reject the high performance goals of their managers. As might be expected, there are substantial differences in the management principles employed by these three managers in comparison with the managers of the offices in the upper-right quadrant.

The managers of the three sales offices (circled in the figure) are not employing group methods of supervision. Their methods of management involve man-to-man interaction. Moreover, they are not applying the principle of supportive relationships; they have, instead, a condescending and exploitive attitude toward their men. The extent to which this is the case is shown by the poor score of these three managers with regard to their application of this principle: out of 40, they rank 38, 37, and 33.

In these three units (circled in Figure 4-5) the men not only reject high performance goals for themselves, but they also feel to a greater extent than do the men in the other units that their sales managers are putting unreasonable pressure on them to produce. Direct, managerial pressure for high performance and high performance goals (i.e., "do it or else") has been found to evoke this feeling on the part of the men quite consistently in many studies and to lead over the long run to low performance. In the light of all these facts, it is not surprising that these three circled units are, as Figure 4-5 shows, among the poorer sales units.

Contrasting sharply with these three sales offices is the one at the extreme right of Figure 4-5. This is the unit in which the men have the highest performance goals of any office. As might be expected from the preceding discussion, the manager of this office applies the principle of supportive relationships well and, in comparison with the other managers, places the greatest emphasis on teamwork and group methods of supervision. He strives hard to build a sales unit whose members pull together toward commonly accepted goals. The men respond by setting and achieving high goals for themselves. This is, as would be expected, one of the top 20 sales offices.

The data in Figures 4-4 and 4-5 point to the following conclusions:

- To achieve and maintain high performance, it is necessary that the subordinates, as well as the superiors of an organization, have high performance goals and have their work well-organized.
- Subordinates are unlikely to set high performance goals for themselves and organize their work well if their superiors do not have such aspirations for each salesman and for the whole office.
- A superior with high performance goals and excellent job organization is much more likely to have subordinates who set high goals for themselves and organize their work well when he uses group methods of supervision and applies the principle of supportive relationships effectively than when he does not.

Building Peer-group Loyalty

The preceding analysis shows that a manager who has high performance goals and excellent job organization but who relies solely on economic needs and direct pressure to motivate his men is very likely to be disappointed by their achievements. The noneconomic motives must be used fully, along with the economic needs, to create high performance goals and establish the level of motivational forces which yield high productivity. Since the principle of supportive relationships and group methods of supervision enable a manager to make effective use of the noneconomic motives, some valuable insights can be obtained by examining how these managerial principles appear to affect the motivations, satisfactions, and behavior of the members of an enterprise.

A substantial body of research findings demonstrates that the greater the loyalty of the members of a group toward the group, the greater is the motivation among the members to achieve the goals of the group, and the greater is the probability that the group will achieve its goals. If the performance goals of such groups are low, they will restrict production; if the goals are high, they will achieve outstanding performance (Cartwright & Zander, 1960).

These findings suggest that a sales manager needs to know how to develop high group loyalty among his men as well as how to assist them to establish performance goals commensurate with their potentiality. How, then, can a manager proceed so as to develop high group loyalty in his organization?

Results bearing on this question are shown in Figure 4-6. The loyalty of the men toward each other in a unit was measured and is called "peer-group loyalty score." This score is plotted along the vertical axis of Figure 4-6. The 40 sales offices were divided into four groups of 10 each on the basis of the extent to which the sales manager is applying the principle of supportive relationships, as shown by the "Sales Managers' Supportive Behavior Scores." (This is the same variable as was used on the vertical axis in Figure 4-3.) The four bars in Figure 4-6 present data for these four groups of 10 sales units each.

The bar on the right in Figure 4-6 shows the mean (average) peer-group loyalty score for the 10 sales units whose sales managers are doing the best job of applying the principle of supportive relationships. The left-hand bar in Figure 4-6 shows the results for the 10 units whose managers scored lowest on applying the principle of supportive relationships. The intermediate bars show average peer-group loyalty scores for the intermediate groups of 10 sales offices each. A marked relationship is evident in Figure 4-6 between the managers' supportive behavior scores

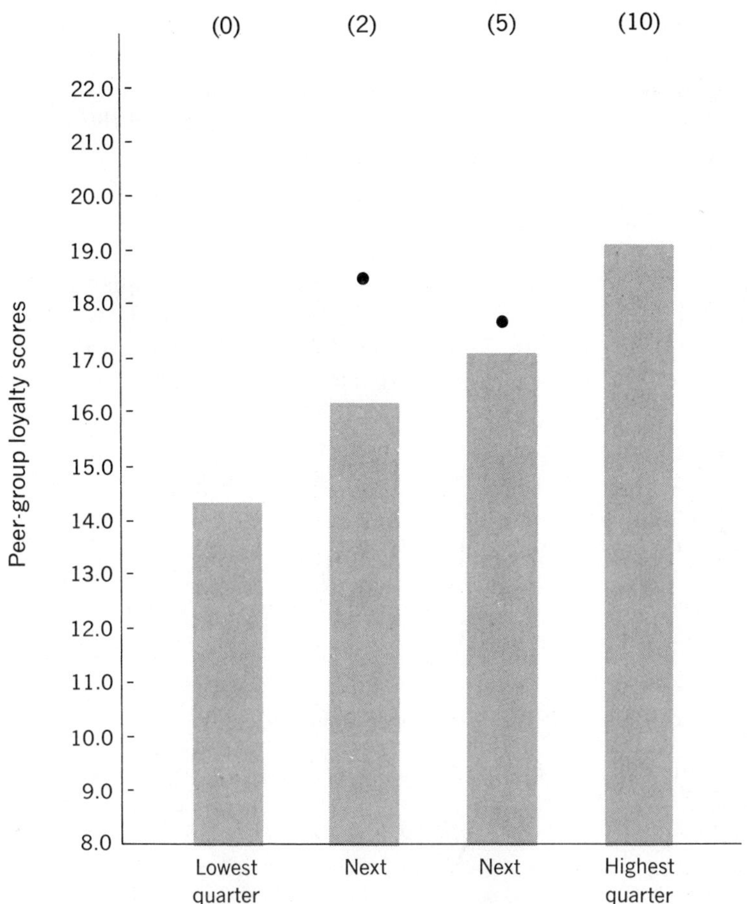

Fig. 4-6. Relation of salesmen's peer-group loyalty scores to sales managers' supportive behavior and use of group decision making. (*After Rensis Likert. New patterns in sales management. In Martin R. Warshaw (Ed.), Changing perspectives in marketing management. Ann Arbor, Mich.: Univer. of Michigan Bureau of Business Research, 1962. By permission of the publishers.*)

and the peer-group loyalty scores. In offices whose managers are applying the principle of supportive relationships most effectively, the peer-group loyalty scores are appreciably higher than in the units whose managers received low supportive behavior scores.

Managers who apply the principle of supportive relationships well are also more likely to use group methods of supervision. Both of these ways of behaving contribute to high peer-group loyalty. The number in parentheses above each bar in the figure shows the extent to which the managers in each group of 10 units are using group methods of supervision. In the right-hand bar, 10 of the 10 units are using group methods of supervision, in the next group, 5 of the 10, in the next, 2 of the 10, and in the left bar group, none of the 10.

The large dot opposite a peer-group loyalty score of 17.6, under number (5) in the figure, indicates the mean (average) peer-group loyalty score for the five sales units in that cluster of 10 whose managers use group methods of supervision. Another large black dot opposite a peer-group loyalty score of 18.2, under number (2) in the figure, indicates the mean peer-group loyalty score for the two sales units in that cluster whose managers use group methods of supervision. These scores reveal that in those offices (represented by the two bars in the center of the chart) the managers who use group methods of supervision achieve higher levels of peer-group loyalty than the managers who do not. This is consistent with the data shown by the bars on the right and left.

The data in Figure 4-6 show clearly that a manager who wishes to achieve high peer-group loyalty in his organization would be well-advised to use the principle of supportive relationships and group methods of supervision fully and effectively.

Peer-group Loyalty Is Related to Sales-office Success

An indication of the impact of peer-group loyalty upon productivity is provided when the peer-group loyalty scores of the 13 sales units in the upper-right quadrant of Figure 4-3 are compared with those of the 10 sales offices whose managers' supportive behavior scores are less than 22.00. The mean (average) peer-group loyalty score of *every* sales office in the upper-right quadrant is higher than the highest mean of any of the ten units in the lower part of Figure 4-3. Moreover, all of the 13 are high-performing sales units. Only one of the offices in the lower part of the chart was rated as high-performing, and this is the office later found to be erroneously classified as to its sales management (+?).

A unit with a high degree of group loyalty will strive hard to achieve the goals it has set for itself. We would expect such units to be high in achievement when they set high goals, low in achievement when they set low goals. This is the case, as Figure 4-7 shows. Of the 40 sales offices, those which have higher mean peer-group loyalty scores and higher mean salesmen's performance goals are appreciably more likely to be high-performing sales offices (+) than those which are lower on both of these dimensions. Of the 17 units with peer-group loyalty scores above 16.5 and salesmen's performance goals above 5.5, all but one are high-performing (+).

We can conclude that sales managers who create high peer-group

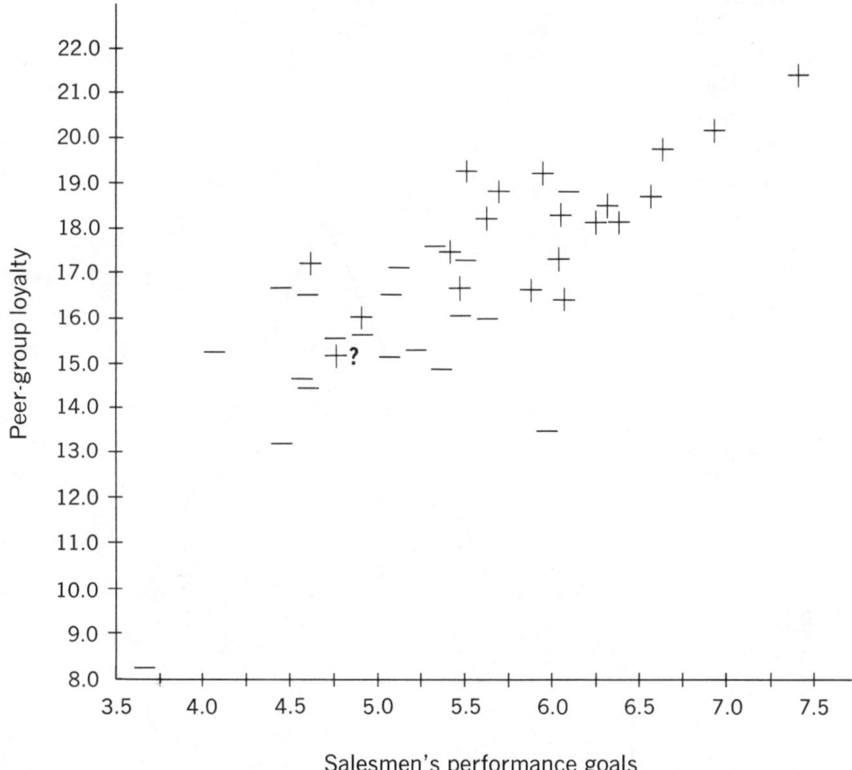

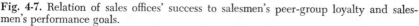

Fig. 4-7. Relation of sales offices' success to salesmen's peer-group loyalty and salesmen's performance goals.

loyalty and high performance goals among their men are likely to have highly successful sales offices. Evidently, the salesmen in such offices aid each other by joint coaching and training and by mutual encouragement and motivation. The salesmen, themselves, are performing leadership functions and contributing thereby to their own success and to that of their sales office. As we shall see, detailed analyses by Bowers and Seashore support this conclusion. The total productivity of each of these sales offices testifies to the value of this situation.

Supportive Behavior and Group Decision Making Contribute to Coordination

In Figure 4-8 the amount of influence exerted by the different hierarchical levels in the organization on the performance of the office is

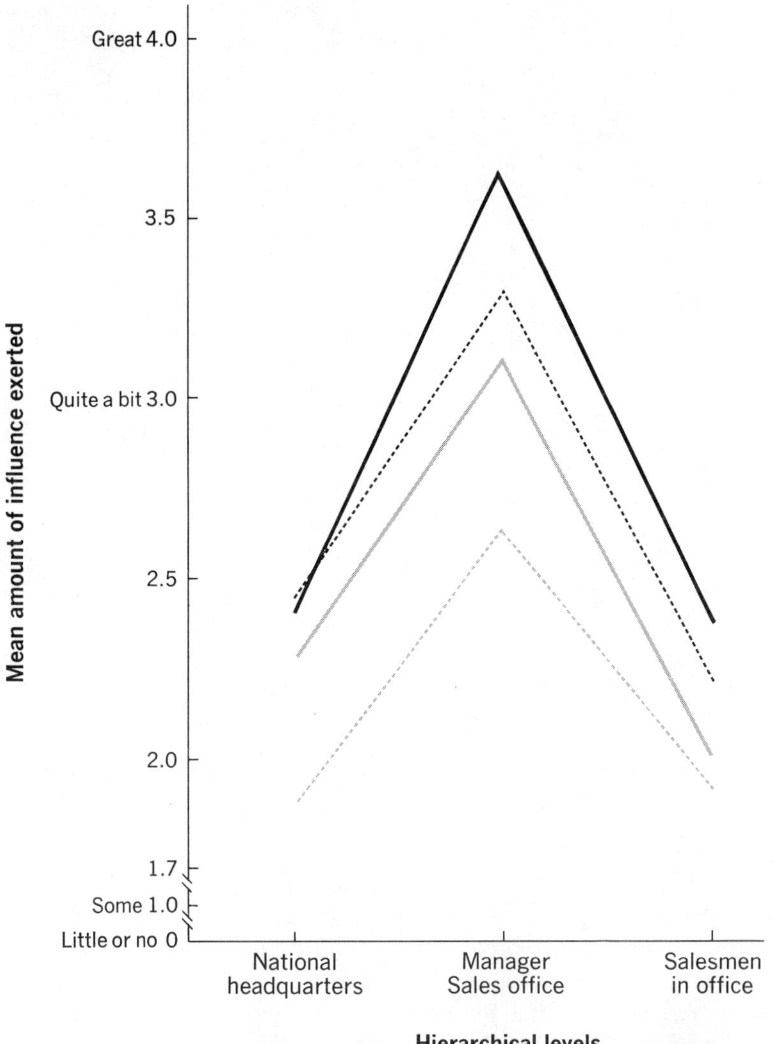

Fig. 4-8. The average amount of influence exercised (as seen by the salesmen) by the different hierarchical levels when the sales offices are clustered on the basis of the managers' supportive behavior scores.

shown for four clusters. These are the same clusters as used in Figure 4-6; i.e., the offices are grouped on the basis of the managers' supportive behavior scores. The sales offices in Cluster I rank highest on the managers' supportive behavior scores; the offices in Cluster IV are the lowest. The data on the amount of influence exerted were obtained from the salesmen in response to the question: "In general, how much say or influence do you think each of the following groups or persons actually has on matters affecting the performance of your sales office as a whole?" (Bowers, 1964; Tannenbaum, 1956; Tannenbaum, 1957).

In addition to the differences in the extent to which the manager applies the principle of supportive relationships (the managers' supportive behavior scores), the clusters in Figure 4-8 differ also, as was mentioned previously, in the managers' use of group methods of supervision. All of the managers in Cluster I use group supervision, five in Cluster II do, two in Cluster III, and none in Cluster IV.

The results in Figure 4-8 show that the more extensively a manager applies the principle of supportive relationships and uses group methods of decision making and supervision, the greater is the amount of his influence and the greater is the amount of influence the men in these offices are able to exert on matters affecting the performance of the sales office. The men's ability to exercise influence, however, is *not* obtained at the expense of the manager's capacity to exert influence. *In the high-influence offices all hierarchical levels can exert more influence: the national headquarters, the managers, and the men.* (This greater amount of total influence is represented by the greater total area under the curve for Cluster I in Figure 4-8. Cluster IV has the least influence and the smallest area under its influence curve.)

As might be expected, the clusters in Figure 4-8 differ markedly in the proportion of sales offices which are high-performing. All of the ten offices in Cluster I are high-performing, six of Cluster II are, three of Cluster III, and none in Cluster IV except the (+?) office which is misclassified as to its sales management.

These data add confirmation to early findings that the more supportively a manager behaves and the more often he uses group methods of decision making, the greater is the capacity of his organization to achieve highly coordinated efforts directed toward accomplishing its objectives and the greater is its success in attaining these objectives (Likert, 1961, Chap. 9).

In an extensive analysis of the influence process in these 40 offices, Bowers (1964) found that the total capacity to exercise influence in an office was correlated with the sales performance of the office (rank-order rho = +.46).

These four clusters differ also in the attitude among the men toward their manager. The men in Cluster I have appreciably more favorable attitudes toward their managers and see him, or their supervisor, more often as a "member of the team" than do the men in units in Cluster IV. The offices in Clusters II and III fall in intermediate positions on these variables.

An Effective Interaction-influence System Is Required for High Performance

As the data on these 40 sales offices reveal, a successful organization, even a relatively small one, is a complex social system. It takes much more than hiring competent personnel, planning well, and issuing orders to achieve outstanding performance. A complex set of interdependent, cooperative relationships exist between the manager and the men and among the men in successful enterprises.

Further evidence is available which demonstrates the value of a tightly knit, synergistic organization in achieving high levels of performance. The extent to which a highly effective interaction-influence system contributes to organizational success is revealed by classifying the 40 sales offices as to the degree of: (1) favorable attitudes in the office toward the manager and (2) favorable attitudes among the men toward each other (peer-group loyalty). When the offices were so grouped into five sets, such relationships as the following are found:

- The managers' supportive behavior scores are appreciably higher in Set I (which has the most favorable attitudes) than in Set V (where the attitudes are least favorable). Correspondingly, all managers in the offices in Set I use group methods of supervision; none does in Set V. The other three sets fall in intermediate positions on the managers' supportive behavior scores and on the use of group supervision. These data point to the necessity of a manager's using group methods of supervision and behaving supportively if he is to develop favorable attitudes toward himself and among his men.
- All the 10 offices in Set I are high-performing; none of the six in set V is high-performing.
- All of the measurements of the communication and influence processes reveal them to be working best in the Set I offices and poorest in Set V. Figure 4-9 shows, for example, for each set of offices, the mean scores of the perceptions by the salesmen of how well the manager listens and of his effectiveness in communicating upward and downward.

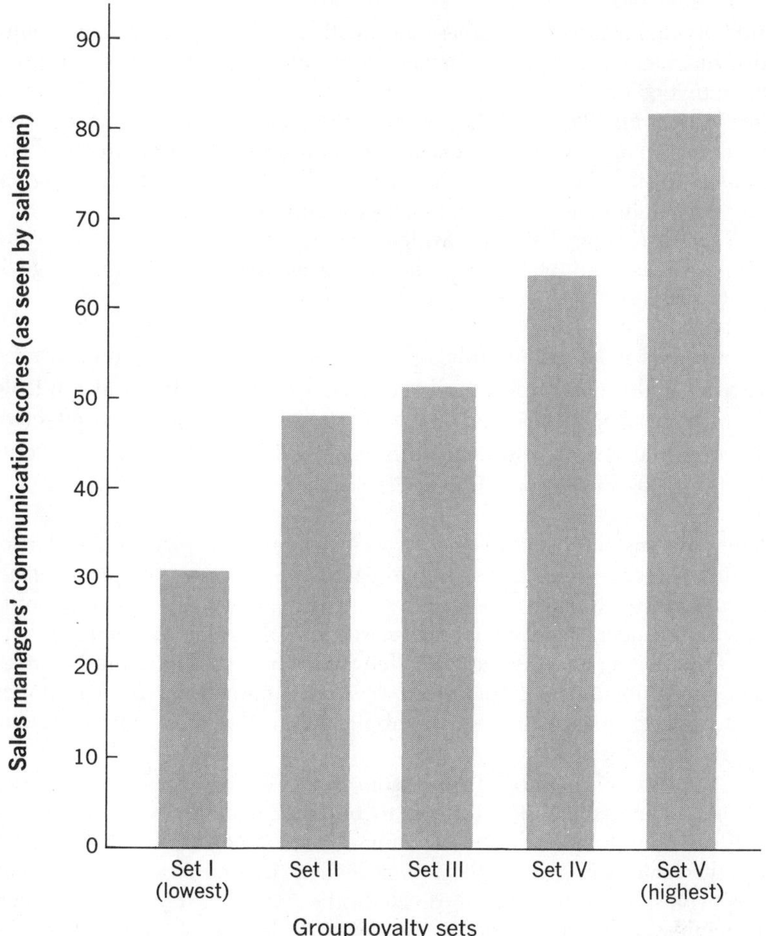

(Sales units grouped into sets on basis of attitudes of salesmen in unit toward sales manager and also toward each other [peer-group loyalty score].)

Fig. 4-9. Relationship of group loyalty sets to sales managers' communication scores.

Findings from 78 Sales Offices

Bowers and Seashore (1964) have extended their study of the 40 sales offices whose data we have been examining to include an additional 38 sales units whose performance covered more of the total range from best to poorest. In reporting their findings for the 78 offices, they propose four dimensions of leadership and then compare the relationship of these dimensions with the performance of the sales office. Their four leadership dimensions are:

1. *Support*—behavior which serves the function of increasing or maintaining the individual member's sense of personal worth and importance in the context of group activity

2. *Interaction Facilitation*—behavior which serves the function of creating or maintaining a network of interpersonal relationships among group members.

3. *Goal Emphasis*—behavior which serves the function of creating, changing, clarifying, or gaining member acceptance of group goals

4. *Work Facilitation*—behavior which serves to provide effective work methods, facilities, and technology for the accomplishment of group goals (Bowers & Seashore, 1964, p. 2).

Their analysis is based "mainly upon an inspection of the intercorrelation matrix for these variables, and secondarily upon partial and multiple correlation procedures designed to assess the joint and separate effect of various combinations of leadership dimensions." The following comments indicate their interpretation (Bowers & Seashore, 1964, pp. 5–6):

1. Our data sustain the idea that group members do engage in behavior which can be described as leadership, and that in these groups, it appears likely that the total quantity of peer leadership is at least as great as the total quantity of supervisory leadership. The groups varied greatly from one another with respect to the degree and the pattern of emphasis in peer leadership behavior.

2. The four dimensions of leadership developed initially for the description of formal leaders appear to be equally applicable to the description of leadership by group members.

3. The supervisor's pattern of leadership (i.e., relative degree of emphasis on each of the four dimensions) tends to be replicated in the leadership behavior of his subordinates; that is, the subordinates tend to provide leadership in much the same way as does the formal leader. This correspondence of pattern, however, is not so great as to preclude the possibility that some compensatory member leadership is occurring. Proof is lacking on this point. The joint effects of peer and supervisory leadership are mixed, with some instances of an additive relationship, some of substitution. None of the tested cases appears to involve a multiplicative relationship.

4. With respect to the issue of relative potency, the peer leadership variables are at least as potent as supervisory leadership variables, and possibly more so, in predicting group achievement of goals.

5. Selective impact on performance clearly occurs. Each of the peer leadership variables and each of the supervisory leadership variables appears to be selective in its impact. For example, the variable "peer goal emphasis" relates significantly to group cost performance, to the group's style of business (larger items, sold to more affluent clients, etc.) and to member satisfaction with fellow salesmen, but it does not relate significantly to such performance variables as volume of business, business growth rate, satisfaction with job. Peer goal emphasis appears in the case of these groups to play a central role, as it is either the best single predictor, or is a significant additive predictor in relation to a majority of our criteria of group performance.

With regard to point 4 in the above conclusions, it is possible that when another variable—time—is considered, supervisory leadership will prove to be the more potent. The importance of time as a variable which influences the magnitude of the relationships found among the causal, intervening, and end-result variables will be discussed in the next chapter.

Irrespective of the influence of time, however, the analysis by Bowers and Seashore provides impressive evidence of the substantial contribution to organizational success of the leadership provided by the nonsupervisory members of an organization. To find that differences in peer-leadership activities among the offices contribute to the differences among them in their performance is all the more surprising when the character of the product is considered. As was pointed out previously, these salesmen are in competition with each other to sell the same product to the same total group of prospects in the same market. They are compensated on a straight commission basis so that any time taken to coach peers or engage in other leadership processes is taken from what would otherwise be time available for income-producing selling for themselves. Nevertheless, time spent on peer leadership yields a more successful sales office and greater income to the salesmen than time spent on selling without such activity.

These findings of Bowers and Seashore are important for another reason (Bowers & Seashore, 1966). A large number of studies, starting with the famous Western Electric Hawthorne project (Roethlisberger & Dickson, 1939), have provided extensive evidence to show that "informal organization and leadership" are present in most enterprises and, as a rule, cause costly reductions in organizational performance because of the restriction of output. Very few studies are available which demonstrate that these peer-leadership processes can result equally well in increased rather than restricted production. Three studies which do so are the Coch and French (1948) experiment, the clerical experiment (Likert, 1961, Chap. 5; Morse & Reimer, 1956), and the study by Patchen (1960). The Bowers and Seashore study adds important evidence to show that peer leadership can contribute substantially to high performance and should be used positively for this purpose rather than being permitted to restrict production through the use of System 1 or 2 management.

Peer Competition Makes Inadequate Use of a Strong Motive

The data from the 40 sales offices, examined at some length in this chapter, along with the additional findings from Bowers and Seashore help to clarify the nature of System 4 management and reveal the sophisticated and effective use that science-based management can make of powerful human motives in addition to the economic needs. The data are particularly valuable in providing an important insight into how the drive for a sense of personal worth can be used more effectively than at present in achieving organizational success.

As a general practice, sales management relies heavily on the economic needs as a source of motivation. This is the case in all of the 100 sales offices of the company in which this study was conducted. The plan of compensation used by all of these offices is the same and is designed to make the most effective use of economic needs. The men are paid on a straight commission basis. But, as the data from these 40 sales offices show, reliance on the economic needs alone yields only mediocre results.

Another widespread practice among sales managers is to seek to reinforce the motivational forces from the economic needs by adding to them those forces which status and recognition can create. Contests and similar competitive procedures are used in an attempt to capitalize on each salesman's drive for a sense of personal worth. The data from these 40 sales offices, as well as results from other studies (Seashore, 1963), demonstrate that this use of the drive can and often does yield high levels of motivation and quite good sales productivity but does not yield the highest levels of motivation or sales performance. There are serious "side effects" from this use of one of man's most powerful drives which are costly to the organization in its efforts to realize its objectives.

These adverse side effects are the motivational forces created among the salesmen in an office to engage in behavior which will help only themselves and to avoid helping those with whom they are competing. Forces are created, for example, against sharing new information with the other salesmen, against telling them of better appeals, better answers to objections, better sales strategies, new markets, etc. These motivational forces also act to restrain each salesman in other ways. If he sees one of his office mates wasting time with "busy work," he is delighted. He does *not* encourage him to get out and make the calls that yield sales. Similarly, neither he nor his fellow worker feels any motivation to help the other on a tough sales problem or to ask for help. Competitive procedures pit salesman against salesman and reward each economically and with status for keeping what he knows to himself.

Although these negative forces arising from competition often may have their full impact tempered, because most members of an organization like to receive warm, friendly, supportive reactions from their colleagues, this tempering is not sufficient to yield the high levels of cooperative motivation which can be attained from making a more sophisticated use of the drive for a sense of personal worth.

The findings in this chapter show that the most successful sales managers are discovering and demonstrating that the drive for a sense of personal worth and importance when used to create competitive motivational forces yields productivity and sales performance appreciably short of the best. The best performance, lowest costs, and the highest levels of earnings and of employee satisfaction occur when the drive for a sense of personal worth is used to create strong motivational forces to *cooperate* rather than *compete* with one's peers and colleagues. The use of this motive in ways which yield cooperative rather than competitive relationships appears to yield stronger motivational forces oriented toward achieving the organization's objectives and is accompanied by positive rather than negative side effects. Subordinates aid each other and share leadership tasks rather than putting immediate self-interest ahead of long-range self-interest and organizational success.

The strong motivational forces created by competition can be used without incurring its negative consequences when the enterprise operates under a System 4 model. For example, the individual can compete with his own past record or with "par for the course." Even better, the entire sales office can compete with its own past record and with current goals the group has set for itself.

All that has been said in the preceding paragraphs about the motivation of salesmen is, of course, equally applicable to sales managers. Contests and the pitting of office against office, district against district, or region against region are all less sophisticated ways to apply the drive to achieve and maintain a sense of personal worth and importance and yield, on the average, poorer performance than applying this basic motive through science-based methods of decision making and managing.

Summary

The findings presented in this chapter are from a sales organization. They are consistent with data from many other studies. The overall consistency in the general pattern of findings indicates that the conclusions as to the nature of System 4 management have wide applicability. The nature of the specific procedures for applying System 4 management in a particular firm will vary depending upon the nature of the work and the traditions of the company. The basic principles of System 4 management, such as those examined in this chapter, are the same, however, for all situations.

The interrelationships among some of these key variables can be portrayed graphically in a useful although oversimplified form, Figure 4-10. The three kinds of variables shown in this figure are the causal, intervening, and end-result variables. These were defined early in Chapter 3 and are discussed more fully in Chapter 8 and Appendix III.

The causal variables have two essential characteristics: (1) they can

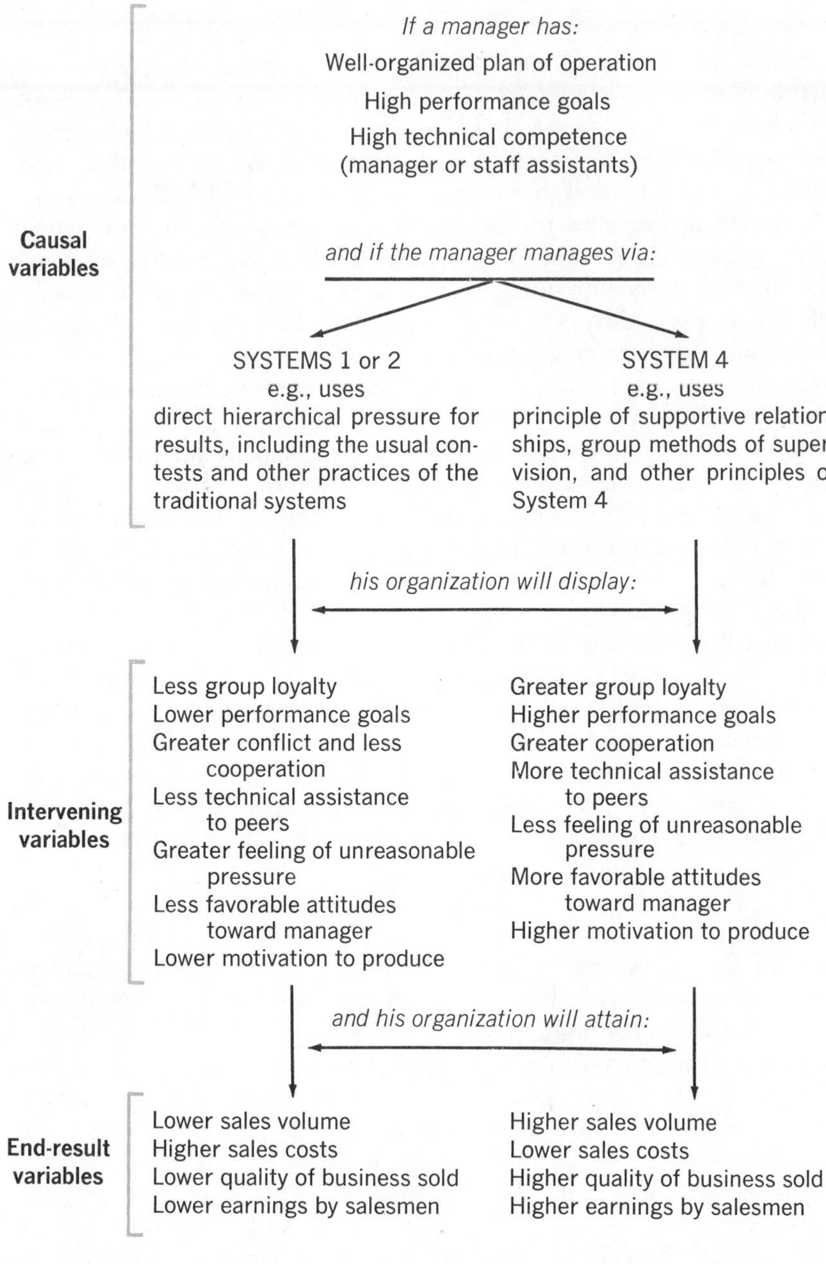

Causal variables
If a manager has:
Well-organized plan of operation
High performance goals
High technical competence (manager or staff assistants)
and if the manager manages via:
SYSTEMS 1 or 2
e.g., uses
direct hierarchical pressure for results, including the usual contests and other practices of the traditional systems
SYSTEM 4
e.g., uses
principle of supportive relationships, group methods of supervision, and other principles of System 4
his organization will display:
Intervening variables
Less group loyalty
Lower performance goals
Greater conflict and less cooperation
Less technical assistance to peers
Greater feeling of unreasonable pressure
Less favorable attitudes toward manager
Lower motivation to produce
Greater group loyalty
Higher performance goals
Greater cooperation
More technical assistance to peers
Less feeling of unreasonable pressure
More favorable attitudes toward manager
Higher motivation to produce
and his organization will attain:
End-result variables
Lower sales volume
Higher sales costs
Lower quality of business sold
Lower earnings by salesmen
Higher sales volume
Lower sales costs
Higher quality of business sold
Higher earnings by salesmen

Fig. 4-10. Sequence of developments in a well-organized enterprise, as affected by use of System 2 or System 4. (*After Rensis Likert. New patterns in sales management. In Martin R. Warshaw (Ed.), Changing perspectives in marketing management. Ann Arbor, Mich.: Univer. of Michigan Bureau of Business Research, 1962. By permission of the publishers.*)

be modified or altered by members of the organization; i.e., they are neither fixed nor controlled by external circumstances; (2) they are independent variables; i.e., when they are changed, they cause other variables to change, but they are not, as a rule, directly influenced by other variables.

The level or condition of the intervening variables, as shown in Figure 4-10, are produced largely by the causal variables and in turn have an influence upon the end-result variables. Attempts by members of the organization to improve the intervening variables by endeavoring to alter these variables directly will be much less successful, usually, than efforts directed toward modifying them through altering the causal variables. Similarly, efforts to improve the end-result variables by attempting to modify the intervening variables will usually be less effective than changing the causal variables.

The end-result variables reveal the final outcome and reflect the influence of the intervening variables upon them. The complex interrelationships among all these variables (shown schematically in Figure 4-10) are discussed more fully in Chapter 8.

Figure 4-10 indicates direction of causality and the influence of an especially important variable, time. The great impact of this variable has been largely ignored by both operating managers and social scientists, with unfortunate consequences both for company operations and for the development of organizational theory, as we shall see in the next chapter.

Chapter 5

TIME: A KEY VARIABLE IN EVALUATING MANAGEMENT SYSTEMS

Social scientists engaged in research on management and organizational performance initially expected to find a marked and consistent relationship between the management system of the leader, the attitudes and loyalties of his subordinates, and the productivity of his organization. A number of studies done in the decade following World War II revealed a variety of relationships among these variables and led me to publish the following in 1955: "On the basis of a study I did in 1937, I believed that morale and productivity were positively related; that the higher the morale, the higher the production. Substantial research findings since then have shown that this relationship is much too simple" (1955, p. 45).

Some studies (Parker, 1963) have found no relationship between the system of management and the productivity of the organization. Other studies have reported a sizable relationship (Katz, Maccoby, & Morse, 1950; Likert & Willits, 1940) between leadership style and output. Many studies find a positive relationship between employee attitudes and productivity; i.e., the more favorable the attitudes, the higher the productivity. Other research projects, however, have found a negative relationship, the poorer the attitudes the greater the productivity (Morse & Reimer, 1956). In reviewing and summarizing the relationships between the attitudes of employees and their productivity, various reviewers (e.g., Brayfield & Crockett, 1955; Herzberg, Mausner, Peterson, & Capwell, 1957; Miller & Form, 1964) have concluded generally that the various studies taken together show no consistent, dependable relationship among the variables.

These generally unexpected research findings which show widely different and often inconsistent patterns of relationship among the leadership, attitudinal, and productivity variables raise an important question.

NOTE: This chapter draws extensively upon R. Likert & S. E. Seashore, Making cost control work. *Harvard Business Rev.*, 1963, 41 (6), 96–108.

What accounts for the failure to find consistently the expected relationship among these variables?

Several factors which appear to be responsible were discussed at length in *New Patterns of Management* (pp. 13, 68–76, 91–95) and need only be mentioned here. These include (1) the difference between the leader's report of his behavior and his actual behavior; (2) inaccurate or inadequate measurements of productivity; (3) the influence of the subordinate's values, expectations, and skills upon his perception of his superior's behavior and his response to it, (4) the effect of the manager's capacity to exercise influence upward, and (5) time.

The Importance of Time as a Variable

The variable which now appears to be particularly important is time. As so often happens in research, it was the failure to obtain expected results in an experiment which called to the attention of the investigators the importance of this neglected variable. In two separate large-scale field experiments, the Institute for Social Research obtained findings contrary to the predictions which had been made when the research projects were designed. In both instances, evidence emerged in the analyses, or in subsequent developments, to show that the time intervals between changes in the causal variables and the related changes in the intervening and finally in the end-result variables took much longer than the investigators had expected.

The first study showing the importance of time was the large-scale field experiment with clerical workers by Katz, Kahn, Morse, and Reimer (Likert, 1961; Morse & Reimer, 1956; Tannenbaum, 1966). Two experimental programs involving changes in managerial and supervisory behavior were introduced. These two programs were conceptually and operationally quite different. One moved the management systems of two experimental departments toward System 1. The other program moved the management systems of the other two experimental departments toward System 4. Both experimental treatments achieved sizable increases in productivity in one year's time. The increase was 25 percent for the former program; 20 percent for the latter. But the changes in the intervening variables over the year proved to be favorable in one program (participative, i.e., toward System 4) and unfavorable in the other (hierarchically controlled, i.e., toward System 1). The movement of the intervening variables in opposite directions was substantial.

These findings suggest that the two programs differed in the degree to which they were in a state of stable or unstable equilibrium at the end of the experimental year. A reasonable inference is that the hierarchically controlled program was in an especially unstable condition: its productivity had increased appreciably, but the intervening variables, such as the perceptions, motivations, performance goals, and turnover of the personnel, had become decidedly less favorable. The participative program was in a more stable state of equilibrium: its increased productivity was accompanied by favorable changes in the intervening variables.

The expected trends through time, of course, would be toward more stable states in each; i.e., the hierarchically controlled program would be expected to achieve equilibrium either through improvement in the intervening variables or through decreased productivity. Since the causal variables in this program, e.g., direct hierarchical pressure for increased productivity, would be likely to lead to further deterioration in the intervening variables, it is most likely that equilibrium would be achieved by decreases in productivity. The participative program would be expected to attain equilibrium by maintaining and improving its productivity, since the causal variables, e.g., more supportive supervision and greater involvement in decisions related to one's work, would be likely to lead to further favorable shifts in the intervening variables.

The second large field experiment which pointed again to the importance of time was conducted by Floyd C. Mann but has not yet been reported. It involved approximately 250 persons in a service company which operates nationally. Mann was assisted by a highly competent staff man who had previously been in a line position in the firm. He was given training in organizational counseling and change before the experiment started. He and Mann worked intensively with the managerial and supervisory personnel of the experimental department. Their objective was to improve the supervision of the experimental department by changing it toward System 4.

The original planning was based on the belief that sizable changes in management style and results would be achieved in six months' time. Mann withdrew, as planned, six months after the start of the project. Measurements at the end of six months revealed the beginning of improvement in the intervening variables, e.g., in the perceptions, attitudes, and motivation of the nonsupervisory employees. It required one and one-half years, however, before significant changes in productivity became evident. The increase in productivity of the experimental department in comparison with three other (control) departments proved, nevertheless, to be both substantial (cost savings of over $60,000 per year) and enduring. There was also an impressive improvement in union-management relationships in the experimental department.

In this field experiment, as in the clerical experiment, the time intervals required both before productivity began to increase and before the situation reached a state of relative equilibrium was appreciably longer than those conducting the work had expected. *Changes in the causal variables toward System 4 apparently require an appreciable period of time before the impact of the change is fully manifest in corresponding improvement in the end-result variables.*

Correlations among Variables Indicate Influence of Time

Evidence from other sources also points to the importance of time as a major factor which influences the observed relationships among the causal, intervening, and end-result variables. When measurements of these variables are obtained at a particular point in time, the relationships among them often show a pattern which suggests that time is an important dimension affecting these relationships. For example, when the correlations among all the different causal, intervening, and end-result variables are measured at one point in time, they will often show a pattern which suggests that the closer two variables are in the causal–intervening–end-result sequence—i.e., are likely to occur or change at about the same point in time—the more marked the observed relationships tend to be. The farther apart the variables are in the sequence and the greater the probable time interval between changes in one and changes in the other, the lower the correlations tend to be.

This general pattern is shown graphically in Figure 5-1. The time intervals between the sequence of developments in the causal–intervening–end-result chain are roughly represented in Figure 5-1 by the length of the different arrows. As will be observed, the higher the intercorrelations among the variables tend to be, the shorter the arrows. This means, of course, that the shorter the time interval between any two variables in the causal–intervening–end-result sequence, the higher the correlations tend to be between the variables. The data shown in Figure 5-1 are from Mann, Indik, and Vroom (1963). Other correlation matrixes reveal the same general pattern.

The extensive data required to state *precisely* the trends in the relationships through time among the causal, intervening, and end-result variables for all of the different conditions which affect these trends are not yet at hand. There are, however, enough results available from a large number of studies and experiments to describe these trends in general terms.

Factors Hiding Trends through Time

Complex interaction among variables has tended to obscure the influence of time. A particularly important factor contributing to the complexity of the interrelationships appears to be the direction and magnitude of the changes occurring in managerial behavior. Thus, the trends in the

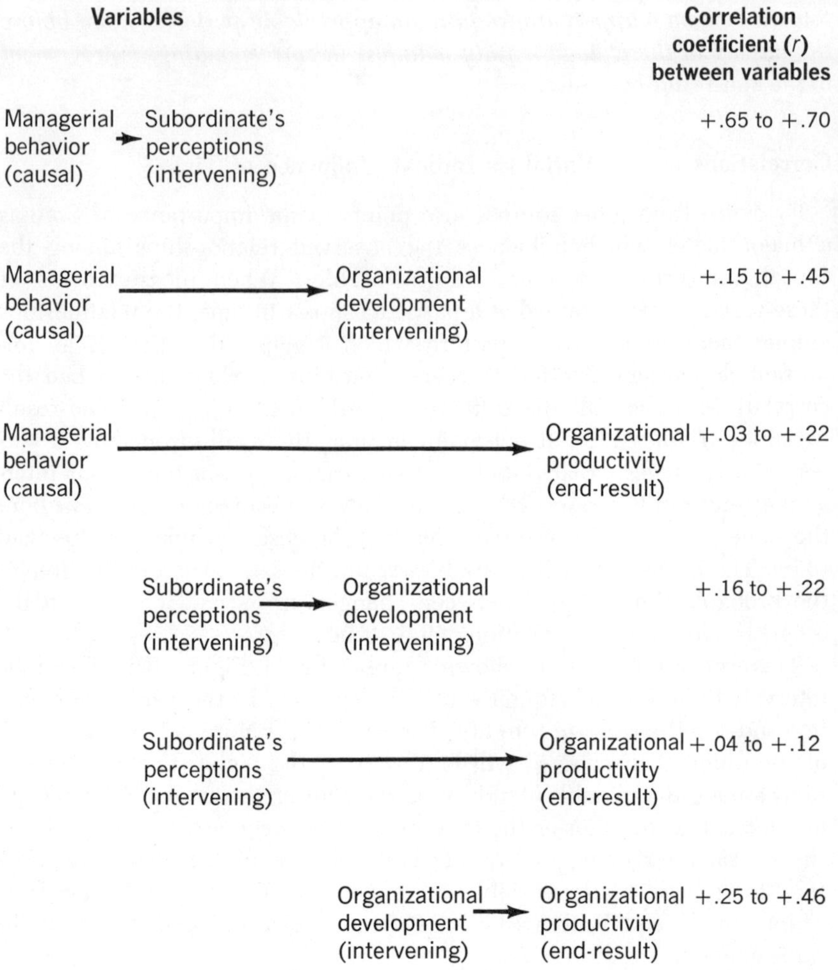

Fig. 5-1. Time intervals among variables related to the magnitude of the correlation between them. (*Data are from F. C. Mann, B. P. Indik, & V. H. Vroom.* The productivity of work groups. *Ann Arbor, Mich.: Institute for Social Research, 1963.*)

relationships among the causal, intervening, and end-result variables are quite different, depending upon the direction of the changes occurring in managerial behavior. One pattern exists when the changes are toward System 1. Quite different trends occur when the shift is toward System 4. It is necessary, consequently, to describe separately the trends through time among the causal, intervening, and end-result variables for each condition, namely, when the shift is toward System 1 and when it is toward System 4.

Shifts in the management system of a firm occur commonly in the firm's efforts to achieve higher productivity and reduce costs. The usual approach to cost reduction involves changes in the direction of tightening hierarchical controls and increasing the pressure for higher productivity and lower costs through such procedures as personnel limitations, budget cuts, and the introduction or tightening of work standards. These changes, as were mentioned in Chapter 2, represent a shift toward System 1.

A very different approach to achieving higher productivity and lower costs involves the kinds of changes introduced by the Harwood management after it had acquired the Weldon plant. These changes, described in Chapter 3, are toward System 4.

Trends through time among the causal, intervening, and end-result variables are obscured also by factors other than the direction of change in the system of management. Some of the more important of these complex, interrelated factors are:

1. The typical cost-reduction procedures, such as setting standards and pressing for higher performance, are usually applied most vigorously and extensively to operations where both product changes and such technological changes as automation occur most often.

2. A much longer time interval than is generally recognized is required before the adverse effects from the usual cost-reduction procedures begin to have an impact. As a consequence, the improvements in productivity and costs caused by automation and technological changes tend to hide, at least for a period of time, any unfavorable trends brought about by the typical cost-reduction efforts.

3. The cost and accounting data, ordinarily available, provide information which obscures the different trends occurring simultaneously in the company. These data reflect only the composite picture of all the developments affecting the productivity and earnings of the company. Some of these developments may be internal and some external to the company; some may be favorable and some unfavorable. So long as the impact on productivity and costs of each causal variable is not measured separately, it is impossible to know from the accounting data alone whether serious, unfavorable developments are being masked by favorable developments of equal or greater magnitude.

4. When the unfavorable trends in productivity, waste, costs, and labor relations caused by the usual cost-reduction procedures finally become evident, there are no measurements which point to the true causes of the adverse shifts. As a consequence, a wrong diagnosis is commonly

made; the wrong causes are blamed, and the corrective steps are often focused on the wrong variables.

Cost-reduction Sequence

The patterns shown in Figure 5-2 represent estimates of the trends which occur, or would occur, if no technological or product changes were made during the period of time examined. That is, the influence of technological and product changes are removed by holding them constant. The figure is a composite based on results from studies and field experiments made in many companies. Some of these studies have been conducted by the Institute for Social Research, some by other research organizations, and some by individual companies. A number have been published; [1] others are not yet in print. Many of those done by companies may never be published. Few of the studies deal with a time interval as long as that shown in Figure 5-2, but enough data are available to permit rough estimates of the trends for the entire period shown. (This chart was first drawn in 1962. Additional results obtained since then support the general pattern of Figure 5-2, but indicate that the time intervals may vary in different situations for reasons discussed subsequently.)

Figure 5-2 is divided into vertical columns which represent time intervals of approximately three months' duration. The horizontal rows in the exhibit represent the different factors that must be weighed in evaluating a cost-reduction program and the management system of a firm. The dotted areas represent improvement; the vertical-line areas represent an adverse trend.

The usual cost-reduction efforts with the shift toward System 1 are generally initiated by decisions at the top of the organization. The efforts of management usually are not limited to a short time period, nor are they limited in scale. They customarily extend over several years and deal with every part of the organization where it is believed that action can be taken. There is likely to be a reduction in personnel, especially in staff departments. In addition, budgets often are reduced and subject to closer control; maintenance and supply activities are often curtailed; activities with uncertain or distant value, such as research and development, are cut back; standards are introduced or extended to more jobs and tightened, and increased pressure is applied to get performance up

[1] See for example: More general summaries or reports: Argyris, 1957; Blau & Scott, 1962; Gellerman, 1963; Kahn, 1958; Katz & Kahn, 1952; Katz & Kahn, 1966; Likert, 1961; March & Simon, 1958; Tannenbaum, 1966; Whyte, 1961. Specific studies: Bowers, 1963; Dunnington, 1963; Guest, 1962; Hood, 1956; Klein, 1963; McAnly, 1956; Mann, 1957; Mann & Baumgartel, 1953; Mann, Indik & Vroom, 1963; Morse & Reimer, 1956; Seashore & Bowers, 1963; Sirota, 1963.

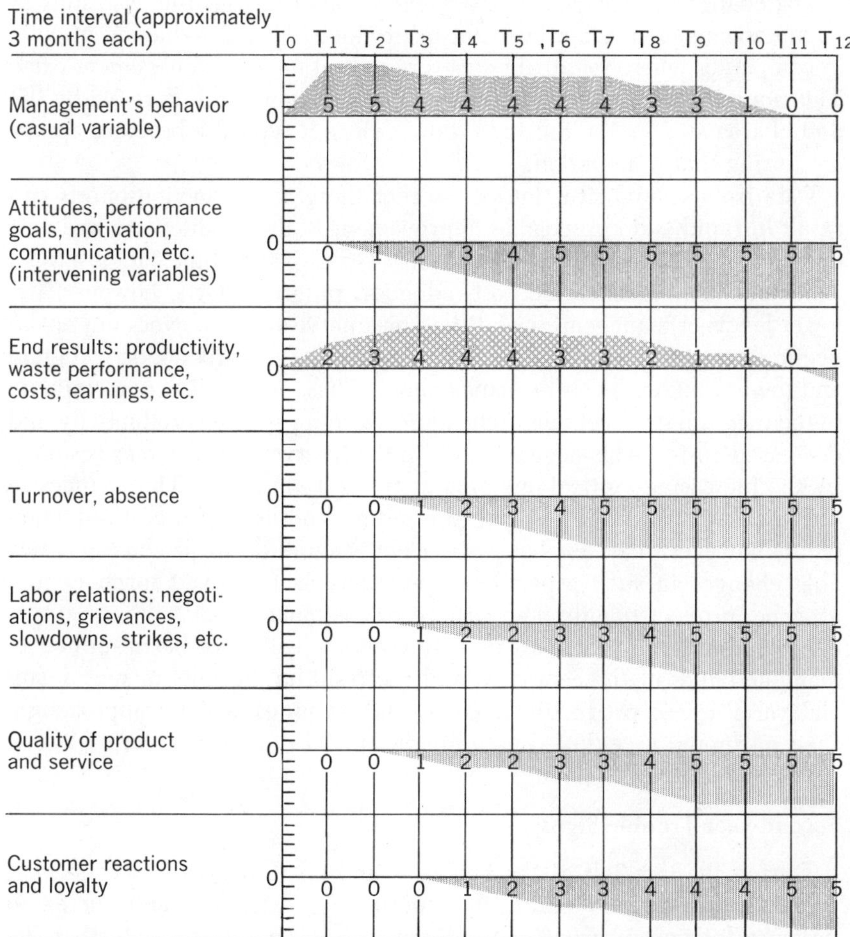

Fig. 5-2. How conventional pressures to reduce costs affect operations in a well-organized System 2 company. (*After Rensis Likert & S. E. Seashore.* Making cost control work. *Harvard Business Rev., 1963,* **41**(*6*), *96–108. By permission of the publishers.*)

to standard. (The *presence* of standards does not seem to be the important fact. The impact comes from *changing* to them, *extending* them, or *tightening* them.) This abrupt change in behavior by top management with its resulting pressures on the organization is shown by the rapid rise in the wavy-line area at T_1 in the first row of Figure 5-2. The duration of the cost-reduction effort is represented by the level of the wavy-line area. A slow decline occurs from a level of 4 at T_7 to zero at T_{11}. (The units of gain or decline are, of course, arbitrary.)

The change in management's behavior from T_0 to T_1 usually results in an almost-immediate improvement in productivity and reduction in costs in companies where reasonably good organization and management exist. This improvement in productivity and costs is shown in Figure 5-2 by the dotted area at T_1 in the third row down, since it typically becomes apparent during that time period.

Data from several situations show that these cost-reduction efforts can result in rapid and appreciable improvement in the productivity and cost figures and that this improvement lasts over a span of time (Figure 5-2).

Several months after the cost-reduction program starts, however, the lower levels of management and the nonsupervisory employees are apt to begin developing hostile reactions toward the cost-reduction program and toward higher levels of management. These reactions are in response to the increase in direct, hierarchical pressure for greater productivity and decreased costs. (This negative shift in the intervening variables is shown by the increasing vertical-line area at times T_2 and T_3.) The changes in the intervening variables during the initial months of the cost-reduction effort, however, may not be of sufficient magnitude to produce measurable changes in such aspects of operations as employee turnover and absence, product quality, and service to customers.

After about one year, cost-reduction efforts will have been applied to many activities of the company, and the resulting benefits in such financial variables as productivity, costs, and earnings will be approaching their maximum (see dotted area for the time T_3 to T_5 in Figure 5-2).

Second-year Trouble Signs

During the last half of the first year and on through the second year of the cost-reduction effort, the continuing, extended, and increased pressure for improvement in productivity and cost causes a further deterioration in the intervening variables. Attitudes, performance goals, work motivation, and the adequacy and accuracy of communication continue to shift in an unfavorable direction. For example:

- There is an increase in the proportion of both supervisory and nonsupervisory employees who resent the direct hierarchical pressure for increased production and view it as "unreasonable pressure." They are apt also to react unfavorably to many of the other related actions taken by management. Anxieties also may arise from fear of unemployment or reduced employment. These anxieties and resentments produce serious changes in attitudes and behavior.

- Confidence and trust in management decline further. Communication, both as sent and as received, becomes more filtered, biased, and distorted. The decision-making processes begin to deteriorate as the information available for company decision makers become less adequate and less accurate.
- The unfavorable trends in the attitudinal, motivational, and other intervening variables begin, in turn, to be manifest in increased turnover and absence, poorer labor relations, more concerted effort to restrict production, and less satisfactory quality of product and of service. The entire organization's capacity to function effectively begins to decrease. The poorer quality of the product and the increased hostility in employee attitudes adversely affect customers, and an unfavorable shift in customer loyalty may begin as early as the last quarter of the year. All these unfavorable developments are shown in Figure 5-2 as vertical-line areas at T_3 and subsequently. The adverse trend grows steadily, as shown in the larger vertical-line area of the figure.

Trends in waste performance during these periods will depend on the attention given by management to quality and waste control. If as much emphasis is placed on keeping waste to a minimum as is placed on achieving high productivity, then waste performance will be about as satisfactory as productivity. If not, then the adverse trend in the intervening variables is likely to cause waste and quality performance to show a similar adverse trend.

Sometime during the second or third year a very important change begins. Although pressure for cost reduction may remain high, the actual performance on costs and productivity starts to drop back from the favorable level achieved during the earlier phases of the cost push. This drop in productivity and earnings stems from several unfavorable developments in the organization: absence and turnover increase (especially turnover among the more able employees); labor relations worsen; grievances increase; slowdowns or wildcat strikes begin to occur; the quality of the product and services decreases, causing customer satisfaction and loyalty to suffer a further slump—with all that means for sales and profits.

About the end of the second year, a further important change begins. The increase in labor difficulties and in turnover among the better employees, and the greater scrap loss, poorer quality, and decreased customer satisfaction stimulate top management to start examining what is happening and why. This may lead to corrective action either at that time, or several months later.

Deterioration and Failure

About the middle of the third year, top management is likely to be compelled to take corrective action and reduce substantially the hierarchical pressure for higher productivity and lower costs. This is often precipitated by the serious labor difficulties or quality-control problems. (In one company, because of warranty problems, distributors did not want products fabricated in a plant with a history of deteriorating employee relations.) If the organizational unit involved is a particular plant or a decentralized division, top management often responds by removing the manager of that operation. The new manager is often selected for his skills in dealing with people and handling human relations problems. Often such a manager is told that his job is to reduce scrap loss, improve product and service quality, and bring a major change in the labor climate. He is expected to reduce grievances, stop wildcat strikes, and correct similar manifestations of serious supervisory and labor dissatisfaction. Pressure for high productivity and cost control is discontinued at this time, since priority is given to these other serious problems.

During the third and fourth years of such a cycle of events, even though the pressure for productivity and cost reduction is removed and attention is focused on improving human relations, there is often little improvement in the intervening variables (attitudes, motivations, performance goals, capacity for effective interaction, communication, and decision making), and little improvement in such matters as turnover, absence, labor relations, restriction of output, quality, scrap loss, and customer loyalty. When hostile attitudes, uncooperative motivations, and distrust of management are widespread and deep-seated, it often requires years for even an extremely competent manager to bring about any substantial improvement. Once middle management, supervisors, and nonsupervisory employees have lost faith in top management, the situation is hard to reverse. The same, of course, is also true of customer loyalty.

Negative Results

While no long-term study using rigorous, quantitative measurements has as yet been conducted to verify the cycle just described and shown in Figure 5-2, nevertheless this cycle conforms, as indicated earlier, to the data obtained in a number of studies, and it conforms also to the experiences of executives who have survived such cycles. The cycle just described shows what is likely to occur if the usual approach to cost reduction is followed and if there are no appreciable changes in the company's product or technology.

Modifications in the pattern may occur for various reasons:

- The duration of the cycle and of its different phases may vary, depending on the history of the organization, the labor climate of the community, the degree of pressure exerted by management to reduce costs, the competitive situation in the industry, and comparable factors.
- The full cycle described is apt to occur only when top management persists in adhering to its original strategy for reducing costs and increasing productivity. In some situations, top management detects the unfavorable developments at an early stage and promptly modifies its approach. When this happens, the general sequence of events is modified accordingly.
- If the company or division is poorly organized and under loose management, the initial response to better organization and tighter management is almost always favorable. Productivity will improve appreciably and so will the other variables. Whether this initial improvement is followed by the cycle described in Figure 5-2 will depend on the extent to which management pursues the cost-reduction steps described above.

This cycle does not appear to occur in all situations in which jobs are timed and standards set. It seems to apply only to those situations in which top management is felt to be *changing* its behavior substantially. Such changes may involve introducing standards, extending standards, pressing for higher productivity, tightening budgets, or taking other similar steps toward aggressive cost reduction.

In those companies where measured work has been used for some time, with or without piece rates, and where there is a well-established process for setting and reviewing standards which all parties involved feel is equitable, the pattern shown in Figure 5-2 does not appear to be present. Employees working under standards may, and often do, have somewhat less favorable attitudes than employees not under standards, but marked shifts seem to occur only in situations where management is changing its behavior by increasing pressure for higher productivity and lower costs.

Effects Are Obscured

If the long-range adverse consequences of the usual approach to cost reduction are as great as Figure 5-2 suggests, why do so many companies continue to use this approach rather than seek better alternatives? Why do they not recognize what is happening? As has been suggested, there appear to be several reasons.

Most cost-reduction programs occur in the context of continuing technological innovation. New products are introduced, automation is extended, production facilities and processes are improved. These generally have immediate and marked effects on the overall cost performance of the company and tend to obscure the slowly developing organizational decay that may be occurring. Even where there is evidence of developing counterforces to cost control, such as less favorable attitudes and increased grievances and other labor difficulties, these adverse developments are often neglected or are attributed to factors other than their true causes. Moreover, signs of growing organizational problems are often overlooked in the face of the certain evidence that cost improvements are in fact being achieved.

It is common, for example, for technological changes and process improvements to result in a gain substantially less than that anticipated on purely technological grounds. Similarly, such programs often take considerably longer than planned. These developments, while sobering, are usually accepted as an inevitable accompaniment of major technological changes and are not diagnosed as signs of serious deterioration in the quality of the human organization. The substantial costs of organizational deterioration are not likely to be recognized or acted upon until accounting procedures provide accurate estimates of the gains which technological improvements should yield. The actual gains could then be correctly evaluated and their deficiencies recognized.

The extent of organizational deterioration is further obscured by the accounting practice of adding to overhead those costs which are incurred when there are slowdowns or strikes. These charges should be handled so that their causes, their magnitude, and their effect on unit costs are immediately evident. If such information were given promptly to top management instead of buried in overhead figures, the likelihood of constructive action would be much greater.

A third reason for the failure to recognize the long-range adverse consequences of the usual approach to cost reduction is the absence of measurements of the causal and intervening variables. A manager's cost reports, which come in monthly or oftener, provide a sensitive barometer of the financial effects of the actions taken under the urgency of a cost-reduction program. These immediate financial results have a compelling meaning. Without measurement, information about the intervening variables concerning the motivation and behavior of his people is harder for a manager to appraise and harder to interpret. If management is to be aware of the events pictured in Figure 5-2, there must be assessment of the causal and intervening variables to make this kind of information available periodically and in a form that illuminates the trend of events. This is likely to require the measurement at regular intervals of all three kinds of variables, i.e., causal, intervening, and end-result, for the same operating units and the full analysis of the interrelationships and trends among these variables.

A fourth reason for the failure to recognize growing organizational problems arises out of the time delay pictured in Figure 5-2. Many of the adverse consequences of crash cost programs appear several months after the effort begins and are not easily associated with their earlier causes. The more drastic consequences, such as loss of key personnel or costly labor difficulties, may not take place until long after the main cost push is past. To discern the connection between events so separated in time is not easy for busy managers under pressure for early results.

The System 4 Approach to Cost Control

What is the sequence of changes which occur when the cost reduction efforts and attempts to improve productivity involve a shift toward science-based management, such as System 4?

This pattern of trends is shown in Figure 5-3 and is based on data pieced together from many different sources. Much of the data have not yet been published. Some are from studies conducted by the Institute for Social Research; other results come from observations by other organizations. The number of employees in the more carefully controlled studies involving a shift toward System 4 has varied from approximately one hundred to several hundred. Most of the projects extend over several supervisory or managerial levels (Bowers, 1963; Coch & French, 1948; French, Ross, Kirby, Nelson & Smyth, 1958; Mann, 1957; Morse & Reimer, 1956; Seashore & Bowers, 1963).

The time intervals and the particular sequence shown represent estimates of the overall pattern. The sequence of developments and the timing will, of course, vary from company to company and by product. It will depend also on management's behavior, as well as on the history and current situation of the company.

When a management seeks to achieve continuous cost control and improvement by applying System 4 management, full use is made of all relevant existing technologies. Effective use is made of work simplification, automation, setting of organizational building and performance goals, measurement of success in achieving these goals, and similar procedures. These resources are used, however, with a fundamentally different set of motivational assumptions and principles from that used in System 1, as Table 3-1 illustrates.

First Signs of Change

The application of this new approach requires that managers and supervisors first learn the relevant principles, master their application,

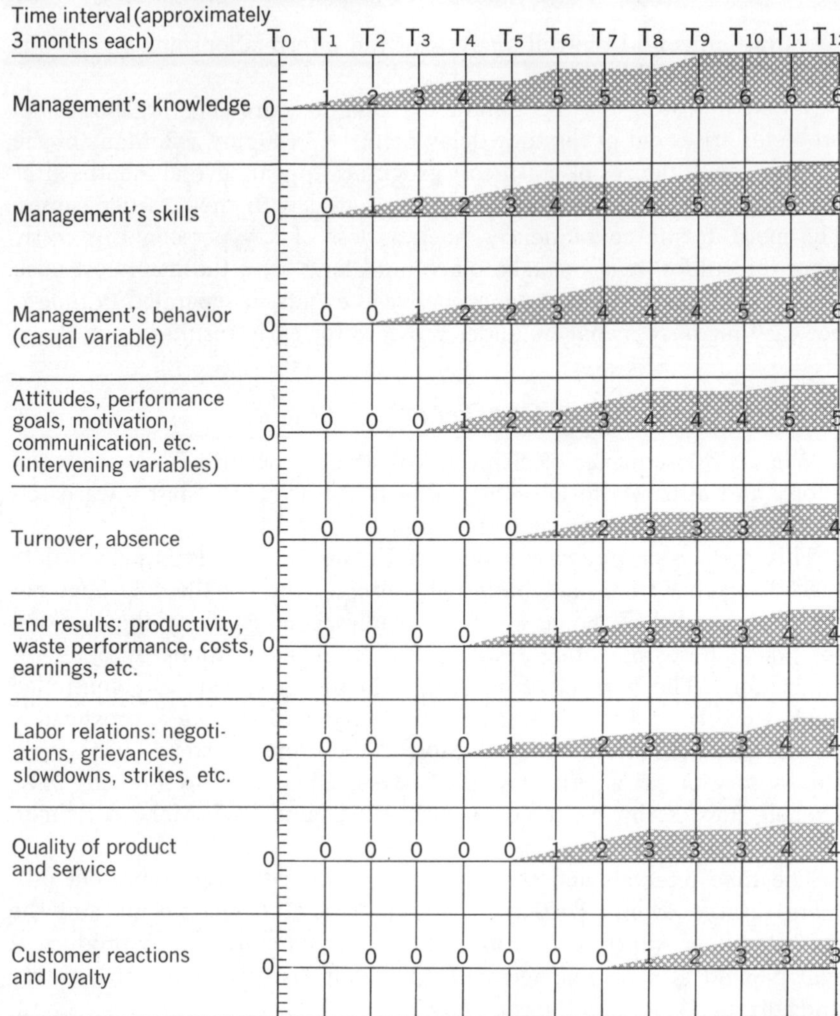

Fig. 5-3. How the shift toward System 4 management improves performance and reduces costs. (*After Rensis Likert & S. E. Seashore.* Making cost control work. *Harvard Business Rev., 1963,* **41**(*6*), *96–108. By permission of the publishers.*)

and develop the behavioral skills to use them on the job. This may require managers to make important changes in their concepts about how to manage and to change some of their attitudes and values (Blake & Mouton, 1964; Bowers, 1963; Bradford, Gibb, & Benne, 1963; Likert, 1959; Maier, 1963; Maier & Hayes, 1962; Mann, 1957; Marrow, 1964a; Rice, 1965; Schein & Bennis, 1965).

Several months are required for this learning and skill development.

Still more time must be spent before all the different levels of management and supervision are applying their new learning sufficiently well for subordinates to become aware of the change in their superiors' behavior. (Some managers, of course, will be already using many of the principles and practices of this new approach, and for them, progress will be faster.) Usually, it will take about a year before subordinates at each hierarchical level experience a sufficient amount of change in a sufficient number of circumstances to be persuaded that the management system of the organization is really changing, that superiors are really behaving more supportively, displaying greater confidence and trust, communicating more adequately, involving subordinates more fully in group decisions about their work, and so forth. When this does happen, the situation as revealed by the intervening variables will show an improvement. (See the dotted area starting about T_4 in the fourth row down in Figure 5-3.)

Steady Gains

As managers and supervisors acquire more learning and skill in applying the proposed system of management and as information from the measurements of the intervening variables helps to guide their actions, their subordinates' experiences and perceptions become progressively more favorable. As a consequence, measurements of the intervening variables show steady improvement during the second year. (Note the wider dotted area in Figure 5-3.)

Improvement in the intervening variables, as reflected in their measurements, means that communication is improving, loyalty is greater, performance goals are higher, the organization is more tightly knit, and the interaction-influence system is more effective. There is greater coordination of effort; decisions are based on more accurate information, and there is greater motivation to achieve the organization's objectives. This improvement in the organization, as shown by the measurements of the intervening variables, is reflected only gradually, however, in improved productivity, waste performance, and reduced costs.

After substantial and continued improvement in attitudes, communication, confidence and trust, performance goals, and so on, the end-result variables begin to reflect increases in productivity and quality and reduction in costs, scrap loss, and waste. The organization begins a concerted effort to eliminate inefficiencies and to improve products and processes. About this time, corresponding improvement in turnover, absence, and labor relations also becomes evident.

The general trend of steady but impressive improvement continues through the third and subsequent years. In other words, although improvement starts slowly with this approach to better management and reduced costs, it continues steadily until highly favorable levels are obtained.

Sometimes reduction in costs must be brought about quite rapidly. When this is the case, the circumstances forcing the rapid cost reduction can be used as "situational requirements." These are the hard facts of life which the firm must recognize and cope with if it is to survive in its present form. Since virtually all members of the enterprise are eager to have it survive in a financially viable form, because of the relation of its success to their own well-being, they usually are quite willing to act fast and drastically to meet whatever financial emergency is threatening. Under such circumstances, the decision-making groups often take more drastic steps than their superiors would take if they were making the decisions by themselves. These decision-making groups also are moved to implement their decisions conscientiously. Although Figure 5-3 reflects the usual rate of improvement, cost reduction using a System 4 approach can occur much more rapidly when the "situational requirements" such as the firm's impending financial failure make it necessary.

Asset Building Is Unrecognized

An ironic fact is revealed by the trends shown in Figure 5-3. Corporate officers and boards of directors as a rule receive no reports to make them aware of the existence of these trends, even when they occur in departments or plants of their own enterprise. This is due to the inadequacies of present accounting procedures and the lack of other measurements to reveal what is really happening in the corporation. In almost every study the Institute for Social Research has conducted, we have found managers whose style of management yielded results more like Figure 5-3 than 5-2. In a large proportion of these cases, top management did not recognize that these managers were *adding* to the income-producing assets of the company rather than leaving them unchanged or liquidating them. Since the contribution of these managers to the income-producing assets and financial success of the corporation was not recognized, they usually went unrewarded both financially and in promotions. Moreover, in many companies these managers experienced difficulty in maintaining their System 4 style of management (Figure 5-3). They found themselves in trouble with their own superiors because they did not put as much hierarchical pressure for increased productivity on their subordinate managers as their own superior desired.

An important conclusion is evident from Figures 5-2 and 5-3 and the related discussion. All of the major organizational variables must be measured over a longer period of time than was thought to be necessary when the field experiments of the Institute for Social Research were initiated. Unfortunately, this was not discovered until after the first two of the more rigorous experimental studies were completed. As a consequence, none of the more carefully controlled field experiments which have been completed to date has continued to measure the causal, intervening, and end-result variables for as long a period of time as we now know is necesasry to explore fully all the developments occurring as this proposed system of management is applied in an organization. All the variables need to be measured for at least three years and preferably five.

Cash from Liquidation Is Not Earnings

The top management of many companies may share the point of view of one company officer who observed that to give a plant manager three to five years for building an effective organization is a long period of grace from full earning requirements. He felt this to be particularly unrealistic if the plant were manufacturing products or using a technology likely to become obsolete within that period of time. As we shall see in subsequent chapters, if the income-producing value of the human organization is taken into consideration, there is no need to give a manager three to five years of grace. When the total income-producing assets of a firm are taken into account, it becomes evident that the science-based management approach to cost control will generally meet current earning requirements in the first and subsequent years. It may not, however, meet the need for short-term improvement in a firm's cash account. If a corporation needs cash, it would do better to liquidate inventories. Inventories can be replaced readily, but highly effective human organizations cannot. Time is required, as well as sizable investments, to rebuild any liquidation of customer loyalty and of the human organization of an enterprise.

Any plant now manufacturing a product or using a process likely to become obsolete in the near future is necessarily going to have to introduce major product or process changes in order to survive. In such circumstances, it is especially important to have an organization capable of making these changes successfully. It would seem desirable for top management, consequently, to help the manager of such a plant build a System 4 organization that is capable of introducing both product and technological changes smoothly, rapidly, and successfully.

This can be done by using the System 4 approach to cost control which, while reducing costs, is simultaneously building a more flexible organization. Such an organization can make more timely, more rapid, and more successful use of automation, technological changes, and product changes than can a System 2 firm (Coch & French, 1948; French, Ross, Kirby,

Nelson, & Smyth, 1958; Mann & Neff, 1961; Ronken & Lawrence, 1952). This flexibility is due to the greater cooperative motivation and more effective communication and coordination present in System 4 organizations.

The motivation of the members of an organization can be crucial in determining whether labor-saving processes—computers or automated equipment—are made to work well or poorly. Supervisory and nonsupervisory employees, if they wish to do so, can make excellent equipment perform unsatisfactorily and with frequent failures. These employees can also, if they desire to do so, rapidly eliminate the inadequacies in new processes or equipment and have the operation running smoothly in a surprisingly short time.

Source of Incompatible Points of View

The general patterns presented in Figures 5-2 and 5-3 provide a basis for understanding how managers can simultaneously hold such contradictory views as (1) management systems more toward System 4, i.e., to the right in Table 3-1, are, on the average, the more productive, and (2) to increase productivity and reduce costs, management should use the usual cost-reduction procedures which involve a move toward System 1. These conflicting views are readily drawn from the extensive accounting reports currently available. As Figure 5-3 reveals, as the management system of a company becomes more like System 4, the long-range developments in the organization are toward higher and higher productivity and lower costs. Hence, as managers observe those departments which achieve long-range, high productivity, they have evidence which supports the view that management systems more toward System 4 are the more productive. Figure 5-2 and the accompanying discussion reveal why managers believe that the usual approach to cost reduction improves earnings, when in fact it usually does not. The results are deceptive, since this approach may improve the cash position of a company but does so by obtaining fictitious, "watered" earnings through liquidating part of the firm's human assets. The income-producing value both of the company's human organization and of its customer goodwill is usually reduced by an amount even greater than the amount of "water" in current earnings.

The contradictory views which managers now hold can exist only so long as the trends and relationships through time among the causal, intervening, and end-result variables are unknown or ignored. As soon as these relationships are known and recognized, an entirely different conclusion emerges, as we have seen.

Systematic data on the trends through time among the causal, intervening, and end-result variables are now being obtained by the Institute for Social Research. Studies will be conducted in a variety of industries, for widely different kinds of work, for different systems of management, and for different patterns of shifts in the management systems. The research will include the effect of all of these factors, since it is known that they exert an influence on the relationships through time among the causal, intervening, and end-result variables.

Major Causes of Lack of Consistent Relationships in Research Findings

Early in this chapter mention was made of the discrepancies in findings obtained by social science investigators in the relationships among such variables as leadership styles (causal), subordinates' attitudes (intervening), and individual or organizational productivity (end-result). The trend patterns shown in Figures 5-2 and 5-3 provide the evidence to help explain a substantial amount of these discrepancies. This can be illustrated by a hypothetical example.

Let us suppose that a researcher collected data on 30 comparable departments or units. The relationships which he might obtain in a particular study among such variables as leadership style, attitudes, and productivity would vary depending upon the mixture among the 30 departments with regard to (1) whether there is a change underway in the management system of any of the departments and the direction of the change, i.e., whether the change is like that in Figure 5-2 or that in Figure 5-3; and (2) where each department is in the time cycle of the change (Figures 5-2 and 5-3).

Before discussing the influence of these conditions, it will be well to point out that other factors, such as variations in the size of the department and in the kind of work being done, can also affect the relationships found in a particular study among the causal, intervening, and end-result variables. Size tends to affect adversely the intervening and end-result variables, the larger the department, the less favorable the attitudes and the poorer the performance. When the departments involved in a study vary in size, consequently, the relationships observed may reflect the influence of the differences in size as much as or more than they reflect the true relationships actually existing among the causal, intervening, and end-result variables. The kind of work done by a department influences the relationships among the variables, since the time intervals between the changes (shown in Figures 5-2 and 5-3) tend to be much shorter for complex and varied tasks, such as research, than for routine, machine-paced operations.

Although both size and kind of work may influence the interrelationships which might be found among the causal, intervening, and end-result variables in a particular study, let us ignore them for the moment to keep our illustration from becoming too complex. As Table 5-1 illustrates, variations in (1) whether a change is occurring in the management system and the direction of the change and (2) the position of each department in the time cycle can yield positive, negative, or no (chance) correlations among the causal, intervening, and end-result variables for our investigator's 30 departments. The relationship he obtains will depend on the mix among the departments of (1) those shifting toward System 1 (Figure 5-2), (2) those shifting toward System 4 (Figure 5-3), and (3) the position of each of these departments in the time cycle (where each falls between T_0 and T_{12}). His data could show that favorable attitudes and high loyalty are associated with high productivity, with low productivity, or that no relationship other than chance exists. Similarly, he could find that System 1 or 2 management is more productive than System 4, or he could find the converse.

In considering the material in Table 5-1, it is necessary to keep in mind that the wavy-line gray area representing changes in management's behavior at the top of Figure 5-2 represents *negative* rather than positive behavior. This area represents direct, hierarchical pressure which is seen by subordinates as threatening and unreasonable behavior. This is violating rather than applying the principle of supportive relationships.

Depending, therefore, upon whether changes are occurring in the management systems of some or all of the 30 departments, the direction of the change, and the point in the time cycle for each department when the measurements were made, our investigator could readily obtain the wide range in relationships which various investigators have in fact reported and which we discussed at the beginning of this chapter. The likelihood of obtaining widely different findings from study to study would, of course, be increased when the influence of such other factors as size and kind of work are added.

Consistent Relationships Exist among Causal, Intervening, and End-result Variables

Table 5-1 and the preceding analysis help to explain the wide variation in results which different social science investigators have found among the causal, intervening, and end-result variables. The interrelationships among these variables are much more complex and are affected by many more factors than was originally anticipated. Nevertheless, as Figures 5-2 and 5-3 and Table 5-1 reveal, the available evidence indicates that there are consistent and dependable relationships among the causal, intervening, and end-result variables. When all of the relevant factors are taken

Table 5-1

Illustrative Interrelationships among such Variables as Leadership Style, Employee Attitudes, and Productivity as Influenced by Time, the Mix of the Departments, and the Character of Change in the Management System Being Used

Assuming data are being collected from 30 departments, any of the following relationships could be obtained among the variables depending upon the conditions as stated below:

I. The intercorrelations among leadership style, attitudes, and productivity would all be positive (high on one variable is associated with being high on the other) if approximately:

10 departments were at $T_8 \rightarrow T_{12}$ in Figure 5-2
10 departments were at $T_8 \rightarrow T_{12}$ in Figure 5-3
10 departments were at $T_0 \rightarrow T_1$ in Figure 5-2
or at $T_0 \rightarrow T_5$ in Figure 5-3

II. The intercorrelations between leadership style and productivity would be negative (high on one associated with low on the other) if approximately:

10 departments were at $T_2 \rightarrow T_7$ in Figure 5-2
10 departments were at $T_3 \rightarrow T_6$ in Figure 5-3
10 departments were at $T_0 \rightarrow T_1$ in Figure 5-2
or at $T_0 \rightarrow T_2$ in Figure 5-3

III. The intercorrelations between attitudes and productivity would be negative if approximately:

10 to 20 departments were at $T_2 \rightarrow T_7$ in Figure 5-2
10 to 20 departments were at $T_0 \rightarrow T_1$ in Figure 5-2
or at $T_0 \rightarrow T_5$ in Figure 5-3

IV. The intercorrelations among leadership style and productivity would be so small as to be negligible if approximately:

10 departments were at $T_0 \rightarrow T_1$ in Figure 5-2
or at $T_0 \rightarrow T_4$ in Figure 5-3
10 departments were at $T_2 \rightarrow T_7$ in Figure 5-2
10 departments were at $T_5 \rightarrow T_{10}$ in Figure 5-3

into consideration, especially time, and the proper analyses made, consistent, positive relationships can be expected among the causal, intervening, and end-result variables in every organization.

As these dependable relationships become clear, managers will have unequivocal evidence concerning the effectiveness of different management systems. This will enable them to improve their art of management and the success of their enterprise by shifting to science-based management.

Improvement in the Control Processes

Recognition that there are consistent, dependable, and marked relationships among the causal, intervening, and end-result variables will profoundly alter the control processes of corporations as well as change their management systems.

All end-result measurements give "after-the-fact" data. This is true of measurements of production, scrap, costs, earnings, and all other financial data. As successful business management has demonstrated, these measurements are valuable. Nevertheless their predictive power is limited. All too often, end-result measurements can be used only to lock the barn door after the horse is stolen. Periodic measurement of the causal and intervening variables can supply "before-the-fact" information. If these data are used, plans will be sounder; programs will be more effective, and the need for emergency action substantially reduced.

Firms using Systems 1 and 2 management, however, cannot make as full use as can System 4 organizations of measurements providing this lead time. The focus in Systems 1 and 2 on direction and control force a concentration of attention on end-result variables. Moreover, it is much more difficult to get accurate information on the causal and intervening variables in a System 1 or 2 operation than in an organization using System 4. As we shall see in Chapter 9, the methods for measuring these variables require the kind of cooperative motivation among members of the organization which System 4, but not System 1 or 2, creates.

The capacity of System 4 to secure accurate information on the causal and intervening variables and the predictive value of these data enable System 4 firms to make use of these measurements which provide lead time. Attention can be concentrated on building a highly motivated, highly effective human organization. The end-result variables are important, of course, and must be watched carefully, but satisfactory costs and earnings will be assured to a much greater extent when the central task of management is perceived as building and maintaining a highly effective interaction-influence system. A most important function of management in System 4 enterprises, consequently, is building and maintaining the human organizations through which all else is accomplished.

A doctoral dissertation completed by Yuchtman (1966) has confirmed the importance of time as a key factor influencing the relationships among the causal, intervening, and end-result variables. He found, for example, that for even a single year, correlations between causal and end-result variables increased over those for a single point in time. Causal variables for the year 1961 produced 13 significant correlations with end-result variables for that same year, and 24 for the following year.

Chapter 6

IMPROVING GENERAL MANAGEMENT BY BETTER FISCAL MANAGEMENT

In *My Years with General Motors,* Alfred P. Sloan, Jr. (1964), reported that of the $33,362,000 General Motors paid for the purchase of the Adam Opel A. G. auto firm in 1928, approximately 60 percent was for the tangible assets and the other 40 percent was for the nontangible assets, including goodwill. Sloan felt that this amount for the nontangible assets was reasonable: "For us to build or equip for manufacturing a new factory in Germany would require at least two or three years before operations could be put on an efficient and profitable basis. The amount paid Opel in excess of net assets would be returned within the time required to start from the ground up" (Sloan, 1964, p. 326).

The payment by General Motors of a sum two-thirds as great as the amount paid for the physical assets of Opel reflects the substantial investments which this and other corporations have in such nonphysical assets as their human organization and customer goodwill. Further evidence of the magnitude of this investment is provided by the prices companies in other industries pay for firms which they acquire. It is not uncommon for corporations to estimate the value of the physical assets of such firms as amounting to no more than 40 to 60 percent of the purchase price. In some situations, the value of the physical assets are reported as being no more than 20 percent of the amount paid for the organization.

There is another way of estimating the size of this investment in the nonphysical assets. Their value is reflected to a considerable degree in the stock market prices. For example, the total shares of one sizable corporation multiplied by the current value of each share amounts to $3.6 billion. The annual report of this corporation shows its net physical and financial assets to be $2.0 billion. Thus the investors who own the corporation place a market value of $1.6 billion on the nonphysical assets. The human resources of this corporation represent a substantial proportion of this $1.6 billion.

Similar computations have been made for more than a dozen large and highly regarded corporations. In all of these firms, the market value (computed by multiplying the shares of stock outstanding times the market price of each share) is much larger than the shareowners' equity as stated in the annual report. The ratio of the latter of these two figures to the former varies substantially and appears to be related, as might be expected, to the nature of the firms' business. This ratio of shareholders' equity to the market value of the firm tends to be relatively small (one-sixth to one-third) for firms which invest substantial sums in research, such as those in the automotive, chemical, electrical, or electronic industries. It is much larger (two-thirds) in such industries as the food chains. Since the shareholders' equity reflects those assets of the firm which are accounted for, the *unaccounted* assets of these firms as a percentage of their market value vary from 35 to 85 percent.

The market value of a firm is much larger than the shareholders' equity, since it takes into consideration all of the resources and income-producing assets of the firm. The assets not reflected in the balance sheet include, of course, not only the value of the human organization and customer goodwill, but also reflect the value of patents, plant, equipment, and land in excess of book value. Some of these exceed book value because of the use of accelerated depreciation, others because of appreciation due to inflation. Nevertheless, the total amount of the assets not covered in the balance sheet of most firms is so large that the actual value of their human organization and of their customer goodwill is clearly substantial. These income-producing resources of corporations are not yet being safeguarded by having accurate, quantitative tabs kept on them.

Income from Liquidation Is Not Earnings

Firms are now basing important policy decisions on something like 25 to 50 percent accounting because of the magnitude of the income-producing assets not yet included in financial reports. When a corporate management's decisions depend upon the trends and changes in one-fourth to one-half of its income-producing assets, the information used to guide policy decisions is necessarily inadequate and often misleading.

An example will illustrate how readily this can happen. Take the case of the following firm:

- Number of shares issued: 50 million
- Current value of share on market: $50
- Market value of firm (50 million × $50): $2.5 billion
- Shareholders' equity: $500 million
- Proportion of income-producing assets accounted for: 20 percent

- Earnings last year: $125 million
- Payroll last year: $350 million

This firm manufactures complex equipment. Some of the key managers of this highly successful company were asked the following question: "Assume that tomorrow morning every position in the firm is vacant, that all of the present jobs are there, all of the present plants, offices, equipment, patents, and all financial resources but no people, how long would it take and how much would it cost to hire personnel to fill all of the present jobs, to train them to their present level of competence, and to build them into the well-knit organization which now exists?" The first spontaneous response was, "If the company faced that situation, we would never make it in today's highly competitive market."

These key managers then went on to say, "It would take us several years and it would cost us at least twice our annual payroll to build the human organization that we have today." Twice their payroll is 2 × $350 million or $700 million.

If a System 2 cost-reduction program were undertaken in this company and if this in turn caused attitudes to become less favorable, confidence and trust to decrease, performance goals to be lowered, restriction of output to increase, and such other shifts to occur as those shown in Figure 5-2, the productive capacity and value of the human organization could readily suffer a 10 percent decrease in one year's time. If, moreover, the value of the human organization is $700 million (twice the payroll), then 10 percent of it is $70 million. This amount ($70 million), in turn, is 56 percent of last year's earnings of $125 million. This shows how a substantial proportion of the reported earnings of a firm for any one year actually could be "watered" earnings whose nature is not detected at the time of the cost-reduction program. Moreover, even though the 10 percent decrease in the value of the human organization caused by the cost-reduction program yielded only a 50¢ return in cash for each dollar of decreased value, which is not improbable, the $35 million obtained in this fashion is still 28 percent of last year's total earnings.

So long as no quantitative surveillance is maintained over a firm's human assets, its management can readily derive a substantial proportion of its earnings in any one year or even in several consecutive years from liquidating these human assets. This, as the above analysis shows, can occur easily without the top management or the firm's shareholders being aware of the spurious nature of much of the income which is being treated as earnings. In addition, as Chapters 2 and 5 have illustrated, omitting 50 to 75 percent of the income-producing assets from the balance sheet encourages decisions which yield spurious short-range gains at substantial long-range costs.

Human Asset Accounting Requires Social-Psychological Data

Accountants recognize the importance and value of the human enterprise and of customer goodwill. Paton (1962, pp. 486–487) states,

> In business enterprise a well-organized and loyal personnel may be a much more important "asset" than a stock of merchandise. . . . Until some scheme is found by which these imponderables of the business enterprise may be assayed and given definite statistical expression, the accountant must continue to prepare the balance sheet as he has been doing. At present there seems to be no way of measuring such factors in terms of the dollar; hence, they cannot be recognized as specific economic assets. But let us, accordingly, admit the serious limitations of the conventional balance sheet as a statement of financial condition.

It is now possible to develop procedures to appraise the current value of a firm's human organization and of its customer goodwill. This requires extensive use of the measurement resources developed by the social sciences. For example, estimates of the current value of a firm's human enterprise will require the sophisticated measurement of the major causal and intervening variables. These variables, and apparently no other variables but these, correctly reflect the current status of the firm's human organization. End-result variables measured at any one point in time or measurements of the trends in these variables do not and cannot yield a correct estimate of the current condition of the human organization. Such end-result measurements actually can be seriously misleading. This fact is demonstrated by the research findings upon which Figures 5-2 and 5-3 are based and is illustrated by the above analysis.

Since accounting methods which will reflect accurately the value of the human assets of a firm require sophisticated use of the measurement resources of the social sciences, improvements in this phase of accounting will not occur until these measurement resources are employed. It will be necessary to collect substantial bodies of data using these methodologies before the current dollar value of customer goodwill or of the human organization of a firm can be computed on a continuous basis. The preparatory research work needed for this human asset accounting will be discussed in Chapter 9.

Prior to the availability of human asset accounting, reasonably accurate estimates of the condition and trends in the human organization of the firm can be obtained through periodic measurements of the causal and intervening variables. Such data, were they continuously available, would reveal whether the human organization is increasing in value, remaining essentially unchanged, or decreasing in value. Comparable trend measurements can be readily made also to reveal shifts in customer loyalty. This information on trends in the value of the human organization and of customer goodwill would do much to fill the present gap in accounting and help greatly in avoiding serious and costly mistakes in policy and operating decisions.

Potential Benefits from Social Science Research

The present lag in the use of the social sciences by industry and government is comparable to the lag in the use of the physical sciences prior to the 1920s. In the mid-twenties the National Research Council established a committee to encourage industry to use research in the natural and physical sciences. During the past three decades, corporate officers have become aware of the importance of the physical, engineering, and biological sciences and have taken steps to see that their companies make good use of these profitable resources. The time appears to be ripe for a similar development with regard to the social sciences.

An extremely small proportion (a fraction of 1 percent) of the total sum spent in the United States on research and development goes to support the social science research related to the art of managing the human enterprise. In spite of these limited funds, the relevant social sciences, particularly social psychology, are making impressive progress both in methodology and in substantive findings. In 1928, for example, there was no well-established, quantitative method for measuring and evaluating that part of the Opel enterprise for which General Motors agreed to pay 40 percent of the total purchase price. The first methods for measuring such variables as attitudes, loyalties, and other intervening variables were published at that time and shortly thereafter (Likert, 1932; Thurstone, 1928; Thurstone, 1929; Thurstone & Chave, 1929).

The methodology and substantitive findings emerging from social science research can make great contributions to management. It is necessary, for example, to draw heavily upon them to develop human asset accounting as well as to provide the measurements needed to help interpret accounting and production data correctly prior to the availability of human asset accounting. Social science research can also provide a sounder body of knowledge as a basis for the art of management. The following propositions and the subsequent discussion suggest the magnitude of these potential contributions:

1. Attitudes, loyalties, motivations, perceptions, and similar kinds of intervening variables can be measured in a rigorous, quantitative manner. Errors involved in these measurements can be computed, and, consequently, the results of such measurements can be interpreted in relation to the magnitude of their errors of measurement. (Chapters 2

and 3 and particularly Table 3-1 have illustrated in relatively elementary ways the kinds of procedures which are available for obtaining some of these measurements. A more extended discussion of the measurement of these variables and of the problems of interpreting the results appears in Chapter 8.)

2. In any organization, the intervening variables change in response to modifications in the causal variables. The intervening variables usually change slowly, unless some dramatic or major event occurs. The general recognition of the stability of attitudes and loyalties and an appreciation that they are not likely to change except in response to modifications in major causal factors are manifest in such concepts as employee goodwill, good union-management relationships, and customer loyalty. The price that corporations pay over and above the value of the physical assets for the companies they acquire also reflects recognition of the stability of attitudes and loyalties. Attitudes are not ephemeral and fleeting; they are relatively stable and change only after the major factors which produce them are altered.

3. A highly productive organization is much more than a conglomeration of strangers. If a firm were to consist of individuals each of whom had excellent aptitude and training for his particular job but knew absolutely nothing about any other member, the productivity and performance of such an organization would be poor. High performance would not be achieved until the individuals had come to know one another well and had learned to work in a cooperative and coordinated manner. Highly productive organizations, as the data examined in Chapters 3 and 4 demonstrate, are tightly knit social systems (Likert, 1961, Chaps. 9–13). Such systems are highly complex and interdependent. Their members possess favorable attitudes and appropriate motivations and have reciprocal understanding and acceptance of their respective roles, functions, and responsibilities. Appreciable time as well as high levels of managerial competence are required to create such synergistic organizations.

4. The highest productivity, best performance, and highest earnings appear at present to be achieved by System 4 organizations. These organizations mobilize both the noneconomic motives and economic needs so that all available motivational forces create cooperative behavior focused on achieving the organizations' objectives. The enterprise is a tightly knit, well-coordinated organization of highly motivated persons. (As social science research makes further substantial contributions to the art of management, science-based systems even more productive than System 4 are likely to be developed.)

5. There is an orderly, systematic, cause-and-effect relationship among the causal, intervening, and end-result variables. The interrelationships

among these variables are highly complex and affected by such mediating variables as time, as was pointed out in Chapter 5. Even though these relationships are complex, it is possible by means of sophisticated measurements and analyses to tell whether a given organization is displaying the trends shown in Figure 5-2 or 5-3. It is also possible to estimate approximately at which time period in Figure 5-2 or 5-3 the organization now falls. Such data can be used also to predict the probable trends or developments which will occur in the organization and in its performance. Since these measurements and predictions are all subject to errors of measurements, they must necessarily be made and stated in terms of probable magnitudes and with probable errors attached to each. These measurements and analyses can be carried out, however, with sufficient accuracy to be highly useful to the organization and its management and to be financially highly profitable.

Social science research findings, as the above five propositions indicate, point to the complex character of the human component of any sizable organization. The dimensions of this human system can be measured and related to the performance of the overall organization. This step is necessary in human asset accounting. Such measurements are necessary also to understand correctly the condition and developments occurring in an organization, as the discussion in the rest of this chapter illustrates.

Superiors Often Are Misinformed concerning Principles Used by Best Managers

Recently, the chief executive officer of a decentralized corporation asked five of his senior staff to describe the management system of the firm's most productive regional vice-president. A lively discussion ensued, as each in turn stated his perception of the leadership principles and practices of this vice-president. Although each of the five persons involved was in a position to be well informed concerning his mode of managing (e.g., one was vice-president of personnel and another vice-president of operations), there was a wide range in points of view. The regional vice-president was seen as using System 1 management by one person and as being close to System 4 by another. The evaluation of the other three individuals fell between these extremes. Each of the five held firmly to his own view throughout the discussion.

This chief executive officer then asked the same question about the least productive regional vice-president. There was far less difference among the five in their perceptions of this vice-president's management style. The general consensus was that he was using System 1 or 1.5 management. Similarly when the question was repeated again about another regional vice-president whose performance was below average, general agreement was rapidly reached as to his style of management.

The contrast between the agreement among these five persons concerning the management system used by the less productive regional vice-presidents and their disagreement over the management system of the most productive vice-president is typical. Orthodox ways of managing, including *laissez-faire*, are readily recognized. The unorthodox styles of the most productive managers are not readily recognized, nor are their major characteristics correctly perceived. The uniqueness of these highly productive management systems makes them difficult to understand and to describe.

Although the specifics with regard to the highest-producing division, department, or plant vary from company to company, the general picture of top managements' inadequate information is much the same in many companies for which the Institute for Social Research has the data. Corporate officers, corporate staff, and top line managers in these companies know from the productivity and cost reports which departments are highly profitable. They also know from grievance and other records that these departments also have excellent labor relations. But so long as measurements of the causal and intervening variables are not regularly available for the department, the accuracy of their information and perceptions typically cease at this point. Lacking accurate information, each senior officer tends to assume that the manager of the firm's most productive department is using the system of management which he, himself, is using. Senior officers who are using System 2, or a style of management close to it, believe that the company's most productive managers employ the same system.

Other circumstances also appear to contribute to senior corporate officers' faulty impressions concerning the management system of their most productive managers. Typically their highest-producing division or department often is at some distance from corporate headquarters. The manager of this division or department visits headquarters periodically and may from time to time express disagreement with the corporate staff concerning the effect of a particular policy or principle upon the productivity of his department. He usually holds firmly to his view and insists that he be permitted to operate his department in accordance with those principles and policies which he feels are essential in achieving high productivity, even though they deviate from the policies set by the corporate staff. He is seen as a man of strong conviction and great firmness. He is recognized also as holding high performance goals for himself and his department. Both the staff and his division officers at headquarters see him, consequently, as a manager who has high performance goals and who vigorously presses his point of view. Their conclusion is reasonable: he must be urging his subordinates to reach high performance goals with the same pressure and unequivocal firmness he uses in dealing with headquarters on matters of policy and on the principles and methods to be used in managing his department. He is seen to be a manager who, with high performance goals, achieves them through firm, hierarchical pressure. He obviously must be a System 2 manager.

This manager of the highest-producing department is well aware that top management holds erroneous impressions about the management system he uses, that he is seen as using System 2 rather than a management style close to System 4. Quite deliberately he does nothing to correct the impression beyond pressing divisional headquarters and corporate staff for those actions required to enable him to manage the way he knows yields superior performance. He is keenly aware that if he attempted to persuade top management that his system of management is more productive than theirs and failed, he would be compelled to stop using his more productive management system.

Another factor at times may be present which contributes to his awareness of the need for caution. He may have been told by a senior corporate officer that he has "black marks" against him for not getting along well with one or more of the men who have been his superiors. Such superiors typically have struggled hard to compel this high-producing manager to give up his System 4 management and use their System 2 model. His refusal to do so is considered to be uncooperative behavior if not insubordination, and he is given a reputation for not getting along well with his superior manager.

There is still another factor which contributes to the erroneous impression held by corporate officers concerning the management style used by their highest-producing managers. It is not uncommon for these managers to do a far better job of *behaving* according to their style of managing than of *verbalizing* it. As a consequence, their explanations are often in part incomplete or inaccurate. This is not intentional. They just happen to be able to manage far better than they can explain or generalize their behavior. The predominance of System 2 concepts in the available literature on management also contributes to the problem these managers have in correctly conceptualizing and verbalizing their managerial principles and practices. The conceptual tools readily available fit System 2 but not System 4.

As a result of all these forces and experiences, the managers of the highest-producing departments typically keep as quiet as possible, are very thankful that they have a good many miles between themselves and corporate headquarters, and not infrequently refuse promotions which would place them in or close to corporate headquarters, since close proximity would make it much more difficult for them to manage in their highly productive style.

Division presidents and corporate staffs at times also contribute to the erroneous perceptions of top corporate officers about the management style of their highest-producing managers. We have seen corporate staffs and divisional presidents in more than one firm withhold from their top corporate officers results of measurements which would correct the faulty impressions held by these top officers. These measurements of the causal and intervening variables were obtained either for or by the corporate staff and accurately revealed the system of management of the corporation's most productive departments. But these data conflicted with convictions held by top corporate officers about the kind of management system which is most productive. These officers believe System 2 or 2.5 is best, but the data showed that their highest-producing managers are using something close to System 4. In these firms, dominated by System 2 management, upward communication by both line and staff understandably has displayed thus far the usual System 2 pattern. It is hazardous to feed important but unsolicited information upward, especially when such information is contrary to views which are strongly held by the higher echelons and which to no small degree proves them wrong. As a consequence, these senior corporate officers have not seen the measurements and are unaware of how seriously wrong they are in their impressions of the management system which yields the best results in their own corporation, as demonstrated by the behavior and results of their highest-producing managers. Until these officers actively seek such data, they are not likely to have the results presented to them.

Poor Communication with the Chief Executive Officer

The motivational forces which block upward communication in organizations using the System 2 pattern of man-to-man interaction, rather than the overlapping group model of System 4, are strong at all echelons, but their effects have the most costly consequences at the very top. Chief executive officers, boards of directors, and heads of government who are confronted with the breakdown of upward communication usually ask, "Why did not my subordinates who knew the facts report them to me?" Unfortunately, this is the wrong question. So long as the man-to-man model of interaction of System 2 is used, these breakdowns will occur, irrespective of who the superior or the subordinates are. The question that urgently needs to be asked by the chief executive officers is, "What is wrong with the management system we are using, which causes these serious failures in upward communication, and what corrective steps should be taken?"

When the correct question is asked and scientific research used to get the answers, corporations, governmental agencies, and all other organizations will be on their way to significant improvement in their upward communication as well as in the management principles they use and the performance results they achieve.

Multiplying the Gain from Highly Productive Departments

The cost to corporations is substantial if incorrect impressions are held by senior officers concerning the management systems of their most productive and profitable departments. These costs take many forms, but some examples will indicate their general nature. Quite commonly senior officers assume that their highest-producing manager is using System 2 management or something close to it. They ascribe his extraordinary performance and results to unusual skill and perhaps also to some unique personality characteristic or aptitude. They do not recognize that the manager is using a more complex management system, which other managers can learn and use with approximately equal effectiveness.

The highest-producing departments in every company of any size represent unique and valuable assets. These departments usually are operating examples of something closer to System 4 than are the other departments. From field experiments in which we have built such System 4 units composed of 100 to 300 people, we have learned that these units are difficult to create and represent an appreciable investment. Corporations would derive substantial financial gains if their top management would use their own highly productive departments in the following manner:

1. Quantitative research could be done to learn why the department is so extraordinarily productive and profitable. Answers could be obtained to such questions as: What principles and system of management are being used? Can these principles be generalized, and can they and the system of management used by the highly productive managers be applied successfully to the entire corporation? If so, what improvements in productivity, costs, and earnings could reasonably be expected?

2. If the answers to the above questions warrant it, research on these highly successful operations could be conducted to learn the full nature of this more productive management system. Corporate policies and standard operating procedures could then be adopted which would foster and encourage the spread of this more effective management system throughout the firm. In addition, the highly productive departments could be used to train younger managers by giving them experience in these departments through rotation.

Very few firms measure the causal and intervening variables regularly, nor do they undertake the social science research needed to discover the fundamental causes responsible for the outstanding performance of their highest-producing departments. Without these data, top management has no way of knowing when new and particularly effective principles of management are being created and used by their most effective managers. It is easy, consequently, for them unwittingly and unintentionally to destroy such valuable assets. Destruction of the management system of the highly productive department usually occurs after the creative manager has left the department and a System 2 manager is put in charge. By using System 2 management and its characteristic authoritarian pressures to achieve production and reduce costs, the new manager often liquidates in one or two years what the previous, highly productive manager spent many years building.

Some System 4 Departments Are Deliberately Destroyed

Sometimes the destruction of a highly productive department is a calculated act. High-producing departments are split and their parts deliberately placed under System 2 managers, who are encouraged to see that all traces of the System 4 management are obliterated. In one situation where we saw this occur, a regional vice-president who had a System 4 department manager reporting to him also had several other departments doing the same kind of work whose managers used System 2. This vice-president knew that his top corporate officers would expect him to improve the performance of his System 2 departments until they were doing as well as his System 4 department. The gap between these departments was appreciable and was growing. He had refused to try to learn System 4 management and had spent his efforts pressing System 2 on his System 4 manager. Not knowing that he and his System 2 managers could readily master System 4 management, he resorted to the only safe action he saw to protect himself. When his System 4 manager was promoted, he split the System 4 department and put the parts under managers he was sure would push the parts back toward System 2. In this manner he destroyed a valuable asset of the company. Corporate headquarters many hundreds of miles away knew that the department had been split and its parts consolidated with other departments, but they were unaware of the real reason for the action and the great loss to the corporation.

Supervisory and nonsupervisory personnel who have experienced System 4 and have then been pushed back to System 2 management find it discouraging and frustrating. Many leave the company when this occurs. Others, if they are not completely discouraged, bide their time and emerge many years hence as creative, highly productive managers moving again toward System 4 management.

System 2 Climate Restrains Improvement in Management System

Senior officers of a corporation often unwittingly handicap many of their most productive managers by policies and standard operating procedures which are established for the firm. For example, orders are issued that all profit centers shall make x percent on invested capital or that wherever the nature of the work permits, measured work will be introduced, standards set, and performance required at the level called for by the standards, or that performance appraisals and reviews are to be conducted by each manager with all of his subordinates. Such actions and policies as these are characteristic of System 1 or 2 management. They aid all managers in the organization who are using System 1 or 2 and seriously handicap all managers who are striving to develop better management principles. These System 2 procedures usually require managers to behave in ways which violate such principles of System 4 as the principle of supportive relationships (Meyer, Kay & French, 1965; Wyatt, 1958). Consistent adherence to System 2 principles and procedures by a corporation creates an organizational climate which seriously restrains the growth and evolution of management practices toward the System 4 model.

After examining all the data revealing the unique character of the management system of their highly productive departments, the senior officers or the board of directors of a corporation may decide either to experiment or not to experiment with a science-based management style, such as System 4. They may decide either to encourage or to discourage attempts by their managers to use principles and methods approaching System 4 management. They should, however, be aware that they are making such a decision, both when it is being made and when it is being reaffirmed. They should have the relevant facts before them when they make such decisions. This requires extensive use of social science research, including periodic measurement of the causal and intervening variables and the analysis of these data in relation to the end-result measurements.

Making Profit Centers Profitable

Basing the compensation of a manager of a profit center largely upon his performance has much to commend it, provided that the compensation formula rewards actual and not fictitious earnings. Compensation systems which reward managers handsomely for fictitious earnings are those which ignore the value of the human organization, do not measure the causal and intervening variables, and pay managers sizable bonuses for achieving specified levels of earnings as a percentage of sales or of return on invested capital. So long as such compensation plans ignore shifts in the causal and intervening variables, they enable a manager who is a "pressure artist" to achieve high earnings over a few years, while destroying the loyalties, favorable attitudes, cooperative motivations, etc., among the supervisory and nonsupervisory members of the organization. Often some of the more able members of the organization choose to leave the company rather than stay in the organization under such management. In one large corporation, for example, where this kind of managerial compensation is used, a study revealed that of the 1,300 carefully screened and selected engineering graduates who were hired over a three-year period, only about one-half of them were still with the company a few years later. The study showed, moreover, that those who had gone were most like the best of the engineers who remained. Turnover was greatest among the most able of those employed.

One serious hidden cost of rewarding managers well for a high current return on sales dollars or invested capital usually does not become evident until many years after the introduction of this form of managerial compensation. This system encourages and rewards behavior by managers which leads to poor labor relations and strikes. Managers are rewarded well when they achieve high levels of current earnings by putting substantial, direct, hierarchical pressure on their organizations. When such pressure leads to hostile attitudes, excessive grievances, and strikes, the managerial compensation system should be recognized as a major cause of the organizational breakdown.

For all practical purposes, managerial compensation plans which reward managers for converting valuable human assets to cash for a fraction of their actual value represent poor financial management. Such plans are even less sound than paying managers a sizable percentage of the dollars they might realize by selling inventory at less than cost while keeping no records on the level or amount of inventory. Inventories are easier to replace than a tightly knit, loyal, highly effective organization.

Boards of directors of corporations with managerial compensation plans which pay handsomely for liquidating the corporation's human assets may not now be aware that some managers of their decentralized divisions or profit centers are exploiting these plans for their personal profit, at the corporation's expense. It is a revealing experience to describe the trends in Figure 5-2 to a meeting of managers in charge of profit centers. When these managers see the data they usually exchange knowledgeable nods and say, "Yes, the data on trends are correct, and we can tell you the men who are milking their units." Unfortunately, such men generally get the reputation of being effective managers who are able to cut costs substantially and are moved by the company every two or three years from one location to another. These moves enable them to keep on earning fat bonuses by converting valuable human assets of the company to cash for a fraction of their value. These managers continue to exploit the company, unless they are kept at one location long enough for the adverse consequences to catch up with them (Figure 5-2).

There is no need for this exploitation of corporate resources to occur. Corporate officers and boards of directors can protect the assets of their shareholders by modifying or discontinuing managerial compensation plans which reward behavior contrary to that in the best interest of the enterprise. An effective modification could be made by linking the causal and intervening variables to the compensation plan and *paying bonuses for excellent earning records only when measurements of these causal and intervening variables show no change or show an improvement.* Basing the managerial compensation on results revealed by human asset accounting (Chapter 9), of course, would be still better, although it will be some time before that is possible.

Summary

Accounting procedures at present ignore a substantial proportion of the income-producing assets of firms. As a result, all levels of management are handicapped by the inadequate and at times inaccurate information now available to them. The costs to the firm from the adverse consequences of this inadequate information are greatest at the highest levels in the corporation. The wrong decisions are made too often on such questions as

- What system of management is most productive and hence should be used by the firm?
- What strategies of cost control yield the lowest costs?
- What system of managerial compensation yields motivation and behavior most nearly in the best interest of the entire organization?

If human asset accounting were added to the usual accounting process, the management of business and governmental organizations would be appreciably improved. Until such accounting is undertaken, however, all levels of management of an enterprise will benefit from having continuously available periodic measurements of the causal and intervening variables for each of the relevant units.

The measurements of these variables must be accurate, must deal with the most important dimensions, and must be correctly interpreted. Some of the problems involved in this complex process will be considered in the next two chapters.

Chapter 7

THE NEED FOR A SYSTEMS APPROACH

A significant fact becomes evident whenever an experienced manager fills out the form which measures the kind of management system used by his organization (see Chapters 2 and 3). If his answers show that the plant or company is using a System 2 organization on some of the items checked, the answers to the rest of the items generally display a System 2 pattern. Similarly, if the manager scores the organization at about 3.5 on some items, he tends to assign roughly the same score to the organization on the rest of the items. Managers, generally speaking, do not believe that an organization using System 1 on some items, uses System 3 on others, and System 4 on still others. A particular organization is generally seen as falling at approximately the same point along the management system continuum on each of the items in the table.

This appears to be true whether the items are of a causal or an intervening character. Managers apparently report the long-run average pattern as they see it, rather than any short-term fluctuations in describing the management systems of their firms. Leadership styles and related organizational characteristics seem to display a remarkably consistent set of interrelationships. System 1 style of leadership results in System 1 organizational characteristics; System 4 style of leadership yields the System 4 syndrome for the intervening and end-result variables. This general pattern was observed in the research findings upon which *New Patterns of Management* was based and was reflected, of course, in the preparation of Table 14-1 of that volume.

The extent to which this observed pattern stands up when tested against the descriptions by managers of many different organizations can be computed readily. The data summarized in Figures 3-2, 3-4, 3-5, and 3-10, along with responses to Table 3-1 by 42 other managers have been used. The answers of each person on each item were compared with his

NOTE: David G. Bowers provided substantial assistance in the preparation of this chapter.

answers on each of the other items in the table. These intercorrelations were computed among all the items in Table 3-1. The resulting correlation matrix is shown in the table in Appendix I.

The data in Appendix I are Pearsonian coefficients of correlation and are a measure of the extent to which the answers to one item are consistent with the answers to the other. If there were perfect agreement, i.e., the highest response on one item also being the highest on the other and so on right down to the lowest on each, the coefficient would have a value of +1.00. If the highest on one item is associated with the lowest on the other, the next highest with the next lowest, etc., the coefficient of correlation would be −1.00. If there is no relationship between the responses on one item and those on the other, i.e., everything is completely chance, the coefficient would be .00. An estimate of the amount of variance in one item which is associated with that in the other can be computed by squaring the coefficient. Thus, a coefficient of correlation of +.50 would indicate that the variance in one item accounts for 25 percent of the variance in the other; if the coefficient were +.70, it would be 49 percent.

In addition to the results for each item, Appendix I includes data for the sum of all the odd-numbered questions (ΣO), the sum of all the even-numbered questions (ΣE), and the total sum for all the items (ΣT). The first 43 items in the table (i.e., items 1 to 43) correspond with the 43 items shown in Table 3-1 (Table 14-1, *New Patterns of Management*). Item 44 is the sum of the odd-numbered questions, item 45 the sum of the even, and item 46 is the total score.

An examination of Appendix I reveals extraordinarily high intercorrelations among the items and between each item and the total score. Apart from the performance items (40 through 43), all the correlation coefficients between an item and the total score are greater than +.73. There is also an unusually high correlation (+.97) between the sum of the odd- and the sum of the even-numbered questions. This yields a very high corrected split-half reliability coefficient (Spearman-Brown), namely +.98. When these data were factor analyzed, only one dominant factor emerged with which the total score correlated +1.00.

The extremely high intercorrelations shown in Appendix I immediately raised questions as to whether spurious factors might be contributing to the high interrelationships observed. High intercorrelations were expected, but the magnitude of the correlation coefficients proved to be so large as to cause one to search for other conditions contributing to their size.

An obvious possibility is the headings at the top of each page of the Table 3-1 and of the answer sheet (Figure 3-1). These headings are: “Exploitive Authoritative,” “Benevolent Authoritative,” “Consultative,” and “Participative Group.” It is possible that some respondents reacted to these headings and answered in terms of them, rather than responding to the content of each item in the body of the table. This would cause the respondent to check every item in the answer sheet under the headings which he feels describe his organization. Such responses, were they to occur, would contribute to the high intercorrelations shown in Appendix I.

The second condition which may be contributing to these very high correlations is usually called "response set." The content of the alternatives presented in Table 3-1 display for every item in the table the same general relationship from left to right, and this might lead some respondents to develop a general orientation and cause each to place his answers at about the same point from left to right on each item on the answer sheet. Methodological studies have shown that this response set may occur when the content of the items from left to right in a test all display the same general relationship, i.e., from System 1 on the left to System 4 on the right.

A third condition present which contributes to the magnitude of the correlations is the substantial range represented in the answers. This condition does not yield a spurious relationship but does affect the magnitude of the observed association. The actual situations to which these managers were responding varied from a plant verging on System 1 (Weldon prior to 1962, Figure 3-4) to an operation approaching System 4 (Figure 3-10). The greater the variability displayed by each of two distributions, the higher the observed correlation between them will be.

Removing Factors Contributing to High Intercorrelations

Steps were taken to test the extent to which the high intercorrelations shown in Appendix I were spurious and due in part to one of the above conditions. A new form was prepared, which was designed to eliminate the effect of the first two of the above conditions. In this way, the intercorrelations among the items could be obtained with the influence of these conditions removed.

This new form omitted all headings. In addition, the order of the content was reversed on items selected at random so that the System 4 end (participative group) was at the left instead of the right. This occurred on 23 of the 50 items in the form.

The nine items shown in Table 7-1 were used in this new form, in addition to those in Table 3-1. Five of the new items (1*a* through *e*) deal with leadership. The sixth (5*f*) concerns decision making. The seventh (8*a*) deals with the level of performance goals of superiors and the last two (8*b* and *c*) with the adequacy of training. The content of the last three items is such that managers should respond somewhat differently to them than to the other items. These items were added to test whether this would be the case. It is to be expected that in System 4 organizations these three added items would be at the favorable end of the continuum, since the effective application of the principle of supportive relationships would require this condition. This does not apply, however, to the other systems of management. It is possible for an organization or manager using any of the Systems from 1 through 3 to hold various levels of performance goals or to provide various amounts of management training and other training. There is no particular reason to expect a System 3 organization to score higher or lower on these three items than a System 2 organization.

This new form, without headings and with the left to right order of content reversed on 23 items selected randomly, was administered to three different groups of managers. One group consisted of 78 managers, all of whom are in one part of a large company. A second group included 70 managers, all in one plant of a second company. The third group was composed of 61 managers from five companies using the Scanlon plan.

The directions used in administering the form to the first of the above groups were as follows:

"*Instructions:* Please indicate on the line *under* each organizational variable where you feel your organization falls. Do this for each item as defined in the table. Treat each item as a continuous variable from the left end of the line to the right end and place a check mark on each line to show where you feel your organization falls on that item."

To the second and third groups, the instructions were:

"Please place an *o* at the appropriate point on each line to show where, *in your experience*, you feel your organization falls on that item. Each line is continuous from the left end to the right end so place your *o* at that point above the line which best describes your organization.

"If you feel your organization is different today from what it was two or three years ago, place an *x* (either to the left or right of the *o*) indicating where your organization fell on that item previously. If you were not in your present plant or department two or three years ago, please fill in the profile with an *o* on each line and omit the *x* marks."

Most of the managers in the latter two groups gave answers describing both their present organization and their present recollection of what it was two or three years ago. Those who recently joined their organization described, of course, only the way they now see it.

After taking these steps to remove or reduce the influence of the three conditions mentioned above, the intercorrelations among the items for the three additional groups of managers were still sizable. The range

TABLE 7-1

ITEMS ADDED TO THE PROFILE OF ORGANIZATIONAL AND PERFORMANCE CHARACTERISTICS

1. Leadership processes used				
a. Extent to which superiors have confidence and trust in *subordinates*	Have no confidence and trust in subordinates	Have condescending confidence and trust, such as master has in servant	Substantial but not complete confidence and trust; still wishes to keep control of decisions	Complete confidence and trust in all matters
b. Extent to which subordinates, in turn, have confidence and trust in *superiors*	Have no confidence and trust in superiors	Have subservient confidence and trust, such as servant has in master	Substantial but not complete confidence and trust	Complete confidence and trust
c. Extent to which superiors display supportive behavior toward others	Display no supportive behavior or virtually none	Display supportive behavior in condescending manner and situations only	Display supportive behavior quite generally	Display supportive behavior fully and in all situations
d. Extent to which superiors behave so that subordinates feel free to discuss important things about their jobs with their immediate superior	Subordinates do not feel at all free to discuss things about the job with their superior	Subordinates do not feel very free to discuss things about the job with their superior	Subordinates feel rather free to discuss things about the job with their superior	Subordinates feel completely free to discuss things about the job with their superior

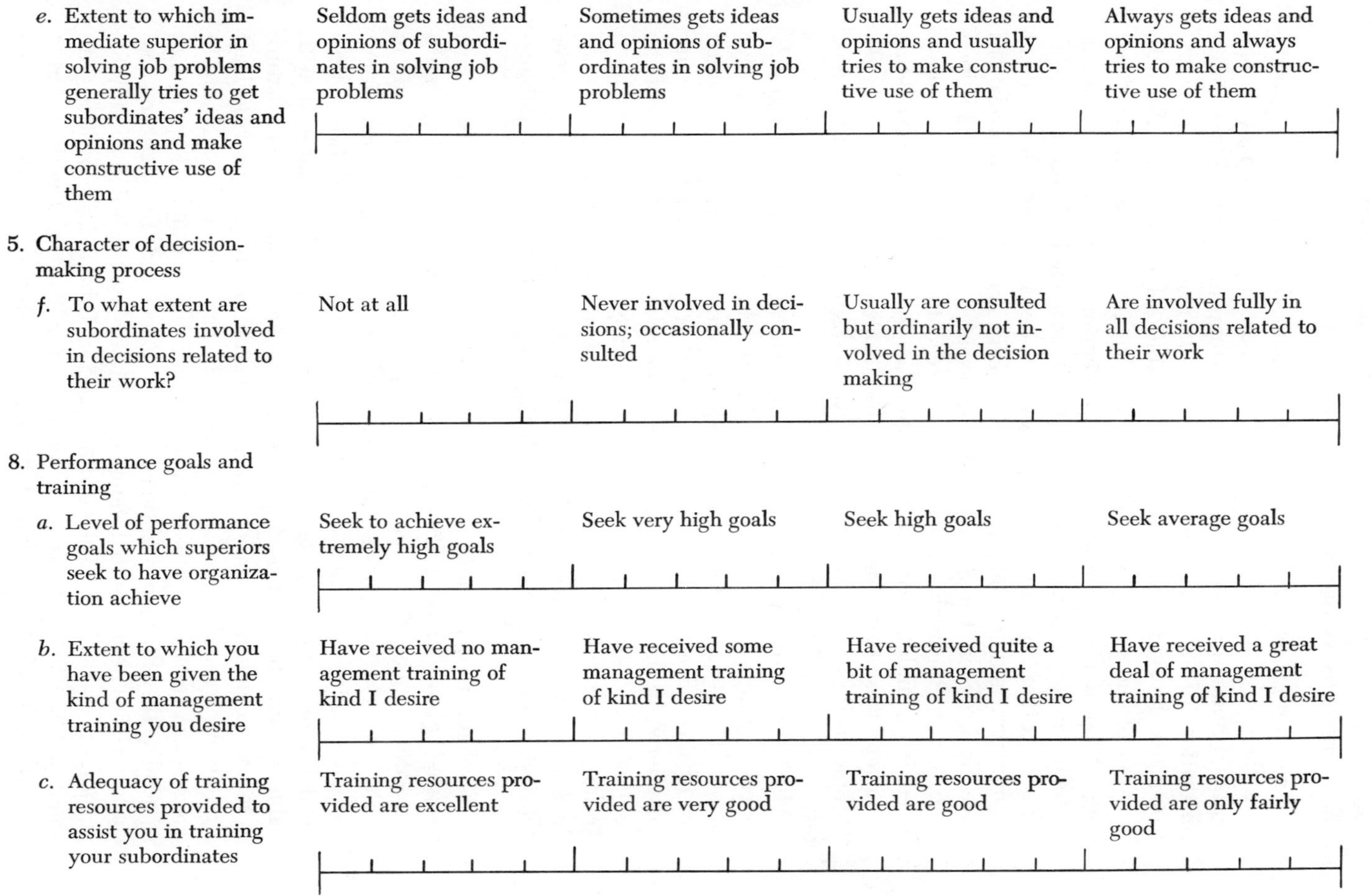

e. Extent to which immediate superior in solving job problems generally tries to get subordinates' ideas and opinions and make constructive use of them	Seldom gets ideas and opinions of subordinates in solving job problems	Sometimes gets ideas and opinions of subordinates in solving job problems	Usually gets ideas and opinions and usually tries to make constructive use of them	Always gets ideas and opinions and always tries to make constructive use of them
5. Character of decision-making process				
f. To what extent are subordinates involved in decisions related to their work?	Not at all	Never involved in decisions; occasionally consulted	Usually are consulted but ordinarily not involved in the decision making	Are involved fully in all decisions related to their work
8. Performance goals and training				
a. Level of performance goals which superiors seek to have organization achieve	Seek to achieve extremely high goals	Seek very high goals	Seek high goals	Seek average goals
b. Extent to which you have been given the kind of management training you desire	Have received no management training of kind I desire	Have received some management training of kind I desire	Have received quite a bit of management training of kind I desire	Have received a great deal of management training of kind I desire
c. Adequacy of training resources provided to assist you in training your subordinates	Training resources provided are excellent	Training resources provided are very good	Training resources provided are good	Training resources provided are only fairly good

was most restricted, of course, for the first of the above three groups, since their responses dealt with only one part of one company at one period of time. As would be expected, this group showed the lowest intercorrelations of the three. For this group of 78 managers, the sum of the scores for the odd-numbered items in Table 3-1 correlated +.81 with the sum of the even items. This means that, even with this restricted range, these items are measuring the perceptions of the system of management of an organization with a split-half, corrected reliability of +.90.

For the other two groups of managers, who described both their present organization and its state two or three years ago, the intercorrelations were much larger. The greater range represented in their answers helped contribute to the higher correlations between the sum of the odd-numbered items and the sum of the even. For one group, this correlation coefficient was +.94; for the other, the Scanlon-plan companies, +.98. This means for these two groups the corrected split-half reliabilities were, respectively, +.97 and +.99.

The data for these three groups have been factor analyzed separately for each group. These three analyses have yielded the same set of five factors. The items added to Table 3-1 and shown in Table 7-1 yielded two of these five factors. One factor consisted of the leaderships items (numbered 1*a* through *c* in Table 7-1). The other factor consisted of the training and of the level of performance items (numbered 8*a* through *c*). As anticipated, this last factor shows that managers' responses to the last three items were somewhat different from their answers to the other items. A report on these factors is being prepared for separate publication.

The data in Appendix I and the split-half reliability coefficients reported above show that there is a substantial amount of intercorrelation among the responses by managers to the original items in Table 3-1. This relationship is sufficiently marked that even with a restricted range, the items yield a high split-half reliability. These relationships among the items indicate that Table 3-1 combined with Table 7-1 can be used as a reliable instrument to measure the nature of the management system of any organization in which there is at least a minimum level of control or coordination; i.e., it is not laissez-faire in character. A revised form of the material in Tables 3-1 and 7-1 appears in Appendix II with two additional items added and the performance-characteristics items omitted. Some of the items are reworded slightly for purposes of clarification. The headings used in Table 3-1 are omitted, and about one-half of the items are reversed from left to right, with System 4 toward the left. The Appendix II form is an improved version for measuring the management system of any organization and is, of course, to be preferred to the original Table 3-1. The Appendix II form can be used to measure the management system of any unit within an organization, as well as that of the total organization.

Management Systems Are Internally Consistent

The results shown in Appendix I and the high split-half reliabilities lead to an important conclusion: the data confirm the validity of the underlying concept used in building Table 14-1 of *New Patterns of Management.* That is, every component part of a particular management system fits well with each of the other parts and functions in harmony with them. Each system of management has a basic integrity of its own. The communication processes of System 1 are compatible with all other aspects of System 1 but are not compatible with any aspect of System 3 or System 4. The same is true of the decision-making processes and the compensation plans. *The management system of an organization must have compatible component parts if it is to function effectively.*

This conclusion has a very important implication: experiments in organizations must involve internally consistent changes. The traditional atomistic research design is not appropriate for experiments involving organizational theory or management systems. Every aspect of a managerial system is related to every other part and interacts with it. The results obtained by altering a single variable or procedure while keeping all others the same usually will yield quite different results from those obtained when that variable is changed along with simultaneous and compatible changes in all other aspects of the management system. The true influence of altering one aspect of a system cannot be determined by varying it and it alone. A test of the effectiveness of the upward communication process of System 4 will yield misleading findings if all the rest of the enterprise is using System 2 methods. *In experiments involving organizational theory and management systems, therefore, a systems approach must be used.* The organic integrity of each system must be maintained while experimental variations are being made.

Maintain System Integrity in Organizational Change and Management Development

When an organization seeks to apply the results of research dealing with leadership, management, and organizational performance, the application must involve a total systems modification and not an atomistic modification. When change is desired, it should be a shift from one coordinated system to another, maintaining all the while the integrity of the system and its component parts. If a company wishes to shift its operations from System 1 or 2 to System 3 or 4, it should plan to modify *all* of its operating procedures: leadership, decision making, communications, coordination, evaluation, supervision, compensation, organizational structure, motivation, etc. *The change should start by altering first the most influential causal variables (see Chapter 8), and there should be systematic plans to modify in coordinated steps all of the operating procedures which now anchor the organization firmly to its present management system.* A well-integrated system of management should emerge.

It is equally important for managerial development activities to apply the systems principle. Unfortunately, this is often not the case. The systems approach needs to be applied fully both with regard to (1) the relationship between the system of management of a company and the content of development programs for its managers, and (2) the internal consistency of the content of management development courses.

In efforts to reduce costs and improve performance, such steps as the introduction of work simplification or job enlargement are often taken. In these circumstances it is not generally recognized that the improved performance realized by the particular step taken is substantially less than the full potential both in magnitude and duration because the action taken is specific and not part of a total, coordinated change in the management system of the firm. The full benefit of such steps will not be obtained unless there is a consistent, coordinated change in the entire management system of the department or firm. This conclusion applies not only to job enlargement and work simplification, but also to such changes as the following:

1. Modification in the compensation procedures including (a) profit sharing, (b) bonuses, (c) stock options, and (d) stock purchase plans.
2. Shifts in assumptions about employees including (a) substituting Theory Y assumption about people for Theory X (McGregor, 1960) and (b) greater use of self-actualization and similar motivational forces.
3. Changes in decision-making, goal-setting, and evaluation procedures including (a) management by objective, (b) management by results, and (c) greater emphasis on self-direction and self-control.
4. Changes in communication practices including (a) emphasis on improved listening and (b) various kinds of communication programs.
5. Introduction of steps to improve lateral and total coordination including (a) product managers, (b) product or business teams, and (c) redefining the jobs of managers so that they actually have two or more superiors.

Most of these kinds of changes usually involve a shift on the part of the organization toward a management system more like System 4 than the one presently used. The nature of this shift is generally not recognized and the particular step taken is usually not accompanied or followed by the other kinds of changes required to yield an integrated, consistent management system. As a consequence, the improvement in the results achieved by the change is significantly less than that which is potentially possible, and often the improvement which does occur may last for only a relatively short time.

Training to bring about cognitive, attitudinal, and skill changes must be compatible with the system of management in which that training is to be used. For example, sensitivity or managerial grid training are essentially System 4 in character and are incompatible with System 2. If such training is given, all components of the management system should reflect System 4 philosophy and practices. The company's organizational structure, its compensation theory and practices, its selection processes, its procedures for establishing objectives and goals and for carrying out control activities must be compatible with its training practices. A company which trains its managers for System 4 and makes them operate in a System 2 environment is selling that training short and will fail to benefit fully from it.

When sensitivity and training in similar System 4 procedures are used by a firm which continues to use System 2, the results may even be harmful. For example, upon returning to their jobs, managers who have received such training often use it to evaluate the behavior of their own superior and his System 2 style of management in terms of the System 4 skills and procedures they have learned. The resulting unfavorable evaluation tends to lead to less favorable attitudes toward their superior and increased skepticism about the company's awareness of what it is doing.

Vaccinating Managers against Change

There is an even more costly consequence of returning to a System 2 operation after training compatible with System 4. Managers generally assume that their company provided the training because it wished to move toward System 4 management. They like the System 4 procedures and start to apply the training back on the job. They may, for example, share confidential company information with subordinates and begin to use group decision making in dealing with job and organizational problems. A better understanding of these problems occurs as the flow of upward information becomes less guarded and more adequate and accurate. Problems which have long been a source of irritation and excessive cost start coming to the surface and are successfully resolved. Enthusiasm grows concerning the effectiveness of the training and the new style of leadership in helping to reveal problems and to improve problem solving and the performance of the department.

About this time some of the long-buried and much more difficult problems become visible because of the more candid upward communication. Their visibility, coupled with the growing courage to deal with them, results in action. One or more of them are tackled, and effective solutions emerge. Some of these solutions, however, require changes in company policy or concurrence by higher levels of management. At this point, the fact becomes painfully clear that the firm is a System 2 organization, and its top management has no intention of changing toward System 4. The action requested is responded to not by joint decision making through a multiple overlapping group structure but by a sharp reminder that subordinate levels in the organization are not expected to raise such issues or recommend such changes in policy. The managers who were applying their training are "slapped down" and are evaluated unfavorably for their behavior. This experience vaccinates such managers against attempting to move toward a science-based system of management. Training managers in System 4 principles and methods and subsequently punishing them for using the training is a potent way to build resistance to change to science-based management in the future.

Management Training Needs to Be Based on a Single System

The systems approach needs to be applied in a second way to management development programs: their content must be internally consistent. Development programs will not be effective when their content draws from more than one system of management, thereby violating the systems principle. It is not uncommon today for a management development program to train managers in the conduct of performance appraisal and review while simultaneously emphasizing the need for managers to be employee-centered and supportive in dealing with subordinates. It is impossible to do both. Rigorous research clearly demonstrates that even when the most approved methods for conducting performance appraisal and review interviews are used, it is not possible to conduct the interview with most managers so that they will feel that they have been treated in a supportive manner. A well-conducted study revealed that the performance review proved to be an ego-deflating experience for 82 percent of the subordinate personnel involved (Meyer, Kay, & French, 1965; Zander, 1963).

A violation of the systems approach occurs in those management development courses which deliberately include principles and procedures drawn from different systems of management. Often such courses are heralded as being eclectic. Stress is placed on the value of picking and using the best from each of the different systems, even though these systems of management are clearly seen as being inconsistent and incompatible. This is as impractical as attempting to graft an elephant's leg on a man. A bizarre creature with little chance of survival would emerge. Research findings show that few managers can achieve effective performance when they attempt to use principles and procedures which so flagrantly disregard the systems approach.

There is merit, of course, in exposing managers to conflicting points of view and in presenting to them results of studies which question current practices. This is intellectually stimulating and valuable and, as studies show, contributes to innovative thinking. When this is done, however, two conditions should prevail. First, it should be made clear to all who participate that the material is intended to stimulate thinking and discussion and that there is no intention that immediate, direct applications will be made. Second, all those managers who are exposed to such stimulation should be given an opportunity, considered adequate by them, to influence the character of the management systems of their companies. To expose managers to new and challenging data and ideas and then to make it impossible for them to make use of their new insights and even penalize them for doing so is highly frustrating. One can safely predict that managers so treated will have their performance adversely affected, and many, especially the more able, will seek a different company with a management system more compatible with their new insights.

The Systems Concept as a Theoretical Orientation

The importance of the systems concept and the value of its contribution as an analytical framework to understanding the dynamics of organizational performance and success have been stressed increasingly in recent years. Discussions which are particularly relevant appear in Emery and Trist (1960), *General Systems Yearbook*, Katz and Kahn (1966, especially Chap. 2), Marrow et al. (1967, Chap. 17), Miller (1955), and Trist, Higgin, Murray, and Pollock (1963). Lewin's field theory (1948; 1951) was, of course, an earlier statement of the systems concept. The limited data reported in the early pages of this chapter add quantitative findings in support of the systems orientation.

Business enterprises, as we have seen in this chapter, are characterized by internally consistent principles and procedures. Consistency is evidently a requirement for success and survival. The need for consistency and a systems approach has widespread implications for organizational research, for attempts to improve organizations by applying research findings dealing with leadership and management, and for management development programs. The application of the systems approach is, however, often hampered because of the lack of accurate information concerning the actual internal state of an enterprise. Measurements are required which reveal clearly the management system and the principles and procedures of a firm and the resulting motivational and behavioral consequences. This is the subject of the next chapter.

Chapter 8

MEASUREMENT

Every organization is in a continuous state of change. Sometimes the changes are great, sometimes small, but change is always taking place. The conditions requiring these changes arise from both within and without. As a consequence, there is never-ending need for decisions which guide adjustments to change. The adequacy of these decisions for meeting an organization's current and developing internal and external situations determines the well-being, power, and future of that organization.

We are coming to recognize with increasing clarity that the capacity of an organization to function well depends both upon the quality of its decision-making processes and upon the adequacy and accuracy of the information used. Sound decisions require accurate information about relevant dimensions of the problem as well as correct interpretation of that information. If the information available for decision making is inaccurate or is incorrectly interpreted, the diagnostic decisions are likely to be in error and the action taken, inappropriate.

The way doctors diagnose an illness illustrates the process. A physician needs two different kinds of information to make a correct diagnosis. First, he must know a great deal about the nature of human beings. This knowledge is based on extensive research which relates symptoms to causes and measurements of body conditions to the health of the organism, thereby revealing the character of the human body's normal and abnormal functioning. This knowledge gives the doctor insights into how the system ought to function, so that he can know what he needs to measure and how he needs to interpret the measurements. The second kind of information needed by the doctor to discover the patient's state of health at any particular time is that revealed by the appropriate measurements and tests made on that patient at that time.

In diagnosing its problems, every organization faces a similar situation. It needs to understand the fundamental nature of its system, the way in which its component parts function, and the adaptive responses it makes to its environment. This basic knowledge is a necessary prerequisite to the determination of what specific measurements should be made for diagnostic purposes and how they should be interpreted.

For purposes of easy reference, let us call these two kinds of information, respectively, information on the *nature* of the system and information on the *state* of the system. By information on the nature of the system, we will mean data which enable us to construct the basic conceptual model of an organization. For our purposes, this will be the measurements needed to build a science-based, organizational model, such as System 4. This model, in turn, tells us what measurements to obtain for diagnosing the state of the system and how to interpret these data. By information on the state of the system, we will mean data which reveal the current situation of the organization, such as the behavior of its leaders, the motivations of its members, its communication and decision-making processes, and its productivity and earnings.

For both purposes, there is urgent need for enterprises to obtain more adequate and more accurate data than are now available to them. The need and importance of obtaining measurements to guide decisions was stressed by Sloan and reported in his *My Years with General Motors*. Wolff (1964, p. 176) summarizes Sloan's emphasis on obtaining facts:

> "An essential aspect of our management philosophy is the factual approach to business judgment," Sloan announced early in his regime at General Motors. And ten years later he was still exhorting his colleagues:
>
> "Notwithstanding that we have the reputation of a fact finding organization, we do not get the facts even now as completely as we should. We sit around and discuss things without facts. I think we should break ourselves of that."
>
> Few of his corporate moves or pronouncements failed, in one way or another, to affirm his unqualified conviction that "the big work behind business judgment is finding and acknowledging the facts."

Sloan made excellent use of facts for the two purposes mentioned previously. He used them to guide the important decisions involved in establishing the corporate structure and the decision-making processes of the General Motors Corporation. He used them also for dealing with policy and operating problems.

Valuable Measurement Resources Are Available but Unused

A series of important scientific developments have occurred during the past quarter of a century of great potential value to administrators in business, government, hospitals, and schools. The social sciences, along with mathematics and statistics, have created methodologies for measuring and analyzing variables valuable both for helping an enterprise decide on which management system to use and for appraising the present state of its human organization. These methodological developments make it possible now to measure the causal and intervening variables with accuracies approaching or exceeding the accuracy of measurement of the end-result variables.

End-result measurements provide, as we saw in Chapter 5, after-the-fact information. They commonly reveal problems when it is too late to take corrective action. End-result measurements, moreover, usually provide neither adequate information about the causes of the undesired results nor the best clues to guide decisions to solve them or prevent them.

Only the causal and intervening variables provide information correctly describing the current internal state of the organization as a human enterprise. Especially important are the causal variables, which provide data enabling one to predict with reasonable accuracy the future trends in the organization.

System 4 Relies on Measurements of the Causal and Intervening Variables

System 4 management recognizes that a highly effective, highly motivated human organization can accomplish with great success almost anything it sets out to do. System 4 management, confident that the desired end-results will be achieved, uses the measurements of the causal and intervening variables to build such human enterprises. This orientation is at sharp variance, as we shall see shortly, with the concepts of System 2 management and with System 2 practices of what is measured and how the information is used. (This discussion is, of course, equally true of System 1 organizations, but to simplify the discussion only System 2 will be referred to, rather than repeating Systems 1 and 2 each time.)

In a System 4 organization, all three classes of variables are measured periodically. The appropriate interval for obtaining these measurements will depend upon the variable involved. Some of the end-result variables should be measured continuously. On the other hand, once a year is usually sufficient for most of the causal and intervening variables, except perhaps during periods of fairly rapid organizational change, when it is desirable to obtain information more often. Obtaining measurements quarterly on a 25 percent sample of the organization may be appropriate in such cases. The sample for such quarterly surveys should be designed to enable measurement of a different 25 percent each quarter. The entire organization will then be covered in one year's time.

The information obtained from each person concerning his behavior, perceptions, reactions, attitudes, and similar variables should be *confidential.* Often it is best to secure such information anonymously. Although individual responses are not identified, the measurements should be obtained in such a manner that *they can be analyzed by operating units down to the lowest levels in the organization.* When these units are so small that the confidentiality of the answers of particular respondents cannot be assured, the data from such small units should be combined with other related small units to maintain the anonymity of the answers. Interpretation and diagnoses can then be made by operating units in terms of cause and effect. Such analyses will reveal for each operating unit the presence of any problems and unfavorable trends requiring remedial action. The information will indicate also the most appropriate remedial steps to take and how best to take them.

System 4 Differs from System 2 in the Use of Measurements

A fundamental concept of System 4 is that the results achieved by an organization are a manifestation of the effectiveness of the interaction-influence system of its human staff. An important focus, consequently, is on building and maintaining a highly effective, highly motivated human organization. Although the end-result measurements are important to a System 4 firm and are watched as carefully as in a System 2 organization, the lead time for corrective action provided by the measurements and by the trends in the causal and intervening variables requires that these variables be given more attention than that given to the end-result data.

In contrast to the System 4 pattern, System 2 management focuses on procedures and outcome. System 2 firms specify the process or work cycle to be used and assign each manager specific objectives. Emphasis is placed on adhering to the standard operating procedures and achieving the designated objectives. Constant inspection of quality, productivity, and earnings is maintained to be sure the outcome is as prescribed. In a System 2 firm, every manager understands that his primary job is to achieve the present goals specified for him. He knows that his performance as measured by the end-result variables must look well continuously. In addition, he is told in an almost "Oh, by the way" manner that his end-result performance should be *accompanied by* favorable supervisory and employee attitudes and good labor relations. Maintaining reasonably desirable attitudes is considered an important responsibility of every manager in System 2 enterprises in order to avoid trouble for the organization, such as loss of good personnel, excessive absence and grievances, work stoppages, and strikes.

This difference between System 2 and System 4 leads, of course, to a basic difference between the systems in the way measurements of the causal and intervening variables are used. System 4 uses them, as we have seen, to build highly effective, highly motivated human organizations in order to produce the desired results. In System 2, the purpose of employee opinion or attitude surveys is to check on each manager to be certain that the attitudes of his department are not becoming seriously unfavorable. Attitude data are collected generally on a plant or company-wide basis in such a way that they cannot be analyzed by smaller operating units. These opinion studies usually obtain few measurements of the causal variables. Even when causal variables are measured, they are not analyzed to reveal their state, nor are the relationships among the causal, intervening, and end-result variables examined.

Such opinion surveys, like a fever chart, may show that the patient has an elevated temperature but tell little of the cause. If management's response to such information is to treat the symptom, the action often accomplishes little and may result in adverse consequences, since the cause is not clear. An additional negative impact from ineffective action is the confirmation of employee's suspicions that such management is not well informed about the human problems of the firm and is making yet another maladaptive attempt to deal with them.

This inadequate use of opinion and attitude measurements in System 2 organizations stems directly from the basic concepts of the system. A central concept is that the job of management is to get high productivity, high earnings, and low costs and if possible, to keep employees happy. This view holds that getting high productivity and keeping employees happy are *two separate and more or less unrelated activities of management,* one much more important than the other. System 2 recognizes that there is less turnover and absence among employees with favorable attitudes and that labor relations are better; hence favorable rather than unfavorable attitudes are preferred. But when a manager has to choose between favorable attitudes and getting production, the choice is clear. Get the production, and then apply some salve to help improve unfavorable attitudes. If one nostrum does not work, try another, but don't worry about employee unhappiness, unless it becomes extreme and labor difficulties prove serious.

The human relations approach to management, which has been fashionable in recent years, is essentially applying salve to System 2 organizations. It fails to deal with the fundamental problems.

An Example of System 2 Use of Opinion Surveys

A very large corporation which measures productivity and performance in a highly sophisticated manner has used this fever-chart approach for many years in measuring employee and managerial attitudes. The attitude surveys in this company were neither designed nor analyzed to reveal cause-and-effect relationships. Even though the questionnaires contained items dealing with causal variables, the analyses always combined answers to several questions, including causal items, into single scores for particular scales. Since these scores could be interpreted only in terms of trends in attitudes and motivation, they brought a sense of frustration when the trends were unfavorable. Managers in charge of operating segments of the corporation were understandably baffled about how to interpret the data to know what constructive steps to take in dealing with any problem the results showed. They made rigorous attempts to derive meaningful clues concerning remedial action but found this difficult because of the lack of causal evidence in the data as analyzed.

Managerial attitudes worsened steadily, as measured by the attitude surveys taken at regular intervals over a span of years. The same development occurred with employee surveys. Both of these surveys have been discontinued on a corporate-wide basis, since they provided few clues for remedial action. Some operating divisions are continuing to use surveys but are modifying the design to obtain better clues concerning constructive steps to take.

This corporation needs sophisticated measurements of its human organization. Its extensive and increasing use of detailed performance measurements of even the smallest operating units is applying powerful forces on its managers to press subordinates for the results specified by top corporate management. The subordinates feel the amount of pressure to be unreasonable. This hierarchical pressure is decreasing confidence and trust, increasing hostile reactions among managers and nonsupervisory employees, and in similar ways is liquidating substantial human assets of the corporation. The available evidence indicates that the attitude surveys which have been discontinued correctly revealed a serious and growing problem.

Until the causal and intervening variables are measured and are used by managers at all levels in this organization for the constructive solution of problems, rather than being used, as are the present performance measures, for inspection, control, and punitive purposes, the corporation will fail to operate at the full capacity of its personnel. Its costs will be greater and its service to customers poorer than need be. Its troubles will continue and may well get worse among managerial as well as nonsupervisory employees. The remedy is a shift from System 2 toward science-based management, such as System 4, with corresponding changes in the measurements obtained and the manner in which they are used.

Opinion Surveys Used as Fever Charts Are Wasteful

Opinion surveys which are analyzed only in terms of such large units as a department, plant, or an entire company are, for all practical purposes, a waste of time and money. They do not yield the needed measurements of the causal variables. Such fever-chart surveys fail to provide the managers and members of each unit and subunit of the organization with the information they need to diagnose their organizational and motivational problems and deal with them effectively.

Even more serious, underlying this use of opinion surveys is the failure to recognize that the performance and output of any enterprise depend entirely upon the quality of the human organization and its capacity to function as a tightly knit, highly motivated, technically competent entity, i.e., as a highly effective interaction-influence system. High productivity, high quality products, high earnings, and successful use of research and development are not accomplished by impersonal equipment or computers. These goals are achieved by human beings. Successful organizations are those making the best use of competent personnel to perform well and efficiently all the tasks required by the enterprise.

Creating the Conditions for Obtaining Accurate Measurements

The capacity of an organization to obtain accurate measurements of the causal, intervening, and end-result variables is greatly influenced over time by the manner in which these data are used. All levels of hierarchy in an organization, except the very top, fear measurements which are used in a punitive manner by their superiors. To protect themselves they tend to resist covertly, if not overtly, the collection of such data. They also try, and often successfully, to distort the measurements in ways to favor or protect themselves. This occurs commonly with the end-result measurements in System 2 organizations. Managers and nonsupervisory employees in many corporations refer to the distortion process as the "fudge factor," "coefficient of fiction," and "Joe Doakes' constant" (Argyris, 1953; Argyris, 1959; Dalton, 1959; Schultz, 1951; Whyte, 1955).

Developments in one large corporation can be used as an example. This firm has become increasingly concerned in recent years with the integrity of its employees. Thefts from the corporation of goods and services total a substantial amount each year. The corporation is also concerned about the ethics involved in the deliberate and successful attempts of their employees to distort the production and performance measurements which the corporation has been using increasingly for inspection and control purposes.

The employees of this corporation, both supervisory and nonsupervisory, have developed a variety of ingenious ways for circumventing the performance measurements. For example, this corporation takes random samples of employee contacts with customers by recording telephone conversations. The recording mechanism is in a small black box and automatically goes on at random intervals to record conversations between an employee and a customer. The employees in one of the units of the corporation observed that whenever the recording unit went on there was a small, audible click. Whoever heard the click promptly alerted the rest of the employees, and the telephone call was immediately taken by one of the most experienced and skilled employees. The performance reports for this unit were outstanding.

This corporation is devoting substantial amounts of time of important staff to this lack of employee integrity and the distortion of performance measurements. Conferences are being held; questions are being asked concerning why these problems exist, what causes them, what should be done to handle these problems constructively, and how to find satisfactory solutions. Unfortunately, this corporation has not yet applied the same objective, scientific approach to this problem as they do to their product research and development. There has been neither a rigorous measurement of the motivational forces prompting their employees to behave as they do nor an adequate, scientific analysis in terms of motivational forces of the alternate solutions the corporation might pursue.

The values of System 2 management still prevail: do not trust employees, tell them what to do, train them to do it properly, and then inspect their behavior to see that they do it. This distrust of the subordinate creates resentment in the subordinate and causes, in turn, distrust of the superior and of the organization. Solutions to this problem will not occur through the use of more elaborate and more innovative inspection procedures. Such steps will, as they have in the past, motivate employees to be equally or even more innovative in finding ways to defeat the inspection procedures.

More constructive alternatives have not yet been tried in any systematic way. The corporation, for example, has not attempted to substitute System 4 management, with its confidence, trust, and supportive managerial behavior, for System 2.

The primary purpose of measurements in System 4 organizations is to provide managers and nonsupervisory employees with information *to help them guide their own decisions and behavior.* These data aid the members of the organization to accomplish both the specific goals they have set for themselves and the broad objectives they have helped to set for the organization. Measurements of all three kinds of variables are eagerly sought when they provide valuable information to help guide decisions and actions and are not used punitively by superiors. All members of the organization want the data and clearly recognize the necessity for the measurements to be accurate. There are strong motivational forces among members to do all they can to assure that the data are accurate and correctly reflect conditions and developments in the organization when the measurements are used for self-guidance. There are, therefore, impressive differences among the different systems of management in their capacity to obtain accurate and undistorted measurements of all variables. Science-based management, such as System 4, can obtain significantly more accurate data than can the other existing systems.

This general conclusion seems to apply equally well to trends in an organization with regard to its management system. If an organization is shifting toward System 4 and its members are aware of this trend, their motivational forces to assure accurate measurements are increased. When, on thc contrary, the trend in the management system of an organization is toward System 1, the motivational forces are to resist the collection of the measurements and to seek to distort the data. Moreover, the greater the trend in either direction and the longer it persists, the greater the changes appear to be in the motivational forces in the predicted direction.

The full potential power of accurate measurements to guide decisions and actions are available to an appreciably greater extent in System 4 organizations, or in firms shifting in that direction, than in System 1 enterprises, or those shifting toward it. The latter have sizable motivational forces in their members to distort the measurements to protect themselves. This prevents the firm from benefiting from accurate information. Moreover, in System 4 organizations, the high levels of confidence and trust which exist enable accurate measurements once obtained to flow to all relevant parts of the enterprise to provide correct information to all persons who have need for it.

Relationships among Causal, Intervening, and End-result Variables

The various dimensions of a firm's human organization and its operation can be placed in a conceptual framework which contributes to their interpretation and helps guide decisions on what to measure. This framework aids in the analysis of the data; it contributes appreciably to the rapid and accurate diagnoses of problems in System 4 organizations, and it is indispensable to firms seeking to shift to System 4 since it focuses their efforts on the key places to introduce change. The variables are grouped into the three broad categories that we have been using, namely, causal, intervening, and end-result. Grouping variables into these categories aids greatly in the correct interpretation of the data and their use for diagnostic and other organizational purposes.

The interrelationships among the three categories of variables in System 2 and System 4 organizations have been discussed in many of the previous chapters and are shown schematically in Figure 8-1. This figure, while

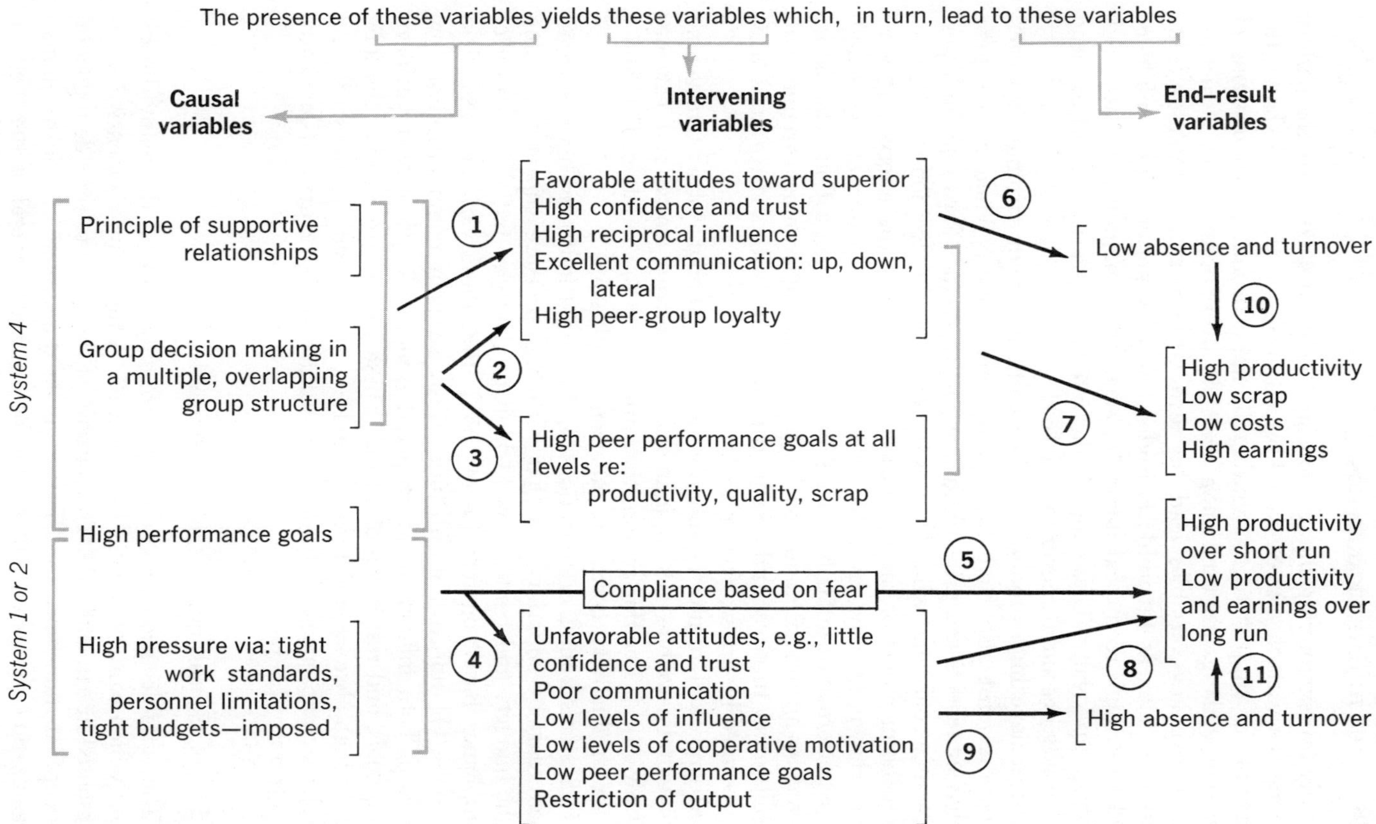

Fig. 8-1. Simplified diagram of relationships among variables for System 1 or 2 and System 4 operation.

grossly oversimplifying the relationships, helps to make clear the pattern among the variables. In System 4 organizations, as the figure shows, the principle of supportive relationships is applied, and group methods of decision making are used in a multiple overlapping group structure. These two key variables lead [as arrow (1) portrays] to intervening variables, such as favorable attitudes toward superior, high confidence and trust, high reciprocal influence, excellent communication, and high peer-group loyalty. These and similar intervening variables, in turn, lead to low absence and turnover [arrow (6)].

To achieve high productivity, low costs, and high earnings, however, superiors must also have high performance goals. When a manager's behavior reflects the principle of supportive relationships and high performance goals, and when he uses the group as the decision-making unit, then the members of the organization will display the intervening variables shown, namely, favorable attitudes toward superior, etc., *and* high peer performance goals for themselves and the organization. This is depicted by arrows (2) and (3). In turn, these intervening variables will result in low turnover and costs and high productivity and earnings, as is represented by arrows (6) and (7).

Absence and turnover probably should be thought of as intervening behavioral variables which influence productivity, costs, and earnings [arrow (10)]. For this reason, they are slightly to the left in Figure 8-1 of the productivity, costs, and other end-result items.

In Systems 1 and 2 organizations, as Figure 8-1 indicates, high performance goals by superiors, coupled with high-pressure supervision using tight budgets and controls, yield high productivity initially because of compliance based on fear [arrow (5)]. But, these variables also yield [arrow (4)] unfavorable attitudes, distrust, poor communication, low levels of both influence and cooperative motivation, low peer performance goals, and restriction of output. These, in turn, result over the long run in high absence and turnover and low productivity [arrows (8) and (9)]. High absence and turnover contribute to high costs and low earnings [arrow (11)].

A List of Causal and Intervening Variables

The variables shown in Figure 8-1 are only a few of the many dimensions which can and should be measured. A much more extensive list is presented in Appendix III. The purpose of this list is to provide a general conceptual framework for all these major dimensions of a firm's human organization and its output. As will be observed, several of the items in Appendix III are concerned primarily with System 4 organizations.

It is valuable to recognize in any diagnosis or analysis of an enterprise which variables are causal, which intervening, and which end-result. Thus, if one wishes to diagnose a problem involving production or earnings (end-result variables) in terms of causal and intervening variables, it is obviously necessary to measure all three kinds. If the relevant causal variables are not measured, as all too often happens, it is, of course, impossible to analyze the problem in terms of such variables. One is then at a loss to know what are the key causal variables which must be changed to improve the situation. In the typical employee attitude surveys, few causal variables are measured and sometimes none at all. Even when causal variables are measured in such surveys, the data are usually collected in such a way that they can be analyzed for large segments of the enterprise only and do not permit analysis by small operating subunits for diagnostic purposes.

The Nature of Causal and Intervening Variables

The causal variables in Appendix III are listed for the organization as a whole and for the superior of each segment or unit. The list obviously does not include all of the causal variables important in affecting organizational success. For example, the condition of the plant, equipment, the amount of working capital, and the adequacy of the technology are not included. The list seeks to cover those dimensions which deal with the quality and productive capacity of the human organization (excluding selection). Moreover, only those items in which the organization or its management has a choice of action are included. If the organization has no choice, the item is not in the causal list. For example, foreign competition, general business conditions, and the international situation affect the end-result variables and may affect the intervening, but these are factors over which the management of a firm can rarely exercise any appreciable amount of influence.

The causal list can be very long, since there are so many ways in which a superior (or organization) can apply or violate the principle of supportive relationships. All the little things a manager does or does not do are apt to reflect this application or violation. When a superior tries to keep grievance channels open because he is genuinely interested in his subordinates and wishes to deal with their grievances in a constructive manner, his behavior usually communicates this orientation to subordinates. When this occurs, he will be seen by them as applying the principle of supportive relationships, and they will respond accordingly. On the other hand, if he intends to do as little as possible about grievances but goes through the motions of keeping grievance channels open as a calculated and manipulative device in an attempt to improve the attitudes and productivity of his department, his subordinates will sense his disinterest in them. Their reactions will reflect this violation of the principle of supportive relationships, and the manager is likely to have more, not fewer, labor difficulties. Virtually all of the contacts between a superior and a subordinate offer the opportunity to apply or violate the principle of supportive relationships. A reasonable number of these ways are listed in Appendix III.

The intervening variables are divided into two broad subcategories: (1) the intervening attitudinal, motivational, and perceptual cluster and (2) the intervening behavioral cluster. These two subcategories merge into one another. There is not a sharp break as the shift is made from the motivational forces to act and some of the resulting action. This is illustrated by the shading from feeling, wanting, and seeking to behaving.

There appears to be much less need for an extensive list of end-result variables, since most companies are now measuring these variables well. Therefore, the list of end-result variables is appreciably less complete than the list for the other two categories and is intended to be illustrative only.

Determining Causality

The lists in Appendix III are derived from the findings of a large number of studies—those done by the Institute for Social Research and by many other researchers. The studies which have been most useful in preparing Appendix III are (1) those of a longitudinal character and (2) the field experiments in which the management style was changed and the resulting changes in the intervening and end-result variables observed. Studies in which measurements were made at one point in time and a large number of correlations computed to examine the relationships among the items have also proved helpful, as have experiments and studies involving small groups.

The causal, intervening, and end-result variables can be thought of appropriately as comprising a complex network with many interdependent relationships. This network concept contributes to an understanding of two important points. It helps to explain the difficulties which are encountered when an attempt is made to classify organizational variables into causal, intervening, and end-result categories. It helps also to account for the deviations often found in particular organizational situations concerning some variables which are not functioning in accordance with the way they have been classified in an overall scheme.

The major items in the causal grouping, such as (1) the character of the organizational structure, (2) the leadership principles employed, and (3) the major assumptions concerning motivation, will prove to be causal in actual operation in most situations. This assumes, of course, that such causal variables are employed in an effective manner. Otherwise their causal impact will be negligible.

Similarly, the major end-result items usually will prove to be only end-result in character. But this may not always be the case. The causal impact which performance can have upon organizational variables has been shown in a study by Farris (1966). "Nothing succeeds like success."

Using data collected from 151 engineers at two points in time, Farris found that a man's performance over a five-year period, 1954 to 1959, predicted more accurately the degree of influence that he was able to exert on his job goals at the end of the five years (1959) than his level of influence in 1959 predicted the quality of his performance over the succeeding five years (1960 to 1965).

The influence question dealt with the extent to which the engineer felt that he could influence the recommendations concerning his technical goals, particularly those recommendations made by the person who had the most authority to establish such goals. Performance was measured by the number of patents and papers, as well as by colleague judgments. The performance measurements covered five-year periods, 1954 to 1959 and 1960 to 1965. The influence variable was measured in 1959 and in 1965.

Farris also found that a man's performance over a five-year period predicted more accurately the degree to which he would be absorbed in his work at the end of the five-year period than the converse. That is, the degree of absorption in his work at the beginning of a five-year period predicted his performance during the five years less well than the performance predicted absorption.

These findings show that the level of an engineer's performance can be a causal variable in determining the extent to which he feels he can exert an influence on decisions affecting his job goals. In Appendix III, however, the level of a man's performance or the results achieved by a department are not treated as causal variables, since they do not meet one of the two conditions stated. To be classified as causal, a variable must be subject to deliberate alterations or change by the organization. This is not the case with these variables. A man's performance or a department's output are not variables which the management of a firm can alter directly. The man, himself, by his actions determines the number of patents he receives. It is not determined by direct company action. The company may create the conditions under which creativity flourishes. In this case, the *conditions* are causal variables, not the man's performance.

The number of patents or papers that an engineer produces can exercise significant influence on his feeling of success. Therefore, steps that an organization or a superior may take to alter a man's sense of achievement or accomplishment are considered causal variables.

In Appendix III, the sense of accomplishment is listed as a causal variable in several instances. For example, the principle of supportive relationships is viewed as a causal variable when the organization gives recognition for excellent performance, when superiors acclaim the achievement of goals, or when high group performance is used to encourage pride in one's organization and aspiration for even greater achievement.

The causal category of Appendix III, therefore, includes only variables subject to control or change by the organization. The procedure used in classifying the variables and preparing the lists was to observe which items, if altered, would, on the average, be followed at a later time by related changes in other items. Those first in the time sequence were viewed as causal; those next, as intervening; and those last, as end-result. Among the intervening variables some are more toward the causal end of the interacting chain; others are closer to the end-result terminal. Changes in the former occur prior to changes in the latter.

The concept of coordination can be used to describe the way the variables were classified. This term refers to the extent to which the activities of different parts of an organization effectively dovetail to contribute to the achievements of an organization. The level of coordination of a firm depends upon such variables as the quality of communication among the relevant units, the extent to which these units can influence and motivate each other, and their capacity to resolve conflicts and differences constructively. Small group experiments, as well as organizational change experiments and longitudinal organizational studies, show that the current condition of the variables contributing to the degree of coordination is determined by the nature of the organizational structure and the interaction processes, i.e., by the extent to which (1) the structure consists of multiple overlapping groups, (2) work problems are handled by group decision making, and (3) the principle of supportive relationships is being applied. These three variables, overlapping group structure, group decision making, and the principle of supportive relationships, can be considered to be causal in influencing those intervening variables associated with effective coordination, such as excellent communication and high capacity among units to influence and motivate each other.

The available evidence provides little reason to believe that when coordination is poor, telling supervisors to communicate more candidly and effectively and telling them to influence and motivate each other to a greater extent will change the organizational structure from man-to-man model (Figure 4-1*a*) to a multiple overlapping group form of organization (Figure 4-1*b*). Nor are such instructions likely to lead superiors to make greater use of group decision making and the principle of supportive relationships. Efforts to improve coordination are most likely to be effective when there is improvement in the causal variables.

Some of the other problems involved in building the list of causal and intervening variables can be illustrated by "communication." This term refers to a variety of different kinds of activities. Some of these are causal, and some are intervening. When the superior uses communication to apply the principle of supportive relationships by providing the subordinate with all the information the latter seeks and needs, the item should be considered causal. On the other hand, communication is intervening in character when it occurs in response to causal factors. For example, whether subordinates are motivated to "yes" the boss or to communicate important information upward (intervening) depends upon the nature of their supervision (causal).

The items in Appendix II can be used also to illustrate this classification process. Items 1, 3, 4, 5, 6, 7, 16, 32, 39, 40, and 41 are causal in character. Items 24, 27, 33, 44, and 46 are largely causal but in some circumstances can be influenced by other items. The rest of the items are intervening.

Causal Variables: The Key to Organizational Improvement

Figure 8-1 and Appendix III are useful guides in all attempts to help an organization shift toward System 4. When an organization is seeking to make such a shift, the efforts to change should be focused initially on the causal variables. Changes brought about in the causal variables will lead in turn to changes in the intervening and end-result variables. Attempts to bring the desired shift in the management system by concentrating on the intervening variables directly will result usually in disappointment and failure.

Efforts to change an organization toward System 4 also need to deal with all those organizational procedures which bind an organization to its present management system. Training in group interaction skills and similar efforts to move an organization toward System 4 are likely to yield disappointing results if steps are not taken to shift all operating procedures toward a System 4 pattern. A company using System 2 management is firmly bound to that system by all of its operating procedures, such as its pattern of setting objectives and budgets, the use of measurement for punitive control, the customary performance appraisal and review process, and its compensation plan with regard to both the way the plan is established and the way it is administered. These and all the other System 2 operating procedures need to be changed to a System 4 model to enable the entire organization to move to System 4.

The character of these procedures in a System 4 firm have been indicated by much of the material in this volume, particularly in Chapters 4 and 10. A volume now in preparation will discuss the nature of System

4 procedures at much greater length and suggest how a firm can develop such procedures tailored to its unique traditions and situation.

Avoid Burying Managers in Data

The tremendous capacity of large computers may tempt those who are handling the measurement program in a corporation to obtain measurements on a large number of the items listed in Appendix III and to report them to the managers of the units involved. This would bury these departments in reports and tables. The time required for the analysis and interpretation of such a mountain of data would cause the results to be ignored due to the time pressures arising from day-to-day operations.

Appendix III, obviously, includes many more items than one needs to measure or report at any one time. The value of an extensive list is that it enables one to be conscious of what he is omitting. Items can be omitted deliberately and for good reasons. A marked relationship between one or two key items and a number of other items is a basis for omission of all but the key items, since in most situations there are relatively stable patterns of interrelations among the items. Knowing these interrelationships, such as those described in Chapter 7, enables one to report only the key variables and be relatively confident of the state of the other related variables. These interrelationships should be checked periodically, however, by including the different items which are related to the key items on a rotating, sample basis with some of these items in each round of measurement. This would permit a frequent check on the stability of the relationships among the items. These analyses are done easily with the aid of computers.

Only the most important variables which have the most marked relationships and which best summarize many other variables need be reported to each operating unit. Each manager and his department need data on only a relatively few dimensions, namely, those which are operationally most important. This would conserve time and focus attention on matters having the greatest influence on the department's performance.

Accurate Measurement Requires Professional Competence

The measurement of the causal and intervening variables is a complex task requiring considerable competence in the relevant scientific fields, namely, social psychology, psychometrics, sociometrics, and statistics. It may appear to be easy to measure these variables accurately when one has a list such as that appearing in Appendix III, but such is not the case. Accurate data are not obtained by merely asking people what they think or how they feel. It takes at least as much sophistication and competence to set up measurements to obtain correct data concerning the causal and intervening variables as is required for accurate accounting. The interpretation of the data and of their use for diagnoses and analyses requires a still greater degree of competence.

The measurements and diagnoses of organizational problems are complex. Moreover, the treatment of symptoms rather than causes can be costly to the enterprise. It would be unthinkable for any modern corporation to have its accounting set up and directed by anyone other than a well-trained accountant. Senior corporate officers should view the measurement of the causal and intervening variables as requiring at least comparable social science training and professional experience. Accurate information correctly interpreted can be too valuable to an organization, and erroneous information too costly, to permit the work to be done by persons lacking the necessary scientific and professional training. In medium-sized and smaller companies, once the measurement program is launched and the analyses and the use of the data reasonably well-established, professional assistance other than occasional consultation may no longer be required.

The subject of measurement, including the correct interpretation of the data and the use of the measurements by means of feedback to guide decisions and to motivate and develop managers, needs to be dealt with at much greater length than has been possible here. It is the topic for another, but as yet unwritten, book.

Chapter 9

HUMAN ASSET ACCOUNTING

Evidence was presented in Chapters 5 and 6 for the necessity of including estimates of the current value of the human organization and of customer goodwill in all financial reports of a firm.

The absence of these estimates for each profit center and for the entire corporation is not due to a lack of interest on the part of the accounting profession (Hermanson, 1964). Cultural lag and the usual gaps in communication among the relevant sciences are the culprits. To create human asset accounting and to make reasonably accurate estimates of its two dimensions—the current value of the human organization and customer goodwill—require close cooperation between accountants and social scientists highly competent in the measurement of the causal and intervening variables.

Such cooperation is now starting. It will require from five to ten years and many million dollars' worth of work to collect the data and to make the computations required before human asset accounting can become fully operational. Sophisticated measurement and accounting procedures should emerge from this work, enabling firms to incorporate in their financial reports reasonably accurate estimates of the current value of the human assets of an enterprise. These procedures will enable a firm not only to know the current value of these resources, but also what changes or trends are occurring from time to time in the magnitudes of these assets. In addition, it will be possible to prepare these estimates for each profit center of the firm and, where appropriate and useful, for any smaller unit within a firm.

Computing a firm's original investment in its human organization is a much simpler problem than estimating the current value of that investment. This is true for the company as a whole and for such units as profit centers, departments, and other subunits. There are several alternate methods for obtaining estimates of the original investment in the human side of an enterprise.

One way is to base these estimates on start-up costs. The problem in many ways is comparable to estimating a firm's current investment in machinery which it has built itself and continues to use for a period of time. The actual cost of building a machine can readily be computed. The human start-up costs of a new plant, unit, or department can be computed similarly, although the task of doing so is more complex and difficult. These start-up costs should include what it has cost to hire and train the personnel and to develop them into a coordinated organization operating in a reasonably satisfactory manner.

Start-up costs can be computed for various kinds of operations and for various-sized units. As these human investment costs become available for the widely different kinds of operations performed by a particular enterprise, they can be used as a basis for estimating the magnitude of the investment a firm has in its human organization—for the entire corporation or for any of its units.

A second way of estimating the magnitude of the investment in the human organization is to obtain data on the costs of hiring and training personnel for each of the many different kinds of positions in the company. The sum of these costs for every person in the firm usually will be substantial. It underestimates, however, the true investment in the human side of the enterprise, since it does not reflect the additional investment made during the period when the members of the firm were establishing effective cooperative working relationships[1] with one another. These cooperative working relationships might appropriately be called the synergistic component. To establish them takes an appreciable period of time and involves substantial costs.

This approach will require a tremendous amount of work if it is done for every kind of position and every member of the organization. The cost and effort of making these estimates can be reduced substantially by probability sampling. Efficient designs will yield estimates closely approximating those which would be obtained were all the jobs and all the positions examined.

Estimating the Current Value of the Human Organization

Although computing a firm's investment in building its human organization or its customer goodwill may be difficult, obtaining reasonably accurate estimates of the *current* value of the human organization is a much more difficult and complex task. It is, moreover, much more important. For the reasons discussed at length in Chapters 5 and 6, it is essential that reasonably accurate information be currently available to all levels of management as to changes and trends in the present value of its human organization. Managers and all other members of the organi-

[1] The nature of these relationships is described on pp. 183–185 of *New Patterns of Management.*

zation and shareholders need to be kept correctly informed on these matters, since the health, profitability, and long-range survival of the enterprise depend upon sound decisions guided by measurements which reflect the current value of its human organization.

Human Asset Accounting

Human assets, as used in this volume, refer both to the value of the productive capacity of a firm's human organization and to the value of its customer goodwill.

The productive capability of its human organization can be illustrated by thinking of two firms in the same business. Both are of the same size and have identical equipment and technology. One, however, produces more and earns more than the other, because its personnel is superior to the other's with regard to such variables as the following:

1. Level of intelligence and aptitudes
2. Level of training
3. Level of performance goals and motivation to achieve organizational success
4. Quality of leadership
5. Capacity to use differences for purposes of innovation and improvement, rather than allowing differences to develop into bitter, irreconcilable, interpersonal conflict
6. Quality of communication upward, downward, and laterally
7. Quality of decision making
8. Capacity to achieve cooperative teamwork versus competitive striving for personal success at the expense of the organization
9. Quality of the control processes of the organization and the levels of felt responsibility which exist
10. Capacity to achieve effective coordination
11. Capacity to use experience and measurements to guide decisions, improve operations, and introduce innovations

The difference in the economic value of the human organizations of these two firms would be reflected by the differences between them in present and future earnings, attributable to the differences in their human organizations. Similarly, differences in the value of customer goodwill would be reflected in the differences between them in the ease and costs of making sales, i.e., in the difference in the motivation among customers to buy the product of one firm, rather than that of the other.

Human asset accounting refers to activity devoted to attaching dollar estimates to the value of a firm's human organization and its customer goodwill. If able, well-trained personnel leave the firm, the human organization is worth less; if they join it, the firm's human assets are increased. If bickering, distrust, and irreconcilable conflict become greater, the human enterprise is worth less; if the capacity to use differences constructively and engage in cooperative teamwork improves, the human organization is a more valuable asset.

Since estimates of the current value of a firm's human organization are both necessary and difficult to obtain, it is highly desirable to use several alternate approaches in developing methods for making these estimates. The results from one approach can serve as a check on those obtained from the others. The initial estimates from any procedure, of course, are likely to have relatively large errors of estimate. As the methodology improves, two important developments will occur. The size of the errors will decrease, and the accuracy of estimating the magnitude of these errors will increase. The accuracy of human asset accounting will increase correspondingly.

The essential first step in developing procedures for applying human asset accounting to a firm's human organization is to undertake periodic measurements of the key causal and intervening variables. These measurements must be available over several years' time to provide the data for the needed computations. The data required for the initial computations should be collected at quite frequent intervals, quarterly or even more often.

The optimum frequency for the measurements will vary with the kind of work involved. The more nearly the work involves the total man, such as research and development (R&D) tasks, the shorter should be the intervals between successive measurements, for, as was mentioned in Chapter 5, the time lag between changes in the causal, intervening, and end-result variables is much less for such work than for work which is machine-paced. The sequence of developments (shown in Figure 5-2) requires a shorter time interval for R&D and other complex tasks than for machine-paced or simple, repetitive tasks. Unfavorable attitudes lead much more rapidly to decreased productivity. A scientist who feels resentful toward his organization or manager rapidly becomes unproductive. With machine-paced and similar work, which usually employs only a part of the capabilities of the total man (e.g., hands), a longer period of time is required before the adverse effect of unfavorable reactions and attitudes manifest themselves in the forms of norms to restrict production, of increased grievances and similar developments, and, finally, in lower performance. For this kind of work, consequently, the intervals between periodic measurements can be longer than for professional and other complex work.

The total period of time required for the cycles, shown in Figures 5-2 and 5-3, to reach reasonable equilibrium, of course, will vary also with the kind of work. The cycle reaches a stable relationship much more quickly with complex tasks than with machine-paced and simple, repetitive tasks. Complex tasks require less time to reach stable relationships; machine-paced and similar work require more time.[2]

The measurements of the causal and intervening variables should be obtained for the corporation as a whole and for each profit center or unit in the company for which productivity, costs, waste, and earnings can be computed. After these measurements have been made over a sufficient period of time for relatively stable relationships to develop or for the sequence of relationships to complete their full cycle, the necessary data will be available to relate the causal and intervening measurements to the earnings record. By using appropriate statistical procedures, relationships can be computed among the causal, intervening, and such end-result variables as costs and earnings. The resulting mathematical relationships will enable one to estimate the productive and earnings capability of any profit center, or smaller unit, based upon its present scores on the causal and intervening variables. These estimates of probable subsequent productivity, costs, and earnings will reveal the earning power of the human organization *at the time* the causal and intervening variables were measured, even though the level of estimated subsequent earnings may not be achieved until much later. These estimates of probable subsequent productivity, costs, and earnings provide the basis for attaching to any profit center, unit, or total corporation a statement of the present value of its human organization.

Corporations which have a number of relatively comparable units, such as chain stores, will have a distinct advantage in using the method just suggested. The data from several comparable units will yield more reliable estimates by providing far more observations upon which to base calculations. Moreover, differences among the units can be used as well as changes for any particular unit over time. Based on these differences, computations can be made of the relation of earnings to each pattern of causal and intervening variables using, of course, optimum time intervals. By capitalizing the greater earnings of the better units, estimates of the present value of the human organization can be obtained.

It is probable that after sufficient research has been done and sufficient data and experience obtained, it will be feasible to do human asset accounting in much the same way that standard costs are now used to estimate the manufacturing costs of new products. Another use of standard estimates is the MTM (Methods-Time Measurement) process of setting a standard time for the performance of a particular task. Experience has shown that standard estimates can be used successfully in accounting and

[2] The influence of different kinds of work upon the cycle of relationships among the causal, intervening, and end-result variables is discussed more fully in Chapter 6, *New Patterns of Management.*

in industrial engineering. A comparable process should be equally successful in human asset accounting.

Present Earnings May Yield Incorrect Estimate

Many corporations at present are making estimates of the current value of the human organization and of customer goodwill. This is done whenever a new firm or division is acquired. Every year there are a substantial number of acquisitions. In each instance, an appropriate value has to be placed on the acquired firm. The purchase price generally is substantially larger than the current value of the physical and financial assets and reflects allowances for both customer and employee goodwill. Both the firm which is acquired and the corporation acquiring it make these estimates in arriving at a fair price. An important factor in arriving at these estimates usually is the current and recent earnings of the acquired firm. This approach has to be used cautiously, however, since it contains a source of error which at times can be sizable. If the acquired firm has been using the approach to cost reduction based on personnel limitations, tightened budgets, and tighter standards and is at a point of high earnings but decreasing value of the human organization (e.g., at approximately T_3 to T_6 in Figure 5-2), then an estimate of the value of the human assets based on current earnings is likely to be appreciably inflated.

Estimating the Value of Customer Goodwill

Customer goodwill, like the value of the human organization, is an asset of substantial magnitude in most companies. The sizable costs in opening new markets or marketing new products demonstrate the magnitude of the current value of this asset in most companies.

This asset can vary appreciably from time to time, depending upon the behavior of the firm's management (a causal variable), the resulting motivation and behavior of the firm's personnel (intervening variables), and the corresponding price and quality of product and service provided to customers (end-result variables).

Cash income can be increased for a period of time by selling shoddy products and rendering poor service while charging the usual prices. This income should not be reported and treated as earnings in financial statements, however, since it is actually achieved by cashing in on the firm's customer loyalty. It represents a liquidation, often at a fraction of its value, of customer goodwill. Such "earnings" are as spurious and misleading as those derived from liquidating part of the firm's investment in its human organization.

Customer goodwill, as well as the value of the human organization, should be reflected at its present value in every financial statement. This can be done by drawing upon the methodological resources created by social-psychological research. The same basic concepts and methodology employed in estimating the current value of the human organization can be used to attach dollar amounts to the current value of customer goodwill. Favorable customer attitudes create motivational forces to buy a firm's products. One set of estimates of the current value of these motivational forces can be obtained by methods available for measuring the sales influence of advertising and marketing efforts. A method for obtaining the relevant measurements was published several years ago (Likert, 1936).

Imbalance in Fiscal Management

In considering the desirability and expense of undertaking the work required for human asset accounting, it should be recognized that the present practice of treating, with great precision, a fraction of the firm's assets and completely ignoring assets of roughly the same or greater magnitude represents a serious imbalance. A firm's financial reports would be much more useful and appreciably more accurate if approximately the same level of accuracy were maintained in dealing with *all* of the firm's assets. The equity of the shareholders would be protected far better than at present if there were more balance in the accounting effort.

It is perfectly feasible for a company to establish a balanced effort in their accounting activities without an appreciable increase in their total accounting costs. This can be done by placing all accounting on a sample basis and using sample designs which yield estimates of acceptable accuracy. There would be a substantial reduction in the costs of the usual physical asset and financial asset accounting, and this saving could be used for human asset accounting, i.e., for obtaining estimates of the current value of the human organization and of customer goodwill.

This use of sampling methods in the accounting work would result in small sampling errors in the reports dealing with the physical and financial assets. At present, these reports usually contain no errors due to sampling, since a 100 percent sample is generally used. With sophisticated, weighted sampling designs, however, the sampling errors would be smaller than the other errors which arise from various assumptions, such as those used in handling depreciation and comparable problems.

The facts are clear. If sophisticated sampling methods were applied to physical and financial accounting, the maximum probable error would be so small as to be unimportant in its consequences. If sound sampling methods were used in conducting human asset accounting, physical asset accounting, and financial asset accounting, the errors due to sampling would be negligible, and a firm would have appreciably more accurate fiscal reports than at present. The sampling errors in such financial reports, on the average, would be only a fraction of the size of the errors which now occur in financial reports which are based on 100 percent sampling of the physical and financial assets and no sampling of the human assets.

Interim Steps to Increase the Accuracy of Financial Reports

There is, of course, an interim problem to be dealt with. Even though a firm started tomorrow to do the research required to develop the necessary procedures for human asset accounting, several years would be required before it could be put into effect. In the meantime, however, corporate officers can take an important step which will enable them to safeguard company assets more completely and to improve appreciably the accuracy and adequacy of the information provided them.

The proposed step is to introduce the periodic measurement of the causal and intervening variables and *to have a record of these measurements made a part of every production and financial report.* This should be done for all fiscal and production reports, both those for profit centers and those for the entire corporation.

These measurements would help the board and the other managers of the firm to interpret more correctly the production and financial reports they receive. If there were no changes from one period to the next in the scores on the causal and intervening variables, the financial report could be considered essentially correct, insofar as any changes in the current value of the human organization are concerned. If, however, these measurements of the causal and intervening variables showed an unfavorable shift, then the financial report should be viewed as overstating the actual situation. Under such circumstances the report would reflect a more favorable picture than the actual facts and would include as earnings funds which were really derived from the liquidation of human assets. Conversely, if the measurements of the causal and intervening variables were to reflect a favorable shift, then the financial report would understate the real situation, since management actually would be doing a better job than the report revealed. The true earnings and changes in assets would be more favorable than the financial report showed.

The measurements of the causal and intervening variables can be used in this manner to assure that there are no serious mistakes in the interpretation of the financial and production reports for any unit, profit center, or the entire company. Managers of units which achieved part of their earnings or productivity by liquidating human assets would have their financial and production reports correspondingly discounted. On the other hand, managers who added to company assets by improving their human organization would have their performance records viewed as understating their total managerial performance. Changes in the size and composition of the labor force should be taken into consideration also.

Bankers making loans, investment houses, and others who are interested in the earnings and success of an enterprise should be just as interested as boards and senior officers in having these periodic measurements of the causal and intervening variables available. These data, as we have seen, are essential for the correct interpretation of production and fiscal data.

It is equally important to have similar periodic measurements of customer goodwill accompany financial reports and for the same reasons. These data should be interpreted and used in essentially the same way as the measurements of the causal and intervening variables.

As soon as corporate officers arrange to have the measurements of the causal and intervening variables and of customer goodwill as part of production and financial reports, enterprises will be managed more successfully. Better decisions will be made at all management levels, because these decisions will be based on more accurate facts. Senior officers and boards will not be misinformed, as they may be at present, concerning the management systems used by the managers who achieve the highest earnings year in and year out. With accurate information to guide its decisions, top management would not superimpose a System 2 manager on a System 4 operation and thereby destroy one of their most valuable assets. The present management of large corporations whose previous managements have built great loyalty and high motivation committed to corporate success at all levels in the organization will not be able to show impressive but fictitious earnings over many years' time by progressively increasing the pressure and tightening the controls on their subordinate managers, supervisors, and nonsupervisory employees, i.e., shifting toward System 2 from System 3 or 4.

Probably the most important improvement in fiscal management will be the profound changes which measurements of the human dimensions of an enterprise will bring in the generally accepted concepts of how a corporation or department should be managed to be financially most successful. The cold hard facts of accurate measurements will wipe out many of the erroneous concepts which are widely held today but which are based on incomplete accounting and short-run financial analyses of only a portion of a firm's total assets.

The Opportunity Is Limited

The opportunity to use measurements of the causal and intervening variables during the interim period in the manner suggested will be affected by the management system of the firm and trends in this system. As was pointed out in Chapter 8, cooperative motivation is necessary to obtain the most accurate measurements of the causal, intervening, and end-result variables over any period of time. A firm's capacity to use the interim steps suggested, therefore, will be influenced by its management system and the trends in this system. Companies which are using System 4 or are shifting toward it will have the cooperative motivation required for measurements to be accurate. Firms shifting toward System 1 or using System 1 or 2 will be unlikely to have such cooperative motivation.

Firms striving to use a science-based management system will have a distinct advantage over other companies in the adequacy and accuracy of the information made available to them to guide decisions and to evaluate results.

Chapter 10

ACHIEVING EFFECTIVE COORDINATION IN A HIGHLY FUNCTIONALIZED COMPANY

A science-based theory of organization, such as System 4, offers modern industrial society new resources to cope with complex organizational problems. It provides formal solutions to organizational difficulties which cannot be solved within the framework and concepts of traditional organizational theory. At present these problems are often handled by means of informal solutions which are at variance with the formal organizational theory of the firm. Coordination will be discussed as an example of the capacity of System 4 to provide better formal solutions than can System 2 to the difficult problems of organizing and managing a highly complex, technologically based, modern enterprise.

Virtually every large company faces, in more or less serious form, the problem of whether to organize on a functional basis or on a product or geographical basis or to try some compromise solution. The requirements of both specialization and low unit costs achieved by large-scale operations (economy of scale) press for a functional form of organization. But it is not easy for a large, highly functionalized organization to achieve effective coordination. New products emerging from research, for example, do not move from research to development to manufacturing to marketing with the speed and coordination required to capitalize on the large demand for a new and useful product.

Unfortunately, major trends are aggravating this already serious problem of how to achieve coordination in a highly functionalized company. New knowledge and methodologies are being created at a rapidly accelerating rate as the national expenditures for research and development increase. Because of the limits of human capacity, more, not less, functionalization is required to make effective use of these new resources. Increases in functionalization, in turn, make effective coordination both more necessary and even more difficult.

The increased volume of research contributes in another way to these trends. To use research (R&D) effectively, an organization must change. Many different kinds of changes are required in products, in technologies, in markets, in the organizational structure, and in many other ways. But the readiness and willingness to change are virtually never the same among the different members and parts of the organization; thus every change involves stresses, differences, conflicts (Kahn, Wolfe, Quinn, Snoek, & Rosenthal, 1964). Effective ways of resolving these differences constructively and with reasonable rapidity must be found if the changes are to occur smoothly and with a minimum of delay, thus enabling the new products and services to be marketed at a time when they are most profitable.

The difficulties created by a functional form of organization have caused many companies to turn to a product form of organization, or a regional form. Decentralization on a product basis has been widely used to meet the problems created by functionalization. But as decentralization solves some problems, it produces others. With decentralization, some of the gains of specialization are lost; economies of scale are often sacrificed, and new problems of coordination are created. For example, a company producing industrial goods with 10 different sales organizations representing their different decentralized divisions must provide coordination of the efforts of those sales departments so that purchasing agents are not irritated by excessive calls.

Decentralization is becoming, moreover, an inadequate solution as technologies become more complex and ever more extensive functionalization becomes essential. Decentralization, furthermore, does not eliminate differences among staff or among departments; it merely changes the relationship of who differs with whom about what.

Large governmental agencies as well as business enterprises are suffering from the failure of current efforts to solve the complex problems of coordination caused by extensive functionalization. This failure is preventing government, as well as industry, from which full use of the new knowledge created by the extensive research which it is supporting. As a consequence, large Federal agencies are not realizing a full return on their substantial research expenditures in the physical and biological sciences and cannot do so until they can solve this organizational problem.

Attempts to find a creative and satisfactory solution have been seriously restrained by the limitations imposed by the currently accepted formal organization theories upon which Systems 1, 2, and 3 are based. As we shall see, so long as a company or governmental agency is bound by these traditional theories, it is unlikely to solve this important management problem.

The Requirements of a Satisfactory Solution

A satisfactory solution requires an organization which can have extensive functionalization and which can also resolve differences and achieve efficient coordination on a product or geographical basis. This usually will necessitate effective coordination horizontally as well as vertically. To meet these requirements, an organization will need to have two or more channels of decision making and coordination, with at least one occurring via the functional lines and the other via the product or geographical line. Many persons in such an organization will have two or more superiors.

This organization will need to have decision-making and influence processes sufficiently effective to reach first-rate decisions and to achieve highly motivated, coordinated behavior directed toward efficiently attaining the organization's goals. These decision-making and influence processes must be able to achieve coordination in spite of initial and often substantial conflict coming through two or more channels or lines.

At least four conditions must be met by an organization if it is to achieve a satisfactory solution to the coordination-functional problem.

1. It must provide high levels of cooperative behavior between superiors and subordinates and especially among peers. Favorable attitudes and confidence and trust are needed among its members.

2. It must have the organizational structure and the interaction skills required to solve differences and conflicts and to attain creative solutions.

3. It must possess the capacity to exert influence and to create motivation and coordination without traditional forms of line authority.

4. Its decision-making processes and superior-subordinate relationships must be such as to enable a person to perform his job well and without hazard when he has two or more superiors.

These four conditions are not and cannot be met by a System 1, 2, or 3 organization operating on the basis of currently accepted organizational theory. This is not to say that the highest-producing managers are not operating within System 2 and System 3 companies in such a way as to provide these conditions. They are. But, as we have seen in earlier chapters (also Likert, 1961, Chaps. 2–5), in doing so, these high-producing managers are deviating in fundamental ways from the formal theory upon which their company's organizational structure and standard operating procedures are based.

The Inadequacies of Systems 1, 2, and 3

The formal organization theory underlying Systems 1 through 3 fails to meet these four conditions in that (1) the theory specifies that a person can have only one boss; (2) it calls for managerial procedures and behavior which, on the average, tend to produce competition and conflict between peers and apathy or resentment among subordinates; and (3) it fails to make full use of those motivational forces which must be employed if cooperative attitudes and effective coordination are to be achieved.

The view that a person can have only one superior and should be given orders by him and no one else is based on "hire-and-fire" authority (White, 1963, pp. 36–41). This is a central concept of current, formal, organization theory (Steiglitz, 1962, p. 14).

Hire-and-fire authority and such related concepts as direction and control and the view that a man can have only one boss stem from the underlying motivational assumption of classical management theory. This theory relies primarily on the economic needs of man. The basic motivational assumption of Systems 1 and 2 is that when an organization buys a man's time it obtains control over his behavior. When this assumption first was made, it probably was valid. Lack of income often meant in those days lack of food and shelter and even, perhaps, loss of life. But today this assumption is no longer valid and is totally inadequate as a basis upon which to base an organizational theory.

As many studies have demonstrated, supervision based on economic needs and reliance on coercive, *have to* motivation produces apathy or hostility in the subordinate toward the superior and toward the organization and its objectives (Argyris, 1957; Katz & Kahn, 1966; March & Simon, 1958; Mathewson, 1931; Roethlisberger & Dickson, 1939; White & Lippitt, 1960; Whyte, 1955). It also stimulates competition and conflict among subordinates who, as peers, strive for recognition and reward from their boss and often "knife" each other in order to get more for themselves. When an organization relies primarily on economic needs, it fails to use adequately those basic human motives which are capable of developing the kinds of cooperative relationships needed to operate productively the highly complex, highly functionalized organizations required by modern industrial technologies.

Fortunately, as research shows, the highest-producing managers in American business and government are, on the average, bound neither by the inadequate motivational assumption of Systems 1 and 2 nor by the systems themselves. They do not reject motivation based on economic needs. They seek to use it more fully than present wage-and-salary plans by providing more clear-cut economic rewards for behavior which helps the organization achieve its objectives. They seek to avoid rewarding behavior which fails to serve the company's objectives or which defeats their attainment, as, for example, salary plans which generously reward managers for liquidating a firm's human assets. In addition to making more effective use of economic needs, these managers strive to use fully the noneconomic motives which yield cooperative attitudes and behavior.

Using their experience and insights, these managers are steadily developing more effective managerial principles. An integration of these principles into a management theory has yielded System 4. This science-based system offers new and more promising solutions to the complex problems of managing and coordinating the highly complex enterprises required by modern technology.

Coordination via System 4

Let us examine the nature of the solutions suggested by System 4 by starting first with the situation in which an individual is responsible, for all practical purposes, to two superiors. How would the operation work as a formal system if he were a member of both a functional work group and a product, or cross-function, work group? These two work groups each consist of a superior to whom he and the other subordinates under that particular superior report. Figure 10-1 shows these two work groups and the overlapping member, M-1c, who reports to two superiors. One work group is the functional-line (e.g., marketing) work group and its superior is M-1. The other work group is the product, cross-function work group with its superior, A-1.

If both of these work groups have high group loyalty and are using group decision making well (Bradford et al., 1963; Maier, 1963; Marrow, 1964a; Schein & Bennis, 1965), subordinates in each work group would be able to exercise significant amounts of upward and lateral influence (Likert, 1961, Chaps. 8, 9, 11, 12). (If these groups are not performing in this way, the superiors of these work groups and, in turn, their own superiors, as we shall see, have some training and organization building to do.) This would mean, of course, that the individual we are consider-

Fig. 10-1. Example of subordinate serving as linking pin for horizontal coordination.

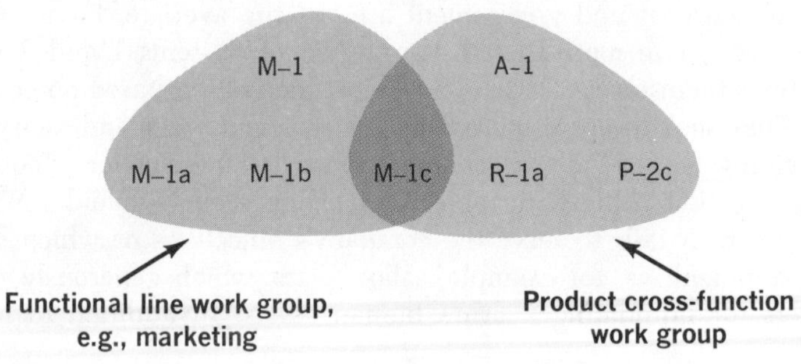

ing (M-1c), who is the subordinate under two superiors, can exert upward influence via group decision-making processes in both work groups. As a consequence, when one superior (e.g., product, cross-function superior, A-1) and the work group reporting to him approach decisions which are incompatible or in conflict with the points of view held or decisions being arrived at by the other superior (marketing department superior, M-1) and his work group, the individual who is in both work groups is obligated to bring such information to the attention of both work groups. This information is relevant data to be used by each work group in its decision making. Even though the chief of one or the other groups may be reluctant to consider such information, the group members are likely to want to do so. They, themselves, are likely to be members of other cross-function work groups and recognize that they, too, sooner or later may find themselves caught in a developing conflict between the two or more work groups of which they are subordinate members. They will wish, consequently, to resolve this conflict constructively and thereby help to create a well-established process and precedent for handling such differences.

Under System 4, both work groups shown in Figure 10-1 will be expected to engage in group decision making in order to resolve the differences. The decision-making processes should strive to create an innovative solution which satisfactorily meets the requirements and opportunities presented by the situations faced by both groups. The focus should not be, as is often the case with System 2 man-to-man decision making, on obtaining a decision favorable to a particular work group or its department, irrespective of how costly it is for the rest of the organization. The primary objective of the decision making of the two work groups should be to discover a solution which will serve the best interests of the entire organization.

Whenever the members of one or both of the two groups display inability to use group decision making sufficiently well to achieve consensus in terms of the best interests of all concerned, the higher-level work groups must provide further training in group processes. This training of the subordinate work groups in group problem solving and related processes should enable all work groups to recognize from their own experience that everyone in the organization benefits when the decision making is focused on discovering the best solutions for the entire organization and that almost everyone suffers when the decision-making processes break down into a bargaining, or win-lose battle.

If the individual (M-1c) were in a System 2 organization and caught in a developing conflict between his two superiors, the situation could be resolved only by getting one or both of his superiors to change their decisions and their expectations regarding his behavior. The individual's only recourse in his attempt to change the conflicting demands on him would be man-to-man interaction separately with each superior. He would have to try to persuade one or both of his superiors to change their decisions in a subordinate-superior discussion with each. Often the requested change would be seen by the particular superior as implying a criticism of him, or as taking sides with the other superior against him. Neither criticism nor taking sides is warmly received. In this System 2 situation, the subordinate's attempts to change the decisions of one or both of his two superiors would not be likely to succeed, and he would be left in jeopardy, unable to satisfy the conflicting demands. It is for this reason that a cardinal principle of System 2 is that a man can have only one boss.

As we have seen, System 4 handles this problem by providing the resource of group rather than man-to-man interaction. With System 4, the individual caught between conflicting demands initiates discussion of the problem in the relevant work groups. Discussion of it takes place there in a much more impersonal way than is possible when the subordinate raises the question personally with each one of his two superiors.

There is impressive evidence to show that, in comparison to man-to-man interaction, a work group which uses effective group decision making with its superior can give him substantially more information which is valuable to him but which may involve criticism of him. It can also present a strong case for a course of action other than the one the superior initially prefers. In group decision making, individual members of the group can "toss the ball" back and forth among themselves and through such group processes communicate safely to the chief information which is important to him, but which no single individual dares communicate in a man-to-man session. This kind of group decision making requires two broadly different kinds of skills. Group members need skill in leadership and in membership interaction processes in order to build and maintain a group efficient both in solving problems and in coping with conflict and differences. Skill is also required in the intellectual processes of problem solving (Kepner & Tregoe, 1965).

When an individual has two superiors, one must be designated to take the initiative on personnel functions, such as salary review and recommendations. In the System 4 model, decisions are reached through consensus, and recommendations or action reflect the combined judgment of the superiors involved. Therefore, it is immaterial which superior is given the responsibility for initiating any necessary actions and for seeing that the decisions or recommendations are implemented. It is merely necessary that one superior be given this assignment.

Applying System 4 to Coordination across Functions

If a company were to seek to handle differences more constructively and to achieve better coordination by shifting to System 4, what would be the structure of the organization and how would it operate?

Figure 10-2*c* illustrates how System 4 can be applied to achieve effective coordination in a highly functionalized manufacturing or continuous-process company. Figure 10-2*c* combines Figure 10-2*b* with Figure 10-2*a* and, in addition, shows three illustrative cross-function work groups. In Figure 10-2*a,* the dotted lines and arrows on the right portion of the work group reporting to each executive vice-president indicate that such groups often include vice-presidents in addition to those shown.

In Figure 10-2*c*, our example includes three executive (or group) vice-presidents who report to the president. One is in charge of the functional departments; another is in charge of product departments, and the third oversees service departments. No attempt is made in Figure 10-2*c* to show a complete organization chart applying System 4 to line as well as cross-function coordination. Only enough is shown to illustrate the application of the theory.

The chart shows one essential characteristic of a company operating under System 4: the organization is made up of multiple, overlapping groups. *The functional line, the product line, and the service line are all parts of a multiple, overlapping group structure.*

In Figure 10-2*c*, a product, cross-function work group to manage the A family of products (e.g., consumer products) is shown under VP A. There is also such a group to deal with the A-1 subfamily of products (e.g., shoes). These cross-function groups are only two of a large number of such lateral, cross-function work groups required to coordinate the efforts of the members of the functional lines to achieve efficient management of each product or family of products. The product, cross-function work group under VP A (VP for consumer products) consists, as the chart shows, of a person from each of the relevant functional lines represented in Figure 10-2*c*. All these persons, e.g., R-1 from R&D, P-2 from production, and M-3 from marketing, come from the divisional, hierarchical level within their line. Each of them is working for his function on the A family of products. Thus M-3 might be the head of advertising in the marketing department and also the linking pin between the marketing department and the consumer products department (the A family of products).

Individual A-1 is the superior in the subordinate product cross-function work group dealing more intensively with one category (the

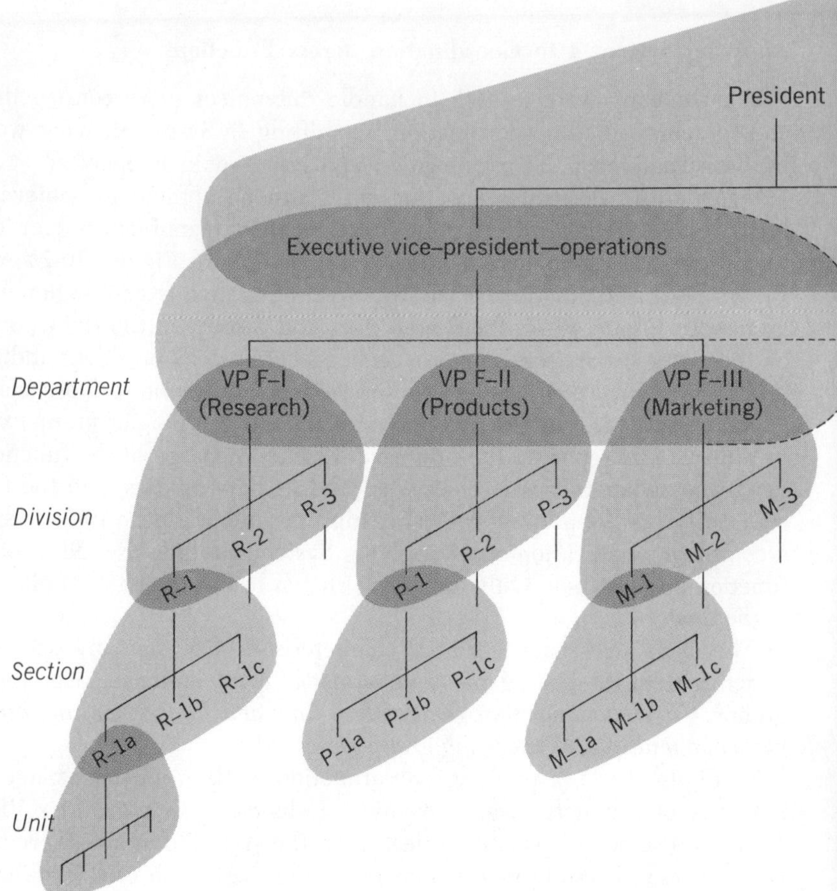

Fig. 10-2a. Vertical, overlapping group linkages

number 1 category, e.g., shoes) of products within the broad A family of products (consumer products). In the cross-function work group under A-1 are persons from the sectional, hierarchical level of each relevant functional line, e.g., R-1a, P-2c, and M-1c. All of them are working on the A-1 products. If M-1 and M-2 (and possibly M-4 and M-5) are in charge of sales regions, then M-1c might be in charge of consumer goods in the M-1 region. He might have been selected to serve as the linking pin between the marketing department and the shoe division (the A-1 family of products), since his headquarters are in the same city as A-1's office. When necessary for effective linkage, relevant persons at his level would join M-1c in meetings of the cross-function group. At

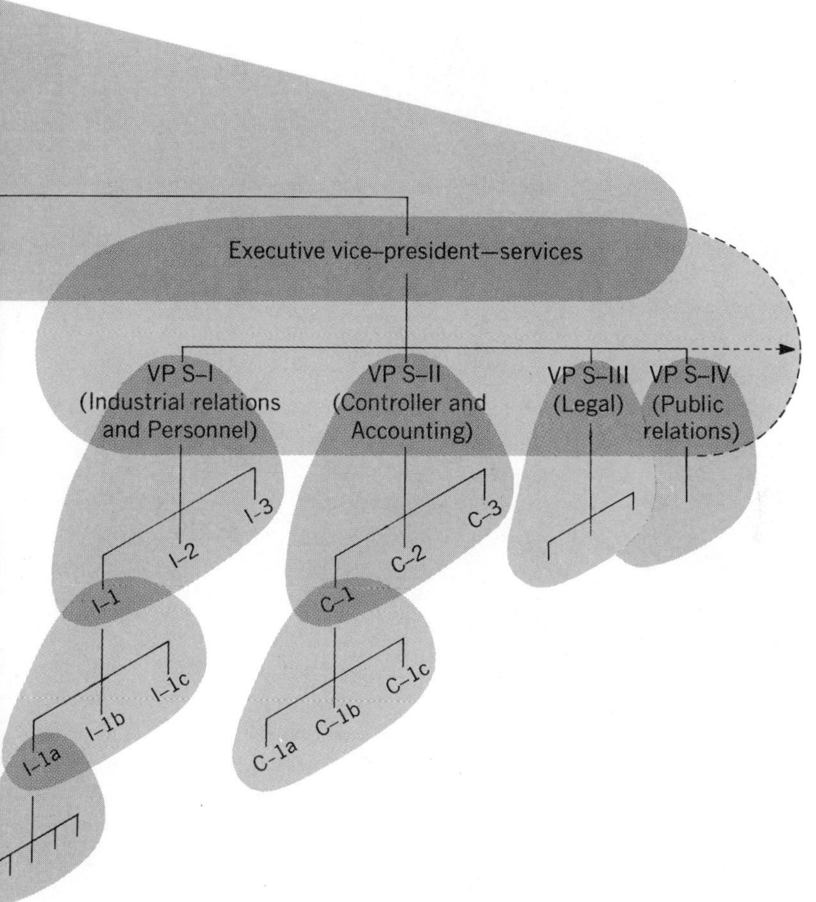

of customary line and staff departments.

other times M-1c could provide the linking interaction by meeting with his peers from the other sales regions.

The subordinate cross-function work group consisting of A-1, M-1c, P-2c, and R-1a is the same as that shown in Figure 10-1. The character of its group decision making was discussed previously.

Each cross-function work group has as its superior a product-family person from the hierarchical level *directly above* that of the other members of the group. Thus, A-1 is at the next higher level from that of the other cross-function members, R-1a, P-2c, and M-1c. This hierarchical-level relationship is as necessary in the cross-function work group as it is in the functional and product work groups, to assure that there will

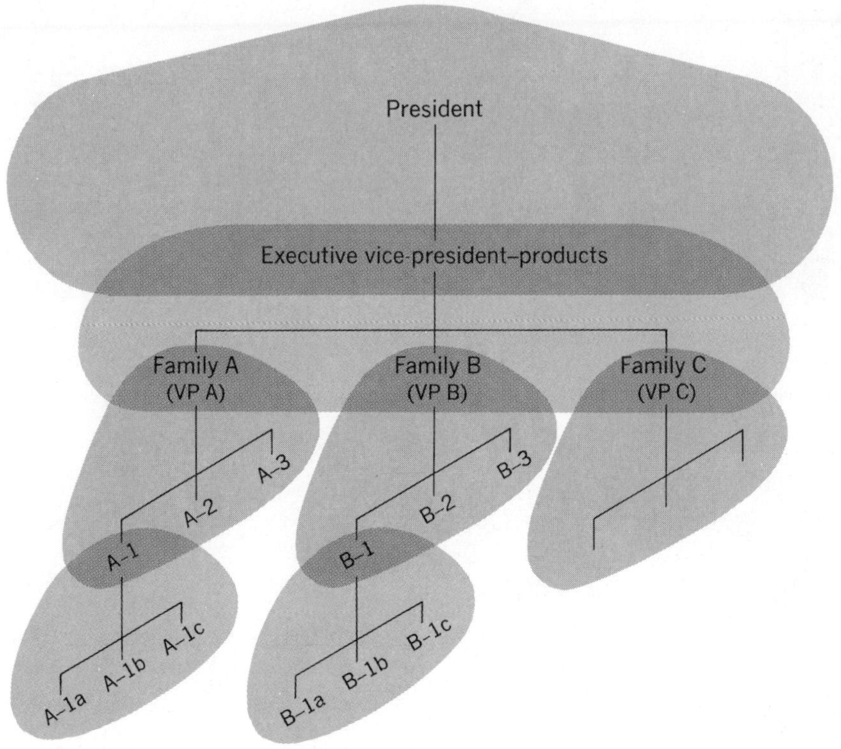

Fig. 10-2b. Vertical, overlapping group linkages of product departments.

be an effective decison-making approach to the solution of problems of lateral coordination as well as to contribute to vertical integration. Without this balance in influence within the decision-making network, the cross-function work group would become impotent in the face of pressures from the functional lines, and the coordination processes would break down. If the decisions on the salaries, promotions, and all such matters of the cross-function work group members were influenced solely or largely by their functional line superiors, the cross-function work groups would have little capacity to deal effectively with the important but difficult problems requiring cross-function coordination.

In the meetings of the cross-function work groups, there may be items on the agenda from time to time which would make it desirable to include one or more of the subordinates of the superior who heads the cross-function group. Whenever this occurs, the relevant product subordinate or subordinates should be included in the meeting on an *ad hoc* basis. Thus, for example, individual A-1 might be invited by VP A to attend a cross-function group meeting when it is working on a problem of direct relevance to individual A-1.

If Figure 10-2*c* attempted to represent the entire organization, it would, of course, contain a large number of product, cross-function work groups. Some of these would be at higher organization levels, some at lower. Those at the higher levels would be dealing with coordination problems for broad families of products or for a product particularly important to the firm. Those at lower levels would be dealing with more specific problems and products. The vertical coordination within a family of products, such as Family A, would be handled by the linking-pin members of the overlapping groups of the product line organization. This vertical coordination would be supplemented, of course, by that of the functional departments.

A Fundamental Requirement

To perform the intended coordination well a fundamental requirement must be met. The entire organization must consist of a multiple, overlapping group structure with *every* work group using group decision-making processes skillfully. This requirement applies to the functional, product, and service departments. An organization meeting this requirement will have an effective interaction-influence system through which the relevant communications flow readily, the required influence is exerted laterally, upward, and downward, and the motivational forces needed for coordination are created.

The necessity for meeting this fundamental requirement is evident when the interaction characteristics of System 4 in contrast with System 2 are recalled. When the superior in a functional department is using man-to-man supervision (System 2), any subordinate of his who serves as a member of a cross-function, product work group will be required to perform as a "representative" of his chief. This, of course, will prevent the subordinate from engaging in innovative group decision making in the cross-function work group. The superior's desire to control by direction (System 2) rather than by involvement and interaction (System 4) usually puts pressure on the subordinate to serve in the role of representative to protect the interests of the superior's department (or division) and carry out his instructions in the cross-function work-group meetings. When the subordinate is in a group meeting as a representative of his chief, he tends to deal with differences in a way which creates a polarized relationship, such as win-lose or bargaining. So long as these circumstances prevail, innovative, cross-function decision making cannot occur, and efficient coordination will not be achieved.

If by any chance the cross-function work group should persuade this

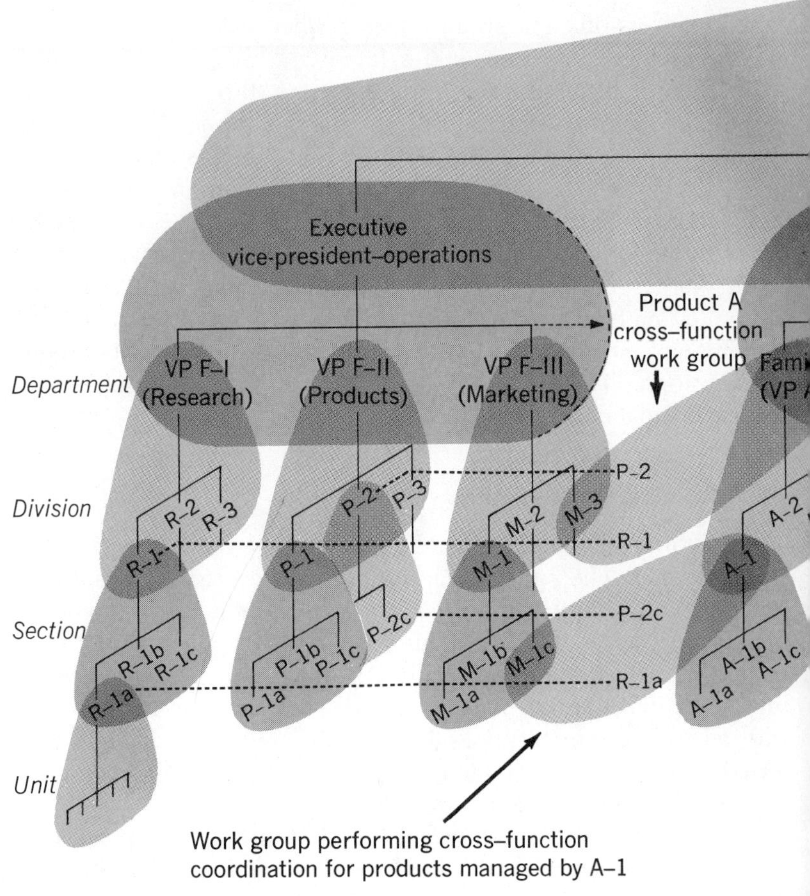

Fig. 10-2c. Multiple, overlapping group structure showing horizontal

subordinate to drop his representative role and take part in group decision making, the subordinate is likely to find himself in a hazardous position. If the decision making is innovative and calls for changes on the part of his functional department, the subordinate is in a difficult spot, because he must persuade his functional superior to change his decision for reasons that may benefit the total organization but may not benefit the department and even may make its work more difficult. The superior's concern with his status and power also may make it difficult for the

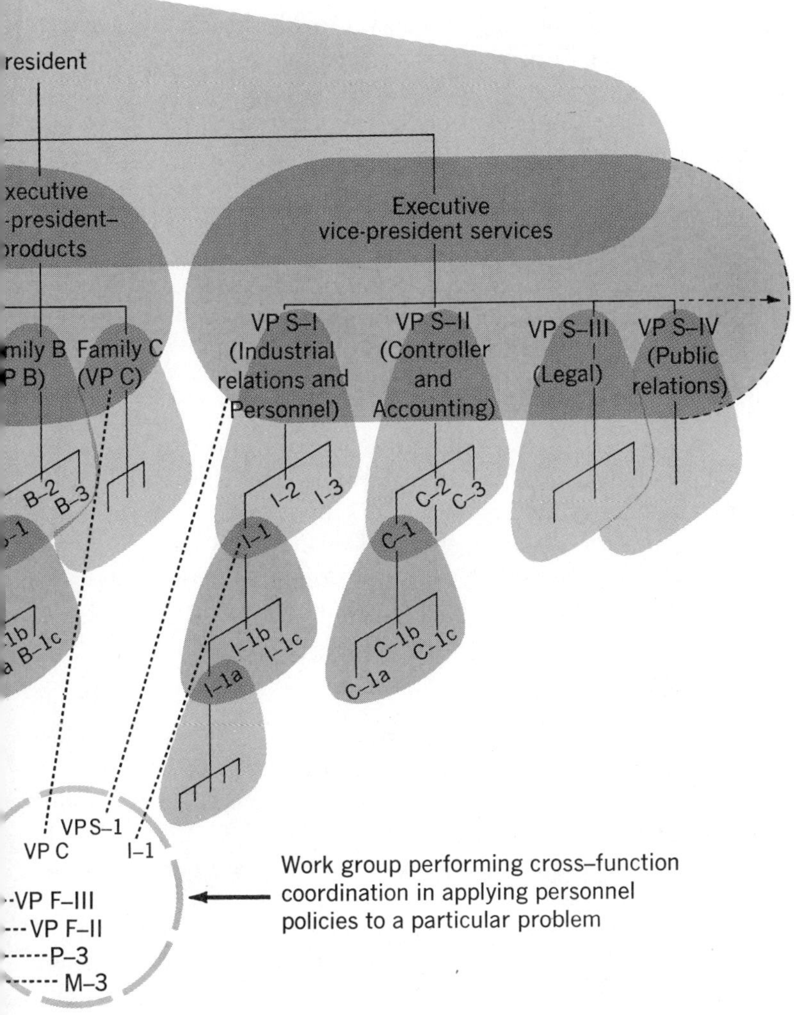

(lateral) linkages as well as vertical linkages, based on adding managers.

subordinate to bring a change in the superior's decision. So long as the functional superior is a System 2 manager, group decision making in cross-function groups is not likely to contribute to lateral coordination.

Communications required for coordination in a changing organization, particularly communications of a challenging and differing character, do not flow upward or laterally rapidly and without distortion in a System 2, man-to-man organizational linkage. Moreover, superior-to-subordinate, man-to-man supervision stimulates competition and win-lose conflict between subordinates and does not formally provide for lateral communication and interaction, except upward and downward through the superior. Lateral communication and interaction may occur through an informal organization. Since such activity is in violation of the formal system, it is less effective, however, than when done as a legitimate part of the formal system. This is equally true with regard to the exercise of influence and the creation of the motivational forces required for cooperative coordination.

If efficient coordination and the resolution of differences are to occur consistently and dependably in an enterprise, it is necessary that System 4's multiple, overlapping group structure be used with appropriate group decision-making skill throughout the enterprise. If anywhere in one of the vertical functional lines, the vertical service lines, the vertical product lines, or in any one of the cross-function work-group linkages a superior uses a System 2, man-to-man pattern of supervision, the coordination processes and the constructive handling of differences will break down at that point and in turn adversely affect all related activities and operations. Polarized interaction, such as win-lose struggles instead of productive decision making, will occur at that point and radiate from that point.

An Example of Cross-linking Roles

Other kinds of cross-function work groups, in addition to product groups, are needed in a large corporation to help facilitate effective coordination. Such a work group is the second kind of lateral, cross-function group shown in Figure 10-2*c*. This group consists of VP C, VP SI, VP FII, VP FIII, M-3, P-3, and I-1. It is only one of many such groups. The rest are not shown.

Let us assume that this cross-function work group is an *ad hoc* committee, created to deal with the problems of organization and compensation involved in setting up jobs to handle a new and prospectively highly profitable product. This product falls under the general direction of the vice-president for the C products. This vice-president wants to be sure that the new positions are filled with especially able personnel, both in his product department and in the related functional departments. This desire is also shared by the vice-president in charge of marketing. Both vice-presidents want to capitalize fully on the potential profitability of the new product. To encourage able people to move into the jobs, these vice-presidents are pressing to have the salary levels for the new positions, especially those for the senior personnel, set somewhat above the established ranges for such jobs. The industrial relations department wants these salary levels to be in line with the established ranges. The job of this *ad hoc* committee is to solve this salary problem in such a way that the goals and wishes of all of its members are met reasonably well. A second job of this cross-function work group is to arrange for the transfer to the new jobs of personnel best equipped to handle the work. To accomplish this objective, they need to develop a plan of action to overcome the resistance of some department heads who do not wish to lose some of their most able personnel.

To cope successfully with such difficult problems, this *ad hoc* work group will need to develop into a highly effective decision-making unit. Full recognition and use of all the relevant situational requirements will be needed in making decisions if consensus is to be reached in the face of sizable differences. Moreover, if the committee's solutions are to be fully implemented, each of the members of the group, through their overlapping memberships in other work groups, must successfully exert the necessary influence through the interaction-influence network of the firm.

Such decision making and the successful implementation of the decisions are not easy. Nevertheless, this appears to be a sound approach to such problems, judging from the experience of a large corporation which has been using, with impressive success, essentially this System 4 approach in one of its major departments. Whenever the *ad hoc* work groups in this department are unable to deal with their problems, higher echelons do not make decisions for them, but focus remedial efforts on the decision-making activities of those work groups in which the breakdowns have occurred. They ask such questions as "What is wrong with the decision-making processes? Why this inability to reach an acceptable solution? Is the structure wrong? Do the people involved lack training in the necessary decision-making processes? Are they trying to protect interests rather than solve problems? What steps do we need to take to develop an effective problem-solving capacity in this group?" When higher echelons start to raise such questions, the work groups struggling with what have been irreconcilable differences usually discover that they can arrive at a mutually satisfactory solution. If such a solution is not reached, higher echelons conclude correctly that they have an organization-building and training job to do. But they do not weaken the organization by taking over the functions of subordinate units and making their decisions.

Applying System 4 to Geographical Coordination

To illustrate further how a science-based theory, such as System 4, can be used to achieve coordination in a firm with high levels of functionalization, it may be useful to examine a quite different kind of organization: the telephone companies. Their technology is so complex that extensive functionalization is advantageous. Telephone companies are usually organized on a functional basis from the top of the company to the local office. The customary organization chart shows a solid line of authority in each functional department, such as plant, traffic, and commercial, from the department head, who is often a vice-president, to the local manager. This extensive functionalization creates the necessity for effective integration, but here the need is for geographical rather than product coordination. In applying System 4 to improve geographic coordination, two essential steps need to be taken. The first step is to shift the company from a System 2, man-to-man pattern of supervision and interaction to a System 4, multiple, overlapping, group–interaction influence pattern. This mode of operation for some of the major functional departments is shown (Figure 10-3*a*) by the overlapping groups superimposed in gray on the chart. Figure 10-3*a* is not complete but shows part of the overlapping group organization for three of the functional departments: com-

Fig. 10-3a. Vertical, overlapping group linkages of customary functional lines of telephone company.

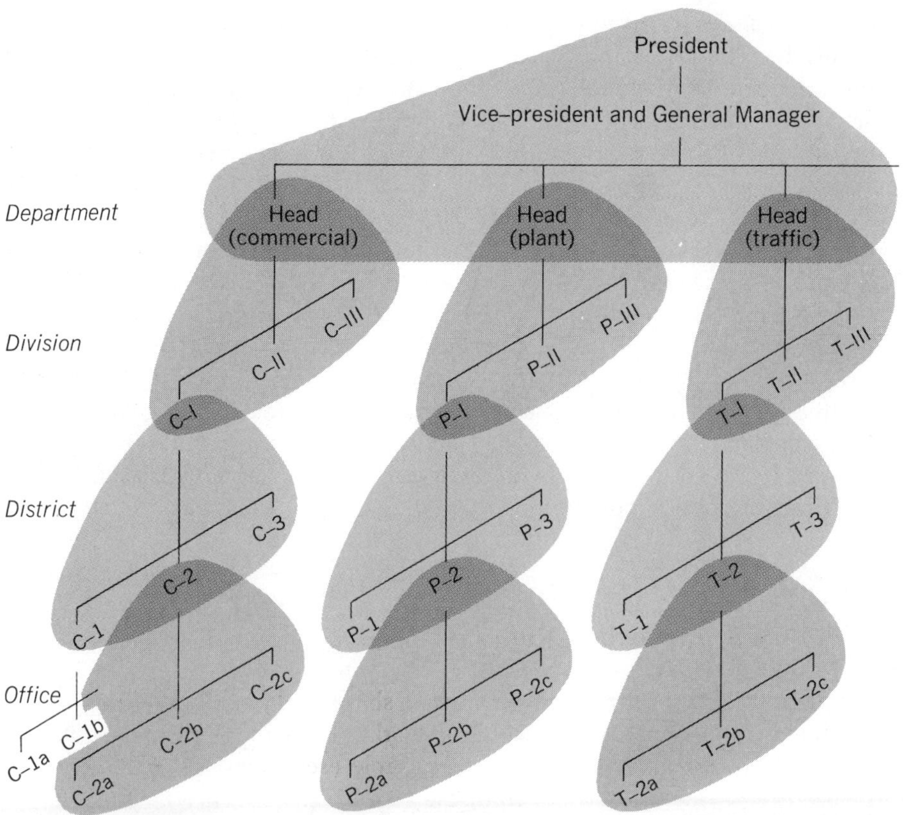

mercial, plant, and traffic. Moreover, the overlapping group structure is shown for only one unit at each hierarchical level.

The second essential step in applying System 4 to help achieve efficient geographical coordination requires the creation of multiple, overlapping, cross-function, geographical work groups. These cross-function groups should be established at every hierarchical level down to and including the office level for each separate geographical operation of any consequence.

These geographical, cross-function work groups could be set up in one of two ways. One, the same plan as presented above for cross-function work groups and shown in Figure 10-2*b* could be used. The organization chart of the company then would be the same as Figure 10-2*c*, and the organization would operate essentially as described previously. Each geographical, cross-function work group would perform in the same manner as the product, cross-function groups described above.

The second way to establish geographical, cross-function work groups would not require the addition of geographical managers (comparable to the product line managers added to the organization shown in Figures 10-2*b* and 10-2*c*). A *new role* would be added to the job of the present functional managers. The relative advantages and disadvantages of each plan, i.e., of adding managers to perform the new role or of adding the role to the job of present managers, will be discussed later. With this second plan, each manager would have a geographical coordinating management role in addition to his functional role. He would serve both as a functional manager and as a geographical coordinating manager. The geographical coordinating role is represented in Figure 10-3*b* by the geographical work groups outlined on the organization chart. This chart, like Figure 10-3*a*, is incomplete. It shows only a small number of the total cross-function work groups but enough to indicate the character of the entire organization.

The proposed organization using this second plan would consist of both the functional work groups (Figure 10-3*a*) and the cross-function work groups (Figure 10-3*b*). Figure 10-3*c* shows the proposed organization by superimposing Figure 10-3*b* on Figure 10-3*a*. Since neither Figure 10-3*a* nor Figure 10-3*b* is complete, Figure 10-3*c* does not show all the different departments of the company, nor does it show all the personnel under each of the department heads represented in the chart. Enough is shown, however, to illustrate the proposed structure and the manner in which it would operate.

Each of the functional department heads shown in Figures 10-3*a*, 10-3*b*, and 10-3*c* is a member of at least three work groups. In the first two, he is performing the usual vertical linking-pin role (see Figure 4-2); i.e., one work group consists of the vice-president and general manager and the

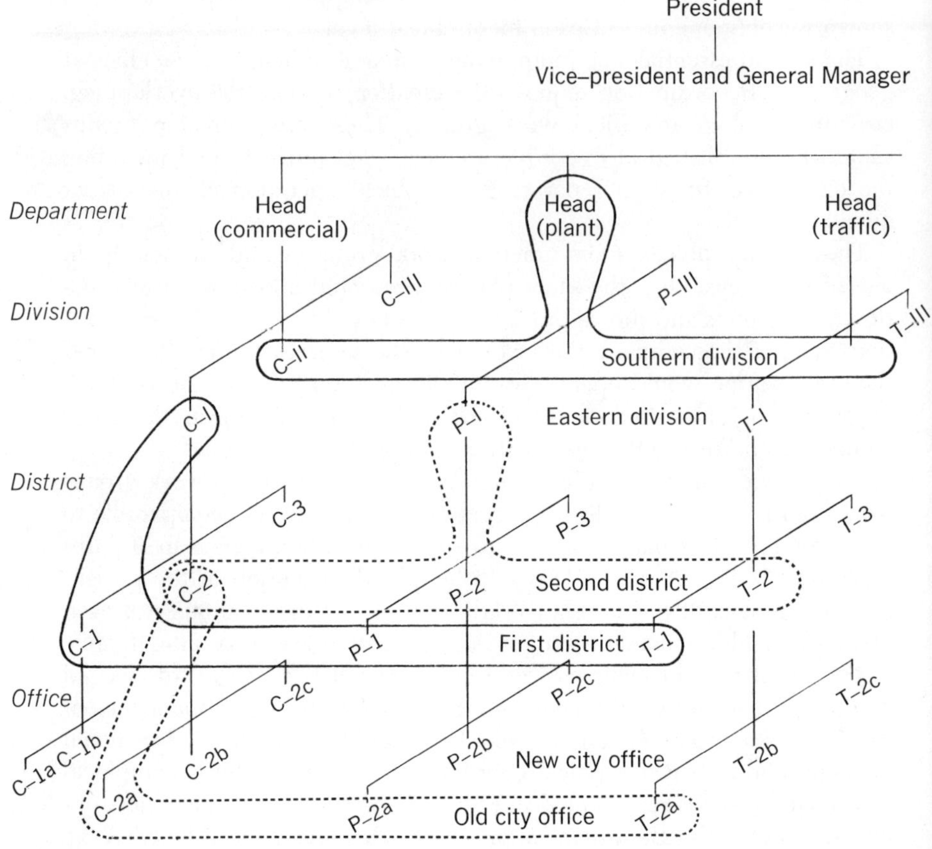

Fig. 10-3b. Cross-function, geographical work groups for lateral coordination in a telephone company.

department heads reporting to him, and the second consists of the department head as superior and the functional managers at the divisional level who report to him (Figure 10-3*a*). The third, a new work group, consists of the department head and all the managers at the divisional level who are in charge of a function and who are in one particular division (see the Southern division and Eastern division in Figures 10-3*b* and 10-3*c*). This third group is a cross-function, geographical work group.

Below the department head level, each manager is a member of at least four work groups. In the first two he is performing the usual vertical linking-pin role. Thus, at the divisional level, manager P-I in the plant department is a member of the following: (1) a functional work group consisting of the plant department head and of all the other plant depart-

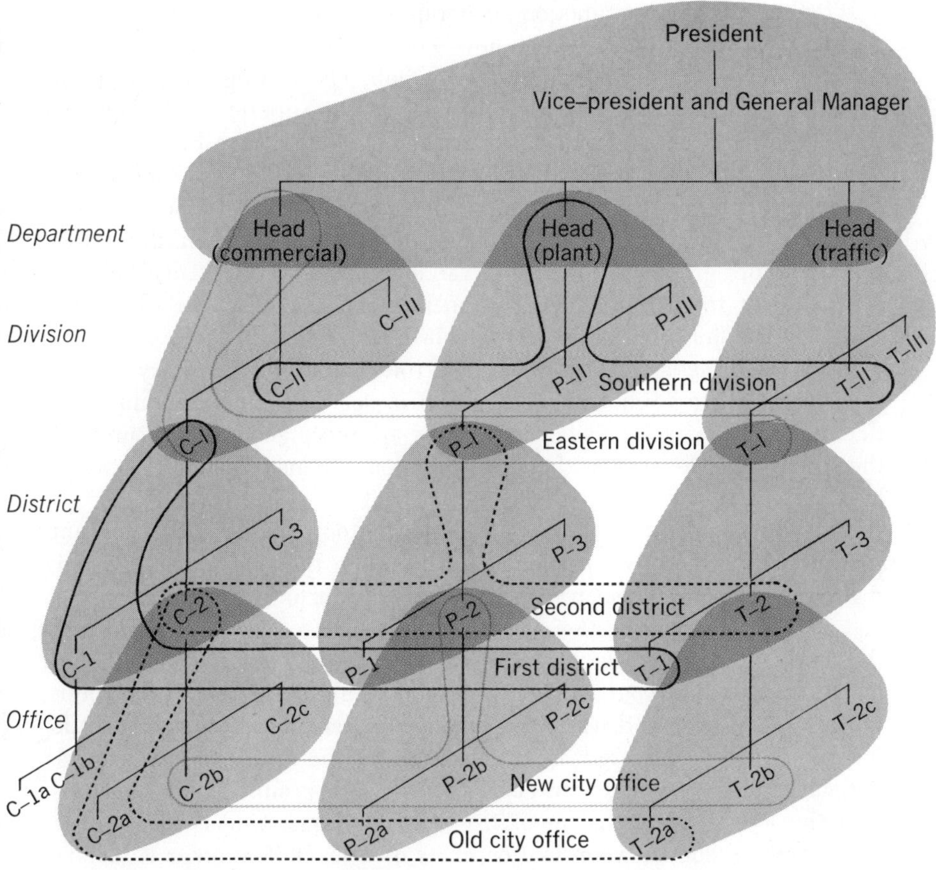

Fig. 10-3c. Multiple, overlapping group structure showing horizontal (lateral) linkages as well as vertical linkages, based on adding roles.

ment managers at the divisional level (in this group, P-I is a subordinate); (2) a second functional work group, of which he is the superior, contains all the plant department managers at the district level who are in his division (Division I); (3) a new cross-function, geographical work group consisting of all the functional managers in his division (Eastern) and one of the functional department heads (Head, commercial); (4) another new cross-function, geographical work group made up of himself (P-I) as superior and all the managers at the district level who are in charge of a function and all of whom are in the same district (Second district). The functional work groups are shown by gray overlays in Figure 10-3*a*; the new cross-function work groups are shown in Figure 10-3*b*.

Whether each cross-function, geographical work group performs as desired depends, of course, upon how well the cross-function work group directly above it in the hierarchy does its job. The linking-pin concept of System 4 indicates that this responsibility of the superior cross-function work group will be performed better when, as is shown in Figures 10-3*b* and 10-3*c*, *a superior from the next higher level is included in each subordinate, cross-function work group.* This provides face-to-face vertical linkage through a responsible, linking-pin person between the cross-function work groups at the two hierarchical levels. This vertical linkage is equivalent to that provided by the product line (Figures 10-2*b* and 10-2*c*) in the first plan of achieving coordination.

When each manager performs a dual role, it may be necessary for the superior in a cross-function work group to serve as a superior in more than one such group. This occurs if there are more geographical units at the subordinate level than there are functional managers at the superior level.

Each cross-function, geographical work group includes all relevant persons who are at that particular level and in that particular division, district, or office. Each such work group should include all persons whose activities and responsibilities will be directly affected by the decisions of the work group. Persons whose responsibilities are not relevant should not be included, of course. Their inclusion would make the work groups unnecessarily large and waste the time of the persons whose activities do not affect, nor are affected by, the decisions of the cross-function groups.

Each of the cross-function, geographical work groups at all levels except the lowest has, consequently, two major tasks. One is to establish and maintain efficient coordination at its own level. The other is to take all the necessary steps to aid the cross-function work groups at all levels below it to perform their tasks well. Especially important will be the skillful coaching, counseling, and training of the cross-function work groups that are immediately subordinate to it and to which it is tied by its members who serve as linking pins.

The training role of the superior group is performed for it in each of the subordinate groups by the member of the superior group who is also a member of that particular subordinate group. Important agenda items for each superior, cross-function, geographical work group, consequently, include, How well is each of the cross-function work groups which report to us performing the decision making and other jobs expected of it? If performance is not satisfactory, how can we, through the linking-pin member from our work group and through the functional subordinates responsible to us, coach, counsel, and assist the subordinate cross-function geographical work groups to perform their coordinating activities well?

Each cross-function, geographical work group, in addition to its two major tasks, has a third role: to watch the quality of group performance in each of the work groups in the functional lines from which one of its members comes. Any time that any one of these work groups begins to perform its group processes poorly, the cross-function work group should, through its linking-pin relationships to higher-level cross-function and functional work groups, see that coaching and training activities are started to correct the group decision-making and group maintenance processes of the ailing group.

Each functional work group has a corresponding role. Each member of a functional work group should observe the quality of group performance in the two cross-function work groups of which he is a member. Whenever one of these cross-function groups fails to perform well its decision-making and coordinating activities, the functional group member observing this breakdown should call it to the attention of his functional work group. Through its linking-pin relationships, this work group should see that the coaching and training required to strengthen the weak cross-function work group is undertaken. This process for recognizing and training weak work groups, both functional or cross-functional, will restore and help to maintain at adequate strength the interaction-influence capacity of the entire organization.

The coaching process needs to reflect the principle of supportive relationships; i.e., it cannot be punitive. It must be supportive and helpful in spirit and in fact if the kind of decision making based on mutual confidence and trust is to be developed. Usually the review of the performance of subordinate cross-function work groups and the coaching and training of their members will be aided if periodic measurements are available of the causal and intervening variables as well as of the end-result variables.

The capacity to bring about improvement in the functioning of a weak work group through alternate channels of communication and influence is an important resource of System 4. System 2 lacks this capability for organizational self-improvement because it does not have the lateral and upward communication and influence resources required.

One of the most important coordinating activities of the cross-function work groups is to see that at each geographic level, decisions are made and problems are solved in terms of what is best for all functions and thereby serve the best interests of the entire corporation. This does not occur in companies which are organized on the System 2 functional basis and, as a consequence, lack cross-function, geographical coordination. Where functional lines are not confronted with the needs of other departments by cross-function problem solving, each functional line at each geographical level all too often arrives at decisions which protect its interests, budget, or performance record but which make the operation of other functions more difficult. Such decisions when viewed from a company-wide point of view are unsound, since they adversely affect costs and service to customers. The cross-function work groups at each geographical level, therefore, have the important responsibility of exerting sufficient influence that decisions and actions are oriented toward serving the entire organization, rather than benefiting a particular functional department.

Cross-function, geographical work groups should meet often enough that they take care of problems promptly and deal with all matters requiring coordination, but not so often that they waste time. The superior in a cross-function work group may often be located in a different community at some distance from the subordinate member of that work group. As a consequence, it may not be feasible for him to attend every meeting of this work group. The superior should attend meetings with sufficient frequency, however, that the group learns to be relaxed, candid, and efficient in his presence.

It will probably be desirable to rotate the superiors periodically among cross-function, geographical work groups. One of the important reasons for doing this is to make clear to all that there is no intention to replace the functional line organization nor to weaken it by the cross-function, geographical, overlapping group organization. Operating experience with this form of organization will provide evidence for the optimum frequency of rotation of the superior members among the subordinate, cross-function groups. This rotation should not be so frequent that it prevents the superior from becoming a fully accepted and effective member of the subordinate group, nor should it prevent him from helping that group to develop into a well-coordinated, decision-making group which recognizes differences and problems, solves them efficiently, and fully implements the decisions. The rotation should, however, be sufficiently often that the cross-function work groups do not weaken or become a substitute structure for the overlapping group organization of the functional lines.

All or many of the managers shown in Figures 10-3*a*, 10-3*b*, and 10-3*c*, in addition to the work groups mentioned, are likely to be members of *ad hoc* or continuing committees performing important tasks for the organization. These committees create additional channels for communication, motivation, and decision making, beyond those provided by the functional-line overlapping groups and the cross-function, geographical work groups. They contribute further strength to the interaction-influence system and to the overall coordination and level of performance of the entire organization.

Create Adequate Coordinating Linkages

The use of System 4 to help achieve efficient coordination requires important changes in the formal structure of a highly functionalized firm and in the manner in which this structure operates. Two major changes are required. First, the cross-function and other linking work groups will be a new, formal structure added to the usual functional structure of the company. Second, all parts of this multiple overlapping group structure will use group decision making rather than man-to-man, superior-to-subordinate direction and control.

The nature of the new, formal structure will depend upon which plan for achieving coordination is used. When the jobs of the present managers are increased by adding roles without adding personnel, the new formal structure will be as shown in Figures 10-3*b* and 10-3*c*. If the plan requiring additional managers is used, the new, formal structure would be as represented in Figures 10-2*b* and 10-2*c*. In general, the decision to add managers (Figure 10-2*c*) or roles (Figure 10-3*c*) will depend upon the work load which the coordination effort introduces. If this load is heavy, it is undesirable to ask each manager to perform both a functional role and a cross-function, coordinating role. Under such circumstances the first plan, shown in Figure 10-2*c*, should be used. We have found it desirable in some circumstances to use one plan at certain hierarchical levels and the other plan at other levels.

In the initial attempts to use System 4 to improve geographical or product coordination, it may be advantageous to start with the plan represented by Figure 10-3*c*. This would give all managers experience in both roles, increase the knowledge of many managers about problems requiring coordination, and increase their appreciation of the importance and difficulty of handling these problems well. On the basis of experience and the work loads encountered, the other plan of organization (Figure 10-2*c*) can be introduced later, if necessary.

In addition to this cross-function linking structure, there is likely to be a need for other linkages as part of the formal organization, especially if the organization is large. If individuals and work groups, widely scattered in the organization, encounter problems requiring lateral coordination and if the existing linkage channels cross many work groups and hence are long and cumbersome, the persons or groups involved should take the initiative in establishing a face-to-face group to provide direct linkage for handling the problems. If it is a temporary problem, it should be an *ad hoc* group. If there are continuing problems, the group should be permanent. When such groups are established, the relevant line organizations affected should be kept informed of the existence and decisions of the cross-linking group. These cross-linking groups and their linking-pin members are a legitimate part of the formal structure in a System 4 organization. (With System 2, such processes are illegitimate, informal structures outside of channels and incompatible with the system.)

The second major change, as mentioned above, deals with the way the formal structure operates. It requires group decision making by consensus in all work groups throughout the organization. Neither the functional work groups nor the cross-function work groups should have the authority to superimpose decisions upon the other. Such use of authority leads to win-lose struggles, resentments, and maneuvering for power rather than to seeking solutions which will be in the best interest of the total corporation. Decision making by consensus should be the basic policy. When it fails, the situation should be handled as suggested; that is, the superior group should not take over the decision making of the ineffective subordinate group but should undertake the required training of the subordinate group and the organization building that is needed. Coordination and productive use of differences should be achieved by group decision-making processes used skillfully throughout the company.

Achieving Decisions Best for the Entire Organization

An important role of cross-function work groups is to see that decisions do not serve the selfish interests of functional lines but reflect the overall needs of the entire organization. The decision-making processes of System 4, in contrast to those of System 2, make this possible.

Problems handled in a System 2, man-to-man interaction pattern are frequently problems of the subordinate and his unit. This is particularly true of problems raised by the lower echelon. The subordinate (*d* in Figure 10-4) presents his problems to his superior and tries to have them solved from the standpoint of what is best for him and for his unit. The focus of the subordinate *d* is to obtain a decision which facilitates effective performance by his unit, even though the decision may be costly to the total organization. If, for example, *d* heads a production operation, he may be seeking approval for a product change which simplifies the manufacturing operation and thereby reduces his costs. He may seek this action even though the product is less acceptable to consumers and hence harder and more expensive for the marketing department to sell.

In this situation, the superior (D in Figure 10-4) is handicapped in any attempt to deal with the problem from a broader point of view by the orientation constantly maintained by the subordinate. The superior is also at a disadvantage, because often he does not possess all the facts,

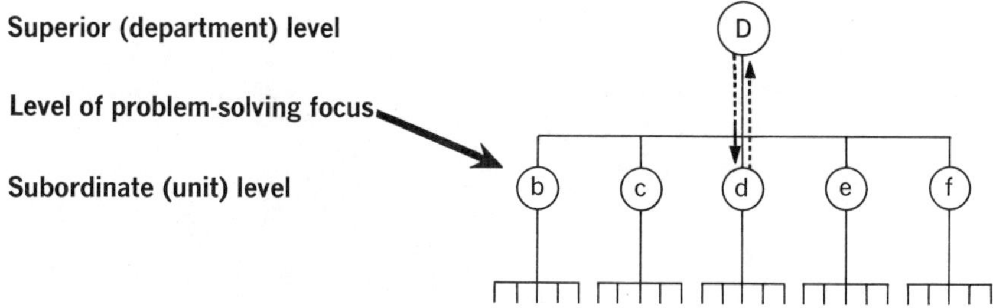

With System 2, man-to-man (D-to-d) decision-making problems, especially those raised by subordinates, tend to be stated, examined, and solved from the point of view of subordinate level; i.e., they serve the interest of the smaller organizational entity at the expense of the well-being of the total organization.

Fig. 10-4. Problem-solving focus in System 2, man-to-man (D-to-*d*) model of interaction and decision making.

information, and technical knowledge which his subordinates have (*b, c, d, e,* and *f* in Figure 10-4) and which are necessary in order to arrive at a solution satisfactory, or at least not detrimental, to the other units affected by the solution (under *b, c, e,* and *f* in Figure 10-4). There are, consequently, forces present in the decision-making processes of System 2 which tend to encourage the statement and solutions of problems focused on what is best for a particular subordinate unit, without proper consideration of the aspects of the problem important to the other units at the same echelon, as well as to the organization as a whole.

When decisions are made by groups, as in System 4, they are made with a broader orientation. Any problem raised for consideration tends to be a problem at the level of the superior and tends to deal with the needs and requirements of that level (department head R in Figure 10-5). If a unit head (e.g., *r* in Figure 10-5) in raising a problem for consideration states it solely from the standpoint of his unit, one of two developments occurs: (1) the superior R, or others in the work group, point out that if the problem deals only with the subordinate unit, that unit should handle it and not raise it for consideration by the superior unit or (2) the problem is restated by the superior R, or other group members, so that it deals with matters of concern to other units as well as to the one which raised it; i.e., the problem is redefined; thus it is of department-wide concern. In solving this department problem, the heads of the various units (*r, s, t, u,* and *v*) add the situational requirements which they face and which a solution must meet to be acceptable. The solution which emerges from such group decision making is one which is deemed best for the entire department and for all of its units. It is not a decision which

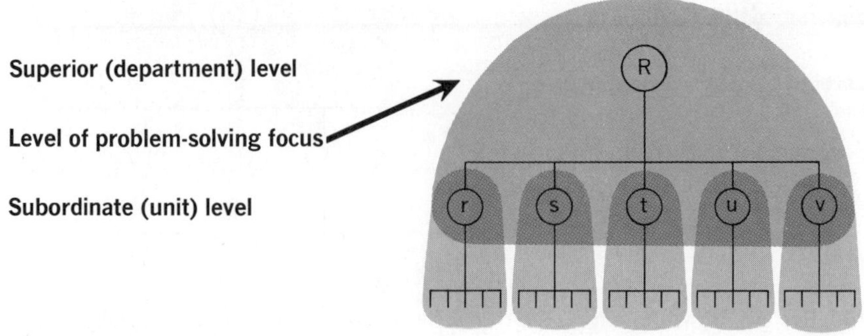

With System 4, problems which affect the subordinate (unit) level only are referred to that level for decision; problems which affect more than one unit are stated as department-wide problems and solved in terms of what is best for the entire department rather than serving the interests of a particular subordinate unit.

Fig. 10-5. Problem-solving focus in System 4, group model of decision making.

meets the requirements of one particular unit (i.e., the unit of *r* in Figure 10-5) while handicapping the other units (those under *s*, *t*, *u*, and *v*).

This difference between System 2 and System 4 occurs at every hierarchical level in the organization. There is, consequently, a multiplying effect of the tendency in System 2 organizations to state problems and solve them in terms of what is best for the subordinate level and in System 4 to deal with and solve problems in terms of what is best for the superior level. As a consequence, with System 4, the decisions and actions which emerge are more likely than with System 2 to be those best for the entire organization.

As the preceding discussion indicates, the network structure of an organization using a science-based theory like System 4 is appreciably more complex than is the usual vertical structure of System 2 and requires greater learning and skills to operate it well. It is not a line, nor a line-staff, form of organization but is a complex grid system with an elaborate, interlaced, organizational structure. It provides powerful resources for horizontal as well as vertical coordination. This complex network, through its alternate linkages, provides, as we have seen, better communication, greater capacity to deal with differences by group decision making, and better coordination than can System 2. It yields a more flexible organization and motivates individuals throughout the company to exercise more initiative in bringing about improvement and change, as well as giving them the means for doing so.

It is well to keep in mind that the best application of System 4 to achieve coordination in any one company is likely to be different from its application in other companies. Each company tends to have its own unique history, traditions, and customs which must be taken into account. But irrespective of the particular application and procedures, the success of the effort to improve coordination will depend fundamentally upon how well the relevant basic principles are followed.

Present Trends Support the Theory

There is growing evidence that attempts to improve coordination in highly functionalized organizations by employing the solutions called for by System 4 are yielding successful results. There are scattered examples indicating that the general approach suggested here is now being used at least partially in a variety of situations and is contributing to effective decision making and coordination. In most of these situations, the approach is not being used on a company-wide basis as a formal system of organization but has been developed by able managers as solutions to particular problems. In many cases, the particular solution is an informal organizational process and is often viewed apologetically as a violation of accepted principles of management. Nevertheless, since the solution seems to work, its use is continued. In some instances, the idea represented by the solution spreads to other parts of the company, but usually not as an accepted, generalized, and formal principle of management.

An example of these developments is found in a company where one of its major divisions tried to improve coordination in order to speed up the manufacturing and marketing of new products. This was done by appointing cross-function, product committees. The committees consisted of one person from development, one from manufacturing, and one from sales. Several of these committees performed group decision-making processes well, and when they did so, the division found that the committees significantly reduced the amount of time required for a new product idea to move from the development stage through manufacturing to successful marketing. This put the company ahead of competition in getting new products on the market at a time when they were highly profitable.

The company tried to extend this committee plan of operation to another division of the company by ordering the second division to establish comparable product committees, with members from development, manufacturing, and sales. The members of these committees lacked training in group decision making, and the order to use the cross-function committees created neither the motivation to try to use them well nor the skill to do so. The members attended the meetings but came as "representatives" from their departments. They engaged in win-lose tactics and were ineffective in speeding up the process of marketing new products profitably. These committees were a dismal failure.

A study of the factors affecting the successful use of research in Scottish electronics companies (Burns & Stalker, 1961; Croome, 1959) yielded results similar to the above example. Most of the companies were small. In several of them, because of a cooperative, informal atmosphere encouraged by the president, there emerged an informal structure for handling problems of coordination. This structure included persons from research, production, sales, and, in some companies, the president himself. By means of this informal structure and use of group decision-making processes, planning for each phase was started in these companies in ample time for the operation to proceed smoothly from one phase to the next. The product design fitted the manufacturing capabilities of the company. Marketing plans and efforts were started in time to sell the product as soon as it became available. These informal activities enabled new products to be marketed in time to be profitable and made the investment in research pay off handsomely.

In other Scottish electronics companies, however, a different pattern was used. The president adhered to his System 2 organization and dealt with the heads of research, production, and sales on a man-to-man basis. He maintained tight control and prevented the development and use of informal channels for dealing with these problems. When decisions were made in the formal, System 2 manner, the head of each successive operation tended to criticize the work done at preceding steps and to point out why the operation would not work as planned at his phase. All the friction which occurs when peers compete and belittle the work of the others to gain the superior's favor were present. This friction caused serious delays in getting new products marketed and often resulted in their being unprofitable. Companies which adhered to this proper use of System 2 found that their investments in research and new products were financially disastrous.

The experience of these Scottish electronics firms indicates that the use of an informal, cross-function, group structure facilitated lateral coordination and thereby made R&D profitable. This was the case, even though this informal structure violated the formal, organizational principles of these firms.

Another illustration comes from a company whose technology is extremely complex. This company has been using project teams to help achieve coordination. The establishment of project teams, however, does not assure the skillful use of group processes. The chief of one team, for example, was not sure that he trusted his subordinates sufficiently to let them tackle a difficult problem as a group. He feared they might recommend a solution which would be easy for them but which would work so poorly that he would be in difficulty with his superiors. As a consequence, he asked each of his four subordinates individually to prepare a report telling him how that individual felt the problem should be solved. The problem involved the work of all four subordinates, since their activities were interdependent. In accordance with his instructions, each subordinate worked by himself and did not discuss the problem with the others. Each prepared a report which handled well aspects of the problem important to him and his section but did not take into consideration the situations or needs of the other three sections. The chief then had four reports with four different solutions and had the problem of selecting among them or combining them in some way.

At this point this work group became involved in a training activity aimed at improving their group interaction skills. This resulted in much more candid interaction among the group members ("leveling") and led the chief to observe in a group meeting that he now had the tough problem of deciding what the solution to the problem should be. He had four separate and conflicting recommendations, since each report had been prepared from the vantage point of that particular subordinate. He concluded it would have been better had he asked the four subordinates to tackle the problem as a group and come up with a single solution. His subordinates agreed and observed that by his instructions to them the chief had made impenetrable the four-inch office wall separating one subordinate from another.

The chief and his four subordinates then did a "back up" in decision making. They did not try to select from among the four solutions already at hand. Instead they started decision making on the problem from the very beginning and went through all the steps of productive group decision making in sequence (Maier, 1963). This included listing all the requirements which a satisfactory solution must fulfill and an innovative search for acceptable choices. As a consequence, they came up with a better solution than any of those recommended by the subordinates working alone. This successful use of group processes led progressively, with additional training and coaching, to its general use by this work group. The chief can now cite impressive evidence for the effectiveness of this procedure. It has gained valuable time on contracts by reducing the period required for the successful accomplishment of important missions; it has resulted also in substantial budgetary saving, as well as sizable bonuses for the corporation for completing projects ahead of contract dates.

Many other examples of the use of group interaction processes to help improve coordination could be cited, but these are sufficient to illustrate what appears to be a growing trend. It is significant that this trend is consistent with and supports the System 4 approach to achieving coordination.

The Need for a Systems Approach

Unfortunately, many of the current efforts at coordination are still largely piecemeal and represent only a partial use of an important insight. In many instances, the particular development represents an *ad hoc* solution, or the use of an informal process at odds with the formal structure and operating procedures of the company, and a violation of the principles upon which both the structure and procedures are implicitly or explicitly based. *Ad hoc* solutions or those achieved via informal organization almost always involve a piecemeal, trial-and-error attack on the problem. An innovative manager may develop procedures and relationships for handling a coordination problem of concern to him, but since this is an individual act, the principles involved in his successful efforts are not generalized and applied to all comparable problem situations in the entire organization. The application usually yields improvement in coordination at only one point.

Ad hoc procedures, such as product teams or product managers, do not spread rapidly in a System 2 company, because they are a violation of System 2 organizational principles. Ames (1963) has pointed this out in his paper on product managers. He says, "The concept (product manager) is an organizational anomaly in that it violates a proven management precept—i.e., that responsibility should always be matched by equivalent authority—and yet it works, if properly applied." The product manager is an anomaly in a System 2 organization, but he is not an anomaly in a firm using System 4.

One way to make such anomalous practices as the use of product managers work well is to use an extraordinarily able manager. A more effective and more permanent solution is to change the underlying system, so that the particular procedure is not an anomaly. Rather than weakening good solutions by grafting them as foreign bodies onto an incompatible host, they can be strengthened by being a part of a congenial system. The solutions, which often work well today in a System 2 firm even though they are incompatible with the system, would work very much better were they used in a system congenial and supportive to them. A firm's effort to achieve efficient coordination would be improved substantially if it used a science-based organization theory, such as System 4, as the formal system for all its operating procedures.

There are important advantages in using a general theory, such as System 4, in efforts to improve coordination within an organization. One is that a theory suggests in a systematic way all the steps which need to be taken. The entire organizational structure can be modified formally in the manner required. The operation of this structure can also be examined at all relevant points to be sure that the most effective interaction processes are being used. This use of a general theory substitutes an integrated, company-wide application for scattered attempts to improve coordination introduced on the initiative of insightful managers. This integrated approach, which takes action at all points where it is required, can achieve better overall results in much less time than piecemeal trial-and-error solutions.

Profitable Use of R&D Requires Science-based Management

In any enterprise which seeks to make profitable use of research in developing new products and technologies, System 2 and many of its widely applied principles are as obsolete as the products and technologies which the results of the R&D replace. The concept that a man can have only one superior is an important System 2 principle, but it is outmoded and should be eliminated in any corporation or governmental agency seeking to realize profitable returns on its research expenditures. This is, of course, equally true of the organizational structure of System 2, with its man-to-man model of interaction and the related communication, decision-making, and coordination processes.

Efficient coordination can be achieved and maintained in large, complex firms or governmental agencies making extensive use of R&D. Differences can be resolved with constructive rather than destructive consequences for the organization. The communication, influence, and motivational processes which develop reciprocal obligations and responsibilities and which yield efficient, cross-function coordination can be established and used to facilitate the successful use of research. A science-based model of organization, such as System 4, provides this opportunity.

Broadening Accountability as a Method of Introducing System 4

A shift to System 4 management is not so drastic as might appear at first glance. In most companies today, because of the changes gradually being brought about by the highest-producing managers, current operations in their actual practice often differ appreciably from their description in the company manuals. These differences between the actual practice and the formal description are, as might be expected, almost always in the direction called for by System 4. Adoption of a System 4 method of operation, therefore, would require less of a shift in actual practice than the company's statement of standard procedures would indicate.

A shift to System 4 can be facilitated by a change in practice with regard to accountability. Under System 2, either the functional line or the product (or geographic) line is held accountable, not both. The managers in this line are given the final authority since, in System 2, a manager cannot be held accountable for results of an operation in which he does not have the last word.

In a System 4 organization, both the functional and the product (or geographic) lines are held accountable for all the results attained by the units reporting to them, thereby achieving a greater total amount of accountability than occurs with System 2. In an international petroleum corporation, for example, the head of operations in a major country or region, such as India or South America, would be held accountable for the sales, costs, and earnings of all the corporation's activities in petroleum, chemicals, and fertilizers in that country or region. In addition, the heads of each of the major functional lines in corporate headquarters, such as petroleum refining, distribution of petroleum products, chemicals, and fertilizers would be accountable for the sales, costs, and earnings of all of the functional operations under his direction, wherever in the world they occurred, i.e., in India, South America, Africa, and elsewhere. It is perfectly feasible to compute the costs and results attained by the operations under each of the various managers in each line and to have these results and trends a matter of record for each.

When the System 4 concept of accountability is used, the performance record of each manager and each member of a work group helps to make clear the contribution of each to the success of the total enterprise. Each will wish to have his record show favorable performance and trends. To accomplish this, each will wish to be able to exert sufficient influence that his knowledge, skills, insights, motivations, and competence are used optimally to achieve successful performance.

When managers use group decision making to devise an organizational structure and operating procedures which enable each manager to exert the influence he feels necessary, whether he is in a functional or product line, the outcome is likely to be a System 4 model of organization, since this model offers a practical solution to the problem they face. With System 4, the managers in both lines have the capacity to exert the influence which each feels he needs to assure the successful performance that his accountability causes him to seek.

Chapter 11

THE NEXT STEP

Several years ago, as head of the research department of the Life Insurance Agency Management Association, I presented a report at the annual meeting of the association describing the findings emerging from our research on the principles of management used by the most successful, in contrast to the least successful, agency managers. The next day I was stopped in the hall by one of the most able agency vice-presidents in the life insurance business. He said to me in the presence of one of my colleagues, "You are a very cruel man."

We both looked at him in amazement. "What do you mean?" I asked.

"Don't you think it is cruel to cut down in cold blood 450 men?"

"Yes," I said, "but who is doing that?"

He said, "You are. If you succeed in what you are doing with your research, you will make obsolete all but about 25 men in the audience that listened to your report yesterday. These 25 or so can adapt and learn the newer ways of managing which your research will show yields significantly better sales performance. The rest will know only the old ways and will be eliminated by the competition of those using the newer and more effective methods of sales management and by the younger men who grow up under them."

We talked about this at some length and then my colleague and I discussed it with the research staff. We found his comments sobering and disturbing.

Over a period of time, as I saw managers improve their performance by mastering better principles and methods of management, there was increasing evidence that he was wrong. My skepticism concerning his pessimistic outlook grew greatly as the results of the clerical experiment became available. Managers and supervisors in this experiment quite generally improved their managerial performance (Likert, 1961, Chap. 5; Morse & Reimer, 1956).

Another impressive instance of improvement occurred in the field experiment conducted by Floyd Mann (briefly discussed in Chapter 6). The division Mann worked with was headed by a manager who was about to be fired because his superiors thought he was doing an unsatisfactory job. Mann did not know this when he started to work with this manager and did not discover it until several years later. The reasons for assigning this manager and this division to the experimental test need not be gone into here, but those responsible for the decision were not seeking to benefit the experiment. The outcome, however, is the significant point. This manager and his subordinate managers began to improve after six months of relatively intensive work, followed by continued coaching and assistance for another year. They shifted from the highest-cost, poorest-producing division among a group of divisions doing comparable work to the highest-producing, lowest-cost division. They held this position for years, and today this manager is considered to be one of the best managers at his level in the company.

This, no doubt, is an unusual case. Not every manager who is about to be fired can be made into one of the company's most successful managers by giving him assistance in shifting toward System 4 management. But the fact that it happened in one of our relatively few attempts to help an organization move toward System 4 illustrates the potentiality managers possess for improvement.

Further evidence demonstrating the capacity of managers to learn better systems of management is provided by the material covered in Chapter 3. The results reported for the Weldon plant are especially relevant, since the improvement was achieved not by replacing managers but by helping them to learn more effective ways of managing. The plant manager and the other managers and supervisors in the Weldon plant showed a remarkable capacity to master better principles and methods of management. They shifted their style of management toward System 4 and achieved more favorable attitudes and better productivity. Moreover, both the employees and the company experienced an increase in earnings. Here again are data to show that managers who seek to do so can readily learn better systems of management.

A manager can change his leadership style most easily when he is in an organization which itself is shifting to System 4 and endeavoring to make full use of it, as, for example, the Weldon plant. When the top management of an enterprise is committed to System 2 and seeks to use it throughout the company, it is extremely difficult for a manager to learn System 4 and to shift to it. If a manager wishes to use System 4 and is in an organization which does not provide the climate and the necessary training and development resources, he should try to encourage his company to consider doing so. If in spite of all his efforts he is unable to persuade the top officers of his company to furnish the climate and training resources needed to develop competence in using System 4 management, he might well give serious consideration to moving to an enterprise which would provide him with all that is required to acquire the knowledge and skills he seeks.

The results of research, as well as general experience, are providing ample evidence that no manager need fear that the introduction of a new management system will make his managerial skills obsolete. Any manager who really wishes to do so can learn to shift the system of management he uses from System 2 to 4 or to other science-based systems. No one can do it overnight, but it can be done gradually over a few years.

Moving to Science-based Management

The Institute for Social Research is working intensively with a limited number of companies in widely different industries helping them to shift to System 4. This is enabling us to learn much more about this system and the most appropriate adaptations for applying it in specific company situations. We are learning much also about the most effective ways to aid a company to train its managers in System 4 principles and procedures. The findings emerging from this work will be published from time to time as they become available.

In the years ahead, management systems superior to any now envisioned will be developed as the science-based body of knowledge grows both in scope and accuracy. Additional research will contribute its part, as will more insightful and systematic integrations of research findings. Firms which wish to make full use of science-based management, both as we know it at present and as it evolves, can start now by moving toward something like System 4. Efforts to move in such a direction will, of course, be facilitated by reasonably full descriptions of the principles and procedures characteristic of this system.

A volume is now in preparation describing fully the nature of System 4 as an example of science-based management. It will present a theory of social motivation and will explore ways of applying the theory in mobilizing fully the noneconomic motives in coordination with the effective use of economic needs. It will describe in some detail the principles and procedures involved in operating a System 4 enterprise, including those dealing with

1. Leadership
2. Organizational structure
3. Decision making
4. Setting objectives and goals
5. Control processes
6. Compensation
7. The productive use of differences and the management of conflict

8. Facilitating innovativeness and creativity
9. Training and personnel development
10. Improving administration in developing countries

This volume also will discuss at length the greater ability of science-based management to cope successfully with the progressively more difficult organizational and management problems being created by the technologies and interdependencies emerging from modern research and development. The emphasis will be on principles and the general nature of System 4 management. This emphasis is necessary, since there will be great variability from industry to industry and from company to company in the specific form in which System 4 is used. Differences in the kind of work, in the traditions of the industry, and in the skills and values of the employees of a particular company will require quite different procedures and ways to apply appropriately the basic principles of System 4 management.

Appendix I

CORRELATION MATRIX FOR ITEMS IN TABLE 3-I

Note: Items 1 through 43 are the items in Table 3-1 and Figure 3-1. Item 44 is the sum of the odd-numbered items 1 through 43; item 45 is the sum of the even-numbered items. Item 46 is the sum of all items 1 through 43 (see Chapter 7). The number of cases upon which these correlations are based is 115.

Column =	1	2	3	4	5	6	7	8	9	10	11	12	13	14	15	16	17	18	19	20
Row = 1	1.00																			
Row = 2	.80	1.00																		
Row = 3	.70	.75	1.00																	
Row = 4	.73	.71	.70	1.00																
Row = 5	.67	.73	.67	.68	1.00															
Row = 6	.70	.76	.74	.71	.73	1.00														
Row = 7	.65	.69	.71	.62	.74	.83	1.00													
Row = 8	.66	.73	.69	.64	.73	.72	.76	1.00												
Row = 9	.61	.65	.64	.62	.75	.68	.70	.74	1.00											
Row = 10	.64	.69	.62	.63	.67	.66	.64	.66	.74	1.00										
Row = 11	.76	.75	.73	.65	.65	.72	.78	.75	.71	.71	1.00									
Row = 12	.70	.73	.66	.70	.62	.67	60	.70	.73	.59	.76	1.00								
Row = 13	.71	.68	.64	.68	.71	.68	.69	.66	.73	.61	.76	.77	1.00							
Row = 14	.56	.59	.56	.52	.56	.67	.71	.68	.72	.66	.69	.64	.70	1.00						
Row = 15	.63	.65	.62	.62	.68	.69	.78	.73	.78	.61	.78	.70	.78	.74	1.00					
Row = 16	.58	.57	.54	.49	.54	.62	.69	.67	.63	.58	.66	.58	.66	.74	.78	1.00				
Row = 17	.53	.63	.56	.50	.50	.70	.69	.61	.61	.60	.67	.55	.61	.71	.65	.63	1.00			
Row = 18	.64	.68	.61	.54	.61	.67	.69	.76	.73	.60	.70	.63	.64	.73	.74	.76	.73	1.00		
Row = 19	.66	.68	.67	.63	.70	.69	.73	.71	.71	.59	.68	.63	.67	.65	.72	.69	.64	.83	1.00	
Row = 20	.71	.74	.70	.65	.74	.80	.79	.76	.73	.68	.74	.65	.72	.69	.79	.68	.67	.77	.75	1.00
Row = 21	.70	.74	.62	.65	.75	.74	.77	.71	.70	.73	.73	.66	.74	.68	.73	.66	.70	.71	.77	.76
Row = 22	.69	.68	.56	.57	.68	.59	.62	.63	.68	.61	.69	.66	.73	.55	.69	.59	.47	.62	.66	.76
Row = 23	.72	.69	.67	.68	.74	.67	.69	.73	.77	.65	.75	.72	.72	.64	.72	.64	.58	.69	.66	.71
Row = 24	.66	.68	.71	.65	.64	.75	.69	.69	.58	.64	.67	.52	.61	.60	.61	.56	.58	.67	.62	.77
Row = 25	.65	.66	.58	.57	.69	.66	.63	.76	.78	.66	.67	.65	.71	.63	.70	.63	.61	.68	.62	.77
Row = 26	.73	.71	.68	.66	.73	.76	.77	.77	.72	.67	.71	.64	.72	.68	.67	.66	.64	.74	.73	.76
Row = 27	.65	.62	.55	.65	.67	.55	.62	.76	.64	.59	.59	.54	.61	.58	.62	.63	.53	.65	.63	.64
Row = 28	.71	.65	.49	.64	.70	.57	.57	.64	.69	.66	.63	.59	.64	.56	.65	.63	.52	.70	.69	.65
Row = 29	.73	.69	.63	.70	.74	.70	.70	.67	.70	.73	.72	.68	.71	.64	.70	.65	.62	.70	.68	.72
Row = 30	.70	.72	.57	.67	.65	.67	.64	.57	.63	.61	.70	.67	.62	.56	.66	.51	.61	.66	.65	.69
Row = 31	.59	.69	.61	.61	.67	.68	.72	.71	.72	.65	.68	.65	.71	.65	.76	.62	.70	.76	.72	.77
Row = 32	.67	.65	.53	.60	.63	.67	.69	.70	.73	.57	.69	.64	.66	.65	.71	.62	.74	.80	.70	.72
Row = 33	.73	.77	.71	.66	.69	.70	.72	.78	.70	.71	.72	.69	.69	.66	.68	.70	.71	.77	.72	.74
Row = 34	.61	.60	.59	.51	.62	.63	.71	.73	.73	.63	.67	.60	.66	.69	.75	.73	.62	.78	.71	.73
Row = 35	.73	.72	.65	.64	.64	.66	.71	.73	.71	.75	.77	.69	.70	.68	.78	.70	.65	.67	.64	.69
Row = 36	.65	.64	.48	.47	.58	.58	.62	.61	.58	.59	.58	.52	.63	.59	.70	.63	.59	.65	.57	.73
Row = 37	.67	.64	.58	.57	.62	.65	.66	.62	.66	.67	.71	.59	.69	.65	.70	.62	.59	.64	.67	.71
Row = 38	.62	.65	.54	.59	.66	.68	.72	.67	.74	.66	.58	.63	.65	.64	.70	.65	.62	.70	.67	.70
Row = 39	.59	.59	.61	.55	.59	.72	.71	.61	.71	.61	.67	.61	.66	.73	.72	.69	.66	.74	.69	.70
Row = 40	.60	.66	.63	.51	.60	.65	.76	.70	.69	.59	.76	.64	.63	.61	.71	.64	.62	.70	.68	.70
Row = 41	.65	.59	.59	.59	.65	.55	.68	.66	.71	.69	.66	.54	.66	.59	.75	.64	.49	.63	.60	.68
Row = 42	.51	.51	.54	.50	.53	.56	.60	.57	.58	.63	.60	.53	.51	.46	.64	.59	.42	.53	.51	.63
Row = 43	.58	.59	.53	.45	.49	.56	.63	.60	.64	.59	.67	.52	.58	.54	.71	.66	.53	.62	.56	.59
Row = 44	.83	.83	.78	.75	.83	.80	.86	.83	.85	.79	.86	.77	.85	.77	.86	.77	.74	.81	.81	.85
Row = 45	.82	.84	.76	.77	.80	.83	.85	.85	.83	.80	.83	.79	.81	.78	.83	.78	.74	.84	.80	.89
Row = 46	.83	.84	.77	.76	.82	.82	.86	.84	.84	.80	.85	.79	.83	.78	.85	.78	.74	.83	.81	.88

	25	26	27	28	29	30	31	32	33	34	35	36	37	38	39	40	41	42	43	44	45	46
1	1.00																					
4	.76	1.00																				
6	.64	.76	1.00																			
9	.69	.75	.77	1.00																		
4	.68	.80	.75	.80	1.00																	
0	.60	.68	.64	.68	.77	1.00																
5	.69	.73	.68	.65	.79	.78	1.00															
9	.72	.74	.68	.73	.74	.71	.77	1.00														
9	.65	.79	.73	.71	.76	.67	.75	.73	1.00													
9	.66	.75	.68	.71	.71	.61	.73	.74	.79	1.00												
6	.64	.69	.68	.73	.71	.68	.66	.64	.77	.76	1.00											
8	.65	.64	.59	.67	.67	.63	.68	.56	.66	.70	.73	1.00										
5	.66	.70	.56	.71	.72	.67	.63	.67	.63	.71	.75	.74	1.00									
9	.66	.73	.62	.66	.72	.66	.76	.67	.73	.65	.64	.72	.66	1.00								
6	.57	.75	.63	.64	.70	.58	.72	.68	.72	.74	.64	.61	.62	.76	1.00							
8	.57	.66	.61	.55	.58	.59	.62	.61	.67	.68	.70	.66	.63	.73	.71	1.00						
3	.69	.67	.63	.66	.68	.57	.63	.55	.67	.69	.73	.74	.65	.66	.61	.64	1.00					
8	.55	.61	.50	.57	.59	.48	.58	.45	.61	.62	.59	.62	.45	.66	.67	.72	.70	1.00				
7	.55	.61	.57	.52	.54	.57	.60	.51	.62	.62	.68	.64	.51	.63	.68	.73	.72	.69	1.00			
9	.80	.86	.78	.80	.87	.79	.83	.80	.86	.81	.86	.76	.81	.81	.80	.78	.82	.67	.74	1.00		
2	.81	.88	.76	.81	.87	.81	.83	.82	.86	.82	.84	.78	.80	.84	.80	.79	.78	.71	.70	.97	1.00	
1	.81	.87	.78	.81	.87	.81	.83	.82	.87	.82	.86	.77	.81	.83	.81	.79	.80	.69	.73	.99	.99	1.00

Appendix II

The table below combines the items from Tables 3-1 and 7-1. Some of the items have been revised for clarification. Two additional items have been added, and the performance-characteristics items have been omitted.

The instructions at the top of the table are a revised draft of the directions. The revisions have proved useful in obtaining measurements of trends as well as of the current situation. The original wording and the results obtained from their use were reported in Chapter 3.

Note that some of the items have the System 1 end at the left, while other items are reversed and have the System 1 end at the right. As was mentioned in Chapter 7, this is to minimize the influence of response set on the answers given.

PROFILE OF ORGANIZATIONAL CHARACTERISTICS

Instructions:

1. On the lines below each organizational variable (item), please place an *n* at the point which, *in your experience*, describes your organization at the present time (*n* = now). Treat each item as a continuous variable from the extreme at one end to that at the other.
2. In addition, if you have been in your organization one or more years, please also place a *p* on each line at the point which, *in your experience*, describes your organization as it was one to two years ago (*p* = previously).
3. If you were not in your organization one or more years ago, please check here _____ and answer as of the present time, i.e., answer only with an *n*.

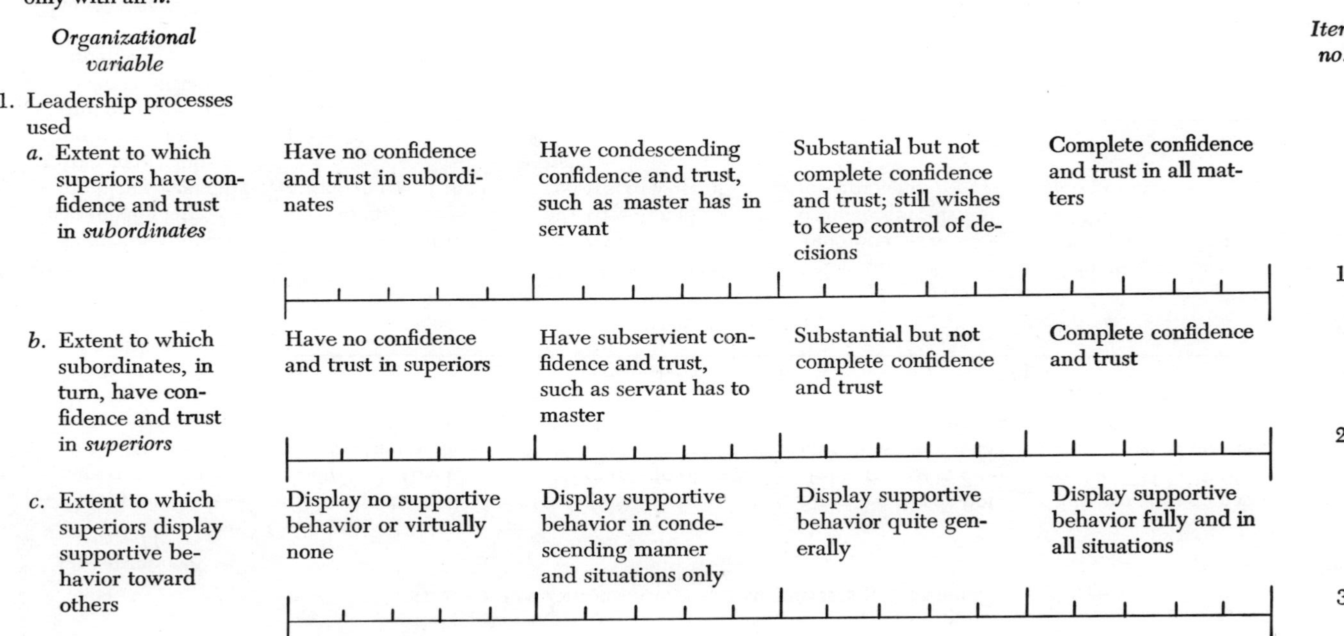

Organizational variable					*Item no.*
1. Leadership processes used					
a. Extent to which superiors have confidence and trust in *subordinates*	Have no confidence and trust in subordinates	Have condescending confidence and trust, such as master has in servant	Substantial but not complete confidence and trust; still wishes to keep control of decisions	Complete confidence and trust in all matters	1
b. Extent to which subordinates, in turn, have confidence and trust in *superiors*	Have no confidence and trust in superiors	Have subservient confidence and trust, such as servant has to master	Substantial but not complete confidence and trust	Complete confidence and trust	2
c. Extent to which superiors display supportive behavior toward others	Display no supportive behavior or virtually none	Display supportive behavior in condescending manner and situations only	Display supportive behavior quite generally	Display supportive behavior fully and in all situations	3

Profile of Organizational Characteristics (*Continued*)

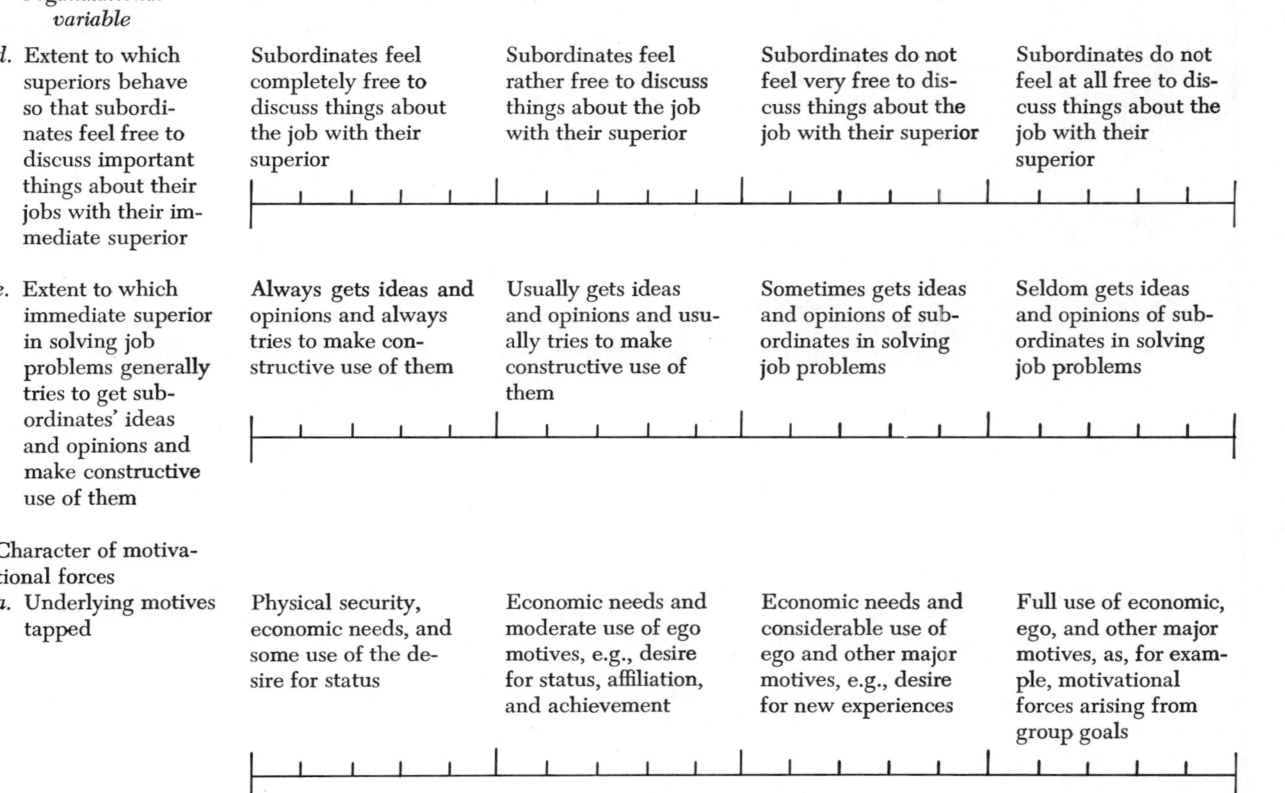

Organizational variable					*Item no.*
d. Extent to which superiors behave so that subordinates feel free to discuss important things about their jobs with their immediate superior	Subordinates feel completely free to discuss things about the job with their superior	Subordinates feel rather free to discuss things about the job with their superior	Subordinates do not feel very free to discuss things about the job with their superior	Subordinates do not feel at all free to discuss things about the job with their superior	4
e. Extent to which immediate superior in solving job problems generally tries to get subordinates' ideas and opinions and make constructive use of them	Always gets ideas and opinions and always tries to make constructive use of them	Usually gets ideas and opinions and usually tries to make constructive use of them	Sometimes gets ideas and opinions of subordinates in solving job problems	Seldom gets ideas and opinions of subordinates in solving job problems	5
2. Character of motivational forces					
a. Underlying motives tapped	Physical security, economic needs, and some use of the desire for status	Economic needs and moderate use of ego motives, e.g., desire for status, affiliation, and achievement	Economic needs and considerable use of ego and other major motives, e.g., desire for new experiences	Full use of economic, ego, and other major motives, as, for example, motivational forces arising from group goals	6

Item					No.
b. Manner in which motives are used	Fear, threats, punishment, and occasional rewards	Rewards and some actual or potential punishment	Rewards, occasional punishment, and some involvement	Economic rewards based on compensation system developed through participation; group participation and involvement in setting goals, improving methods, appraising progress toward goals, etc.	7
c. Kinds of attitudes developed toward organization and its goals	Attitudes are strongly favorable and provide powerful stimulation to behavior implementing organization's goals	Attitudes usually are favorable and support behavior implementing organization's goals	Attitudes are sometimes hostile and counter to organization's goals and are sometimes favorable to the organization's goals and support the behavior necessary to achieve them	Attitudes usually are hostile and counter to organization's goals	8
d. Extent to which motivational forces conflict with or reinforce one another	Marked conflict of forces substantially reducing those motivational forces leading to behavior in support of the organization's goals	Conflict often exists; occasionally forces will reinforce each other, at least partially	Some conflict, but often motivational forces will reinforce each other	Motivational forces generally reinforce each other in a substantial and cumulative manner	9

PROFILE OF ORGANIZATIONAL CHARACTERISTICS (*Continued*)

Organizational variable					*Item no.*
e. Amount of responsibility felt by each member of organization for achieving organization's goals	Personnel at all levels feel real responsibility for organization's goals and behave in ways to implement them	Substantial proportion of personnel, especially at higher levels, feel responsibility and generally behave in ways to achieve the organization's goals	Managerial personnel usually feel responsibility; rank and file usually feel relatively little responsibility for achieving organization's goals	High levels of management feel responsibility; lower levels feel less; rank and file feel little and often welcome opportunity to behave in ways to defeat organization's goals	10
f. Attitudes toward other members of the organization	Favorable, cooperative attitudes throughout the organization with mutual trust and confidence	Cooperative, reasonably favorable attitudes toward others in organization; may be some competition between peers with resulting hostility and some condescension toward subordinates	Subservient attitudes toward superiors; competition for status resulting in hostility toward peers; condescension toward subordinates	Subservient attitudes toward superiors coupled with hostility; hostility toward peers and contempt for subordinates; distrust is widespread	11
g. Satisfaction derived	Relatively high satisfaction throughout the organization with regard to membership in the organization, supervision, and one's own achievements	Some dissatisfaction to moderately high satisfaction with regard to membership in the organization, supervision, and one's own achievements	Dissatisfaction to moderate satisfaction with regard to membership in the organization, supervision, and one's own achievements	Usually dissatisfaction with membership in the organization, with supervision, and with one's own achievements	12

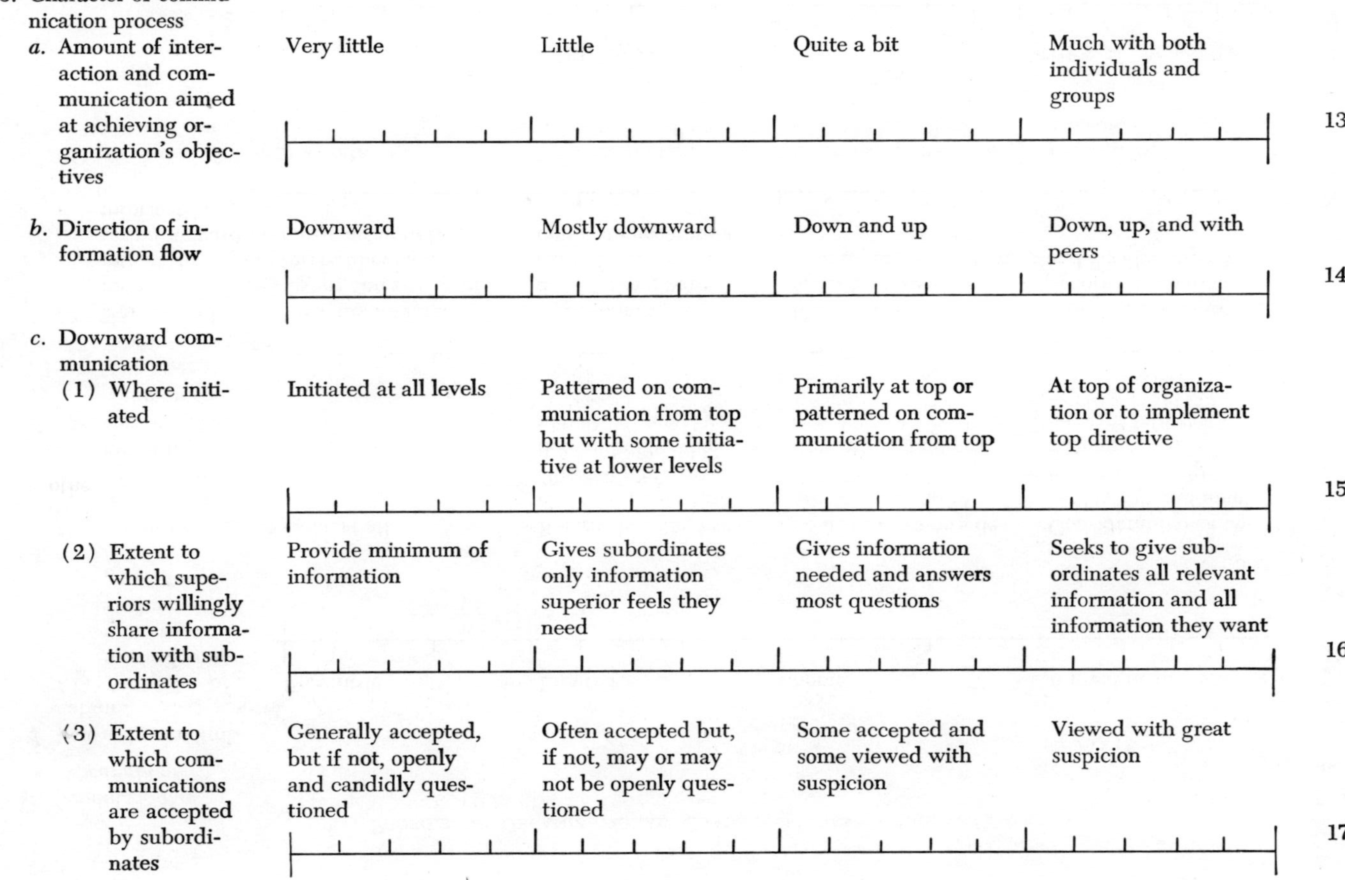

3. Character of communication process					
a. Amount of interaction and communication aimed at achieving organization's objectives	Very little	Little	Quite a bit	Much with both individuals and groups	13
b. Direction of information flow	Downward	Mostly downward	Down and up	Down, up, and with peers	14
c. Downward communication					
(1) Where initiated	Initiated at all levels	Patterned on communication from top but with some initiative at lower levels	Primarily at top or patterned on communication from top	At top of organization or to implement top directive	15
(2) Extent to which superiors willingly share information with subordinates	Provide minimum of information	Gives subordinates only information superior feels they need	Gives information needed and answers most questions	Seeks to give subordinates all relevant information and all information they want	16
(3) Extent to which communications are accepted by subordinates	Generally accepted, but if not, openly and candidly questioned	Often accepted but, if not, may or may not be openly questioned	Some accepted and some viewed with suspicion	Viewed with great suspicion	17

Profile of Organizational Characteristics (*Continued*)

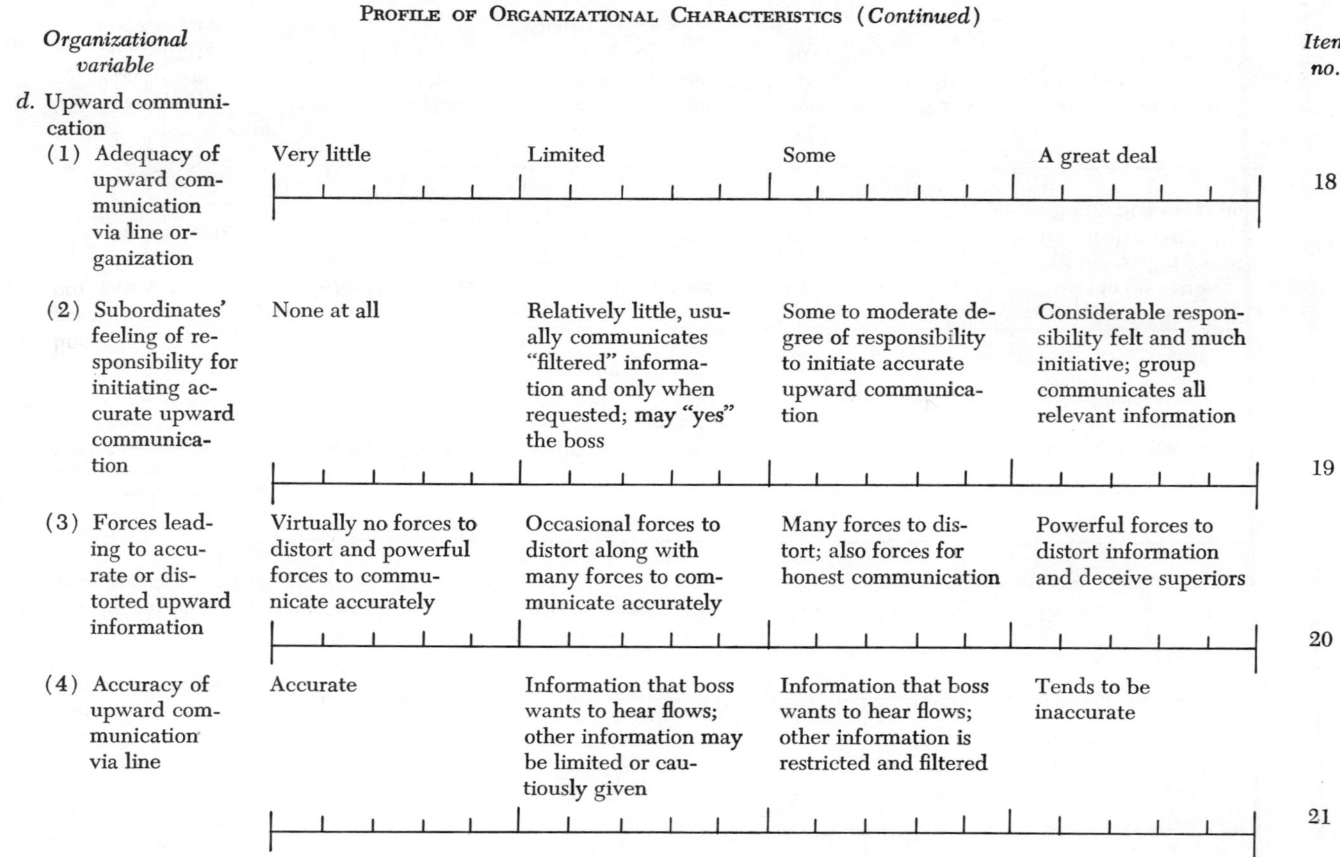

Organizational variable					*Item no.*
d. Upward communication					
(1) Adequacy of upward communication via line organization	Very little	Limited	Some	A great deal	18
(2) Subordinates' feeling of responsibility for initiating accurate upward communication	None at all	Relatively little, usually communicates "filtered" information and only when requested; may "yes" the boss	Some to moderate degree of responsibility to initiate accurate upward communication	Considerable responsibility felt and much initiative; group communicates all relevant information	19
(3) Forces leading to accurate or distorted upward information	Virtually no forces to distort and powerful forces to communicate accurately	Occasional forces to distort along with many forces to communicate accurately	Many forces to distort; also forces for honest communication	Powerful forces to distort information and deceive superiors	20
(4) Accuracy of upward communication via line	Accurate	Information that boss wants to hear flows; other information may be limited or cautiously given	Information that boss wants to hear flows; other information is restricted and filtered	Tends to be inaccurate	21

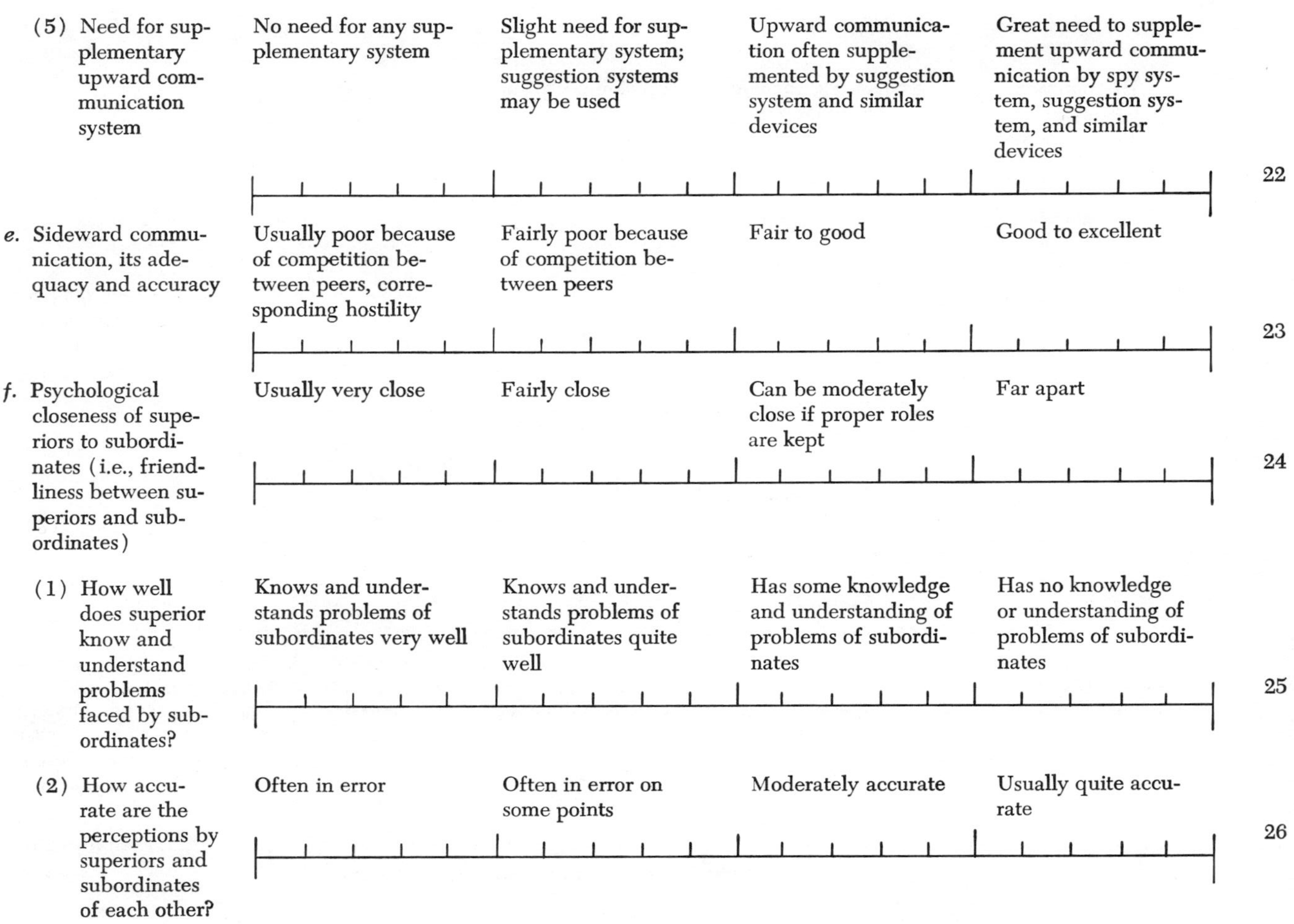

(5) Need for supplementary upward communication system	No need for any supplementary system	Slight need for supplementary system; suggestion systems may be used	Upward communication often supplemented by suggestion system and similar devices	Great need to supplement upward communication by spy system, suggestion system, and similar devices	22
e. Sideward communication, its adequacy and accuracy	Usually poor because of competition between peers, corresponding hostility	Fairly poor because of competition between peers	Fair to good	Good to excellent	23
f. Psychological closeness of superiors to subordinates (i.e., friendliness between superiors and subordinates)	Usually very close	Fairly close	Can be moderately close if proper roles are kept	Far apart	24
(1) How well does superior know and understand problems faced by subordinates?	Knows and understands problems of subordinates very well	Knows and understands problems of subordinates quite well	Has some knowledge and understanding of problems of subordinates	Has no knowledge or understanding of problems of subordinates	25
(2) How accurate are the perceptions by superiors and subordinates of each other?	Often in error	Often in error on some points	Moderately accurate	Usually quite accurate	26

Profile of Organizational Characteristics (*Continued*)

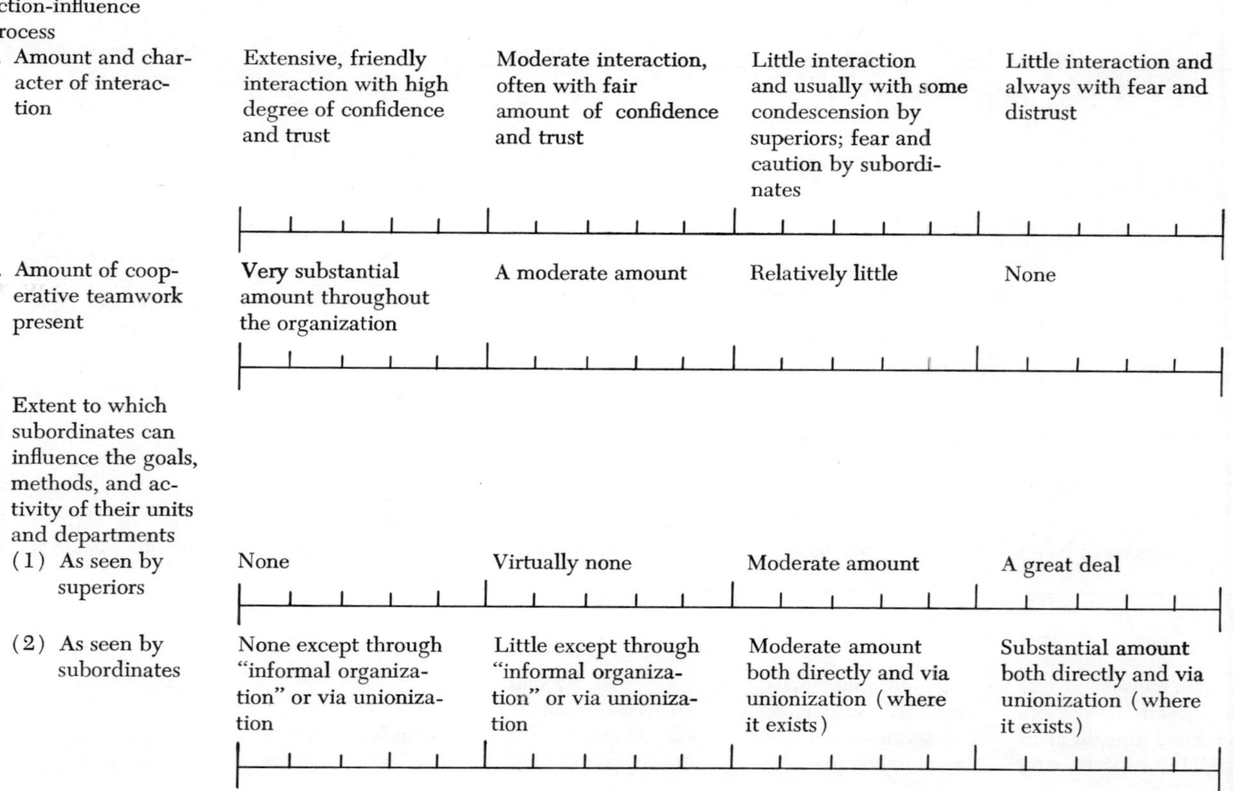

Organizational variable					*Item no.*
4. Character of interaction-influence process					
a. Amount and character of interaction	Extensive, friendly interaction with high degree of confidence and trust	Moderate interaction, often with fair amount of confidence and trust	Little interaction and usually with some condescension by superiors; fear and caution by subordinates	Little interaction and always with fear and distrust	27
b. Amount of cooperative teamwork present	Very substantial amount throughout the organization	A moderate amount	Relatively little	None	28
c. Extent to which subordinates can influence the goals, methods, and activity of their units and departments					
(1) As seen by superiors	None	Virtually none	Moderate amount	A great deal	29
(2) As seen by subordinates	None except through "informal organization" or via unionization	Little except through "informal organization" or via unionization	Moderate amount both directly and via unionization (where it exists)	Substantial amount both directly and via unionization (where it exists)	30

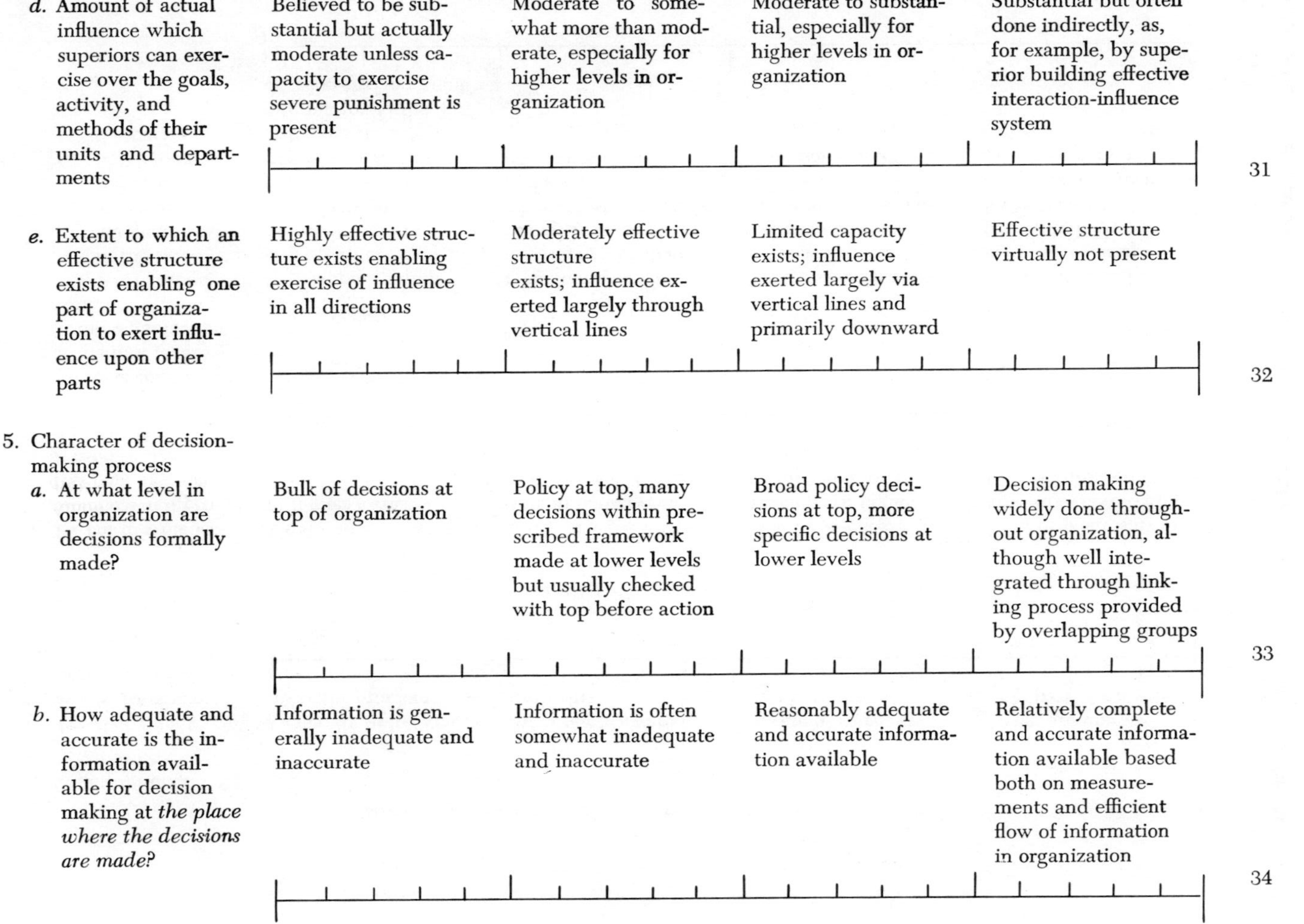

Organizational variable					Item no.
d. Amount of actual influence which superiors can exercise over the goals, activity, and methods of their units and departments	Believed to be substantial but actually moderate unless capacity to exercise severe punishment is present	Moderate to somewhat more than moderate, especially for higher levels in organization	Moderate to substantial, especially for higher levels in organization	Substantial but often done indirectly, as, for example, by superior building effective interaction-influence system	31
e. Extent to which an effective structure exists enabling one part of organization to exert influence upon other parts	Highly effective structure exists enabling exercise of influence in all directions	Moderately effective structure exists; influence exerted largely through vertical lines	Limited capacity exists; influence exerted largely via vertical lines and primarily downward	Effective structure virtually not present	32
5. Character of decision-making process					
a. At what level in organization are decisions formally made?	Bulk of decisions at top of organization	Policy at top, many decisions within prescribed framework made at lower levels but usually checked with top before action	Broad policy decisions at top, more specific decisions at lower levels	Decision making widely done throughout organization, although well integrated through linking process provided by overlapping groups	33
b. How adequate and accurate is the information available for decision making at *the place where the decisions are made?*	Information is generally inadequate and inaccurate	Information is often somewhat inadequate and inaccurate	Reasonably adequate and accurate information available	Relatively complete and accurate information available based both on measurements and efficient flow of information in organization	34

Profile of Organizational Characteristics (*Continued*)

Organizational variable					*Item no.*
c. To what extent are decision makers aware of problems, particularly those at lower levels in the organization?	Generally quite well aware of problems	Moderately aware of problems	Aware of some, unaware of others	Often are unaware or only partially aware	35
d. Extent to which technical and professional knowledge is used in decision making	Used only if possessed at higher levels	Much of what is available in higher and middle levels is used	Much of what is available in higher, middle, and lower levels is used	Most of what is available anywhere within the organization is used	36
e. Are decisions made at the best level in the organization as far as					
(1) Availability of the most adequate and accurate information bearing on the decision	Overlapping groups and group decision processes tend to push decisions to point where information is most adequate or to pass the relevant information to the decision-making point	Some tendency for decisions to be made at higher levels than where most adequate and accurate information exists	Decisions often made at levels appreciably higher than levels where most adequate and accurate information exists	Decisions usually made at levels appreciably higher than levels where most adequate and accurate information exists	37

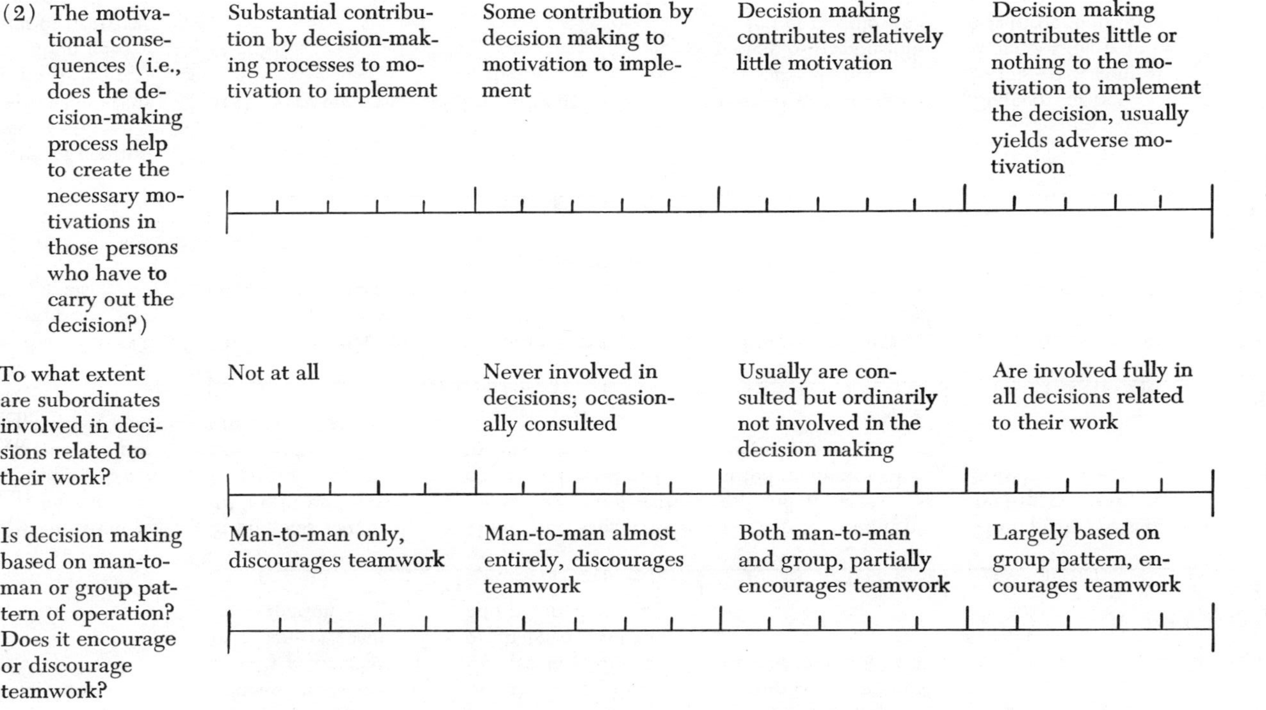

Item					No.
(2) The motivational consequences (i.e., does the decision-making process help to create the necessary motivations in those persons who have to carry out the decision?)	Substantial contribution by decision-making processes to motivation to implement	Some contribution by decision making to motivation to implement	Decision making contributes relatively little motivation	Decision making contributes little or nothing to the motivation to implement the decision, usually yields adverse motivation	38
f. To what extent are subordinates involved in decisions related to their work?	Not at all	Never involved in decisions; occasionally consulted	Usually are consulted but ordinarily not involved in the decision making	Are involved fully in all decisions related to their work	39
g. Is decision making based on man-to-man or group pattern of operation? Does it encourage or discourage teamwork?	Man-to-man only, discourages teamwork	Man-to-man almost entirely, discourages teamwork	Both man-to-man and group, partially encourages teamwork	Largely based on group pattern, encourages teamwork	40

Organizational variable					*Item no.*
6. Character of goal setting or ordering					
a. Manner in which usually done	Except in emergencies, goals are usually established by means of group participation	Goals are set or orders issued after discussion with subordinates of problems and planned action	Orders issued, opportunity to comment may or may not exist	Orders issued	41
b. To what extent do the different hierarchical levels tend to strive for high performance goals?	High goals sought by all levels, with lower levels sometimes pressing for higher goals than top levels	High goals sought by higher levels but with occasional resistance by lower levels	High goals sought by top and often resisted moderately by subordinates	High goals pressed by top, generally resisted by subordinates	42
c. Are there forces to accept, resist, or reject goals?	Goals are overtly accepted but are covertly resisted strongly	Goals are overtly accepted but often covertly resisted to at least a moderate degree	Goals are overtly accepted but at times with some covert resistance	Goals are fully accepted both overtly and covertly	43
7. Character of control processes					
a. At what hierarchical levels in organization does major or primary concern exist with regard to the performance of the control function?	At the very top only	Primarily or largely at the top	Primarily at the top but some shared feeling of responsibility felt at middle and to a lesser extent at lower levels	Concern for performance of control functions likely to be felt throughout organization	44

Item					No.
b. How accurate are the measurements and information used to guide and perform the control function, and to what extent do forces exist in the organization to distort and falsify this information?	Strong pressures to obtain complete and accurate information to guide own behavior and behavior of own and related work groups; hence information and measurements tend to be complete and accurate	Some pressure to protect self and colleagues and hence some pressures to distort; information is only moderately complete and contains some inaccuracies	Fairly strong forces exist to distort and falsify; hence measurements and information are often incomplete and inaccurate	Very strong forces exist to distort and falsify; as a consequence, measurements and information are usually incomplete and often inaccurate	45
c. Extent to which the review and control functions are concentrated	Highly concentrated in top management	Relatively highly concentrated, with some delegated control to middle and lower levels	Moderate downward delegation of review and control processes; lower as well as higher levels perform these tasks	Review and control done at all levels with lower units at times imposing more vigorous reviews and tighter controls than top management	46
d. Extent to which there is an informal organization present and supporting or opposing goals of formal organization	Informal organization present and opposing goals of formal organization	Informal organization usually present and partially resisting goals	Informal organization may be present and may either support or partially resist goals of formal organization	Informal and formal organization are one and the same; hence all social forces support efforts to achieve organization's goals	47

Organizational variable					*Item no.*
e. Extent to which control data (e.g., accounting, productivity, cost, etc.) are used for self-guidance or group problem solving by managers and nonsupervisory employees, or used by superiors in a punitive, policing manner	Used for policing and in punitive manner	Used for policing coupled with reward and punishment, sometimes punitively; used somewhat for guidance but in accord with orders	Used for policing with emphasis usually on reward but with some punishment; used for guidance in accord with orders; some use also for self-guidance	Used for self-guidance and for coordinated problem solving and guidance; not used punitively	48
8. Performance goals and training					
a. Level of performance goals which superiors seek to have organization achieve	Seek to achieve extremely high goals	Seek very high goals	Seek high goals	Seek average goals	49
b. Extent to which you have been given the kind of management training you desire	Have received no management training of kind I desire	Have received some management training of kind I desire	Have received quite a bit of management training of kind I desire	Have received a great deal of management training of kind I desire	50

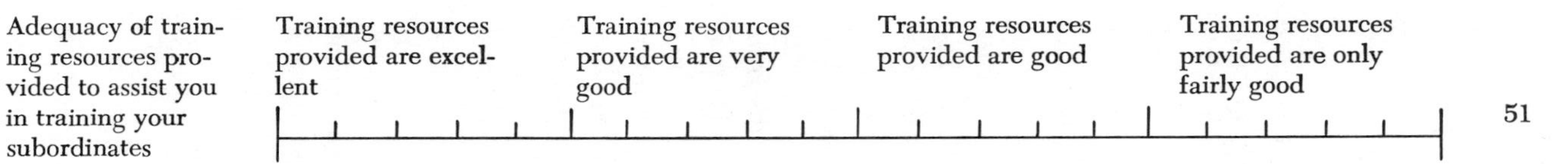

c. Adequacy of training resources provided to assist you in training your subordinates	Training resources provided are excellent	Training resources provided are very good	Training resources provided are good	Training resources provided are only fairly good	51

The table above can be used for other purposes by appropriate modifications in the instructions. In Chapter 2, for example, the table was used to obtain from managers their descriptions of particularly high- and low-producing organizations. The directions below indicate other uses:

Form S Instructions:

On the line below each organizational variable (item), please indicate the kind of organization you are trying to create by the management you are providing. Treat each item as a continuous variable from the extreme at one end to that at the other. Place a check mark on each line to show the kind of management you are using and the kind of organization you are creating.

Form D Instructions:

On the line below each organizational variable (item), please indicate by a check mark where you would *like* to have your organization fall with regard to that item. Treat each item as a continuous variable from the extreme at one end to that at the other.

Appendix III

TABLE OF ORGANIZATIONAL VARIABLES

As we have seen in several of the preceding chapters, it is highly useful for research and operating purposes to have a framework for considering organizational variables. The following table has been prepared for this purpose and presents what is judged to be a common pattern. The approach used in categorizing the variables in the following table was described in Chapter 8.

In employing this table in an enterprise, the appropriateness of this classification of items into causal, intervening, and end-result categories should be tested by obtaining and analyzing periodic measurements from that firm or department. Such analyses will correctly reveal for that particular company or department the actual pattern of relationships which exist among the organizational variables at that time. The highly interdependent, interacting character of most of the organizational variables makes this testing from time to time of the interrelationships among them in a specific situation desirable.

As will be noticed, several of the variables in the table are focused primarily on System 4.

I. CAUSAL VARIABLES (Each variable is a continuum from highly favorable to highly unfavorable. These variables apply to the organization as a whole, to departments or divisions, and, where indicated, to each superior.)

A. Policies, philosophy, and values reflected in behavior

1. Extent to which the principle of supportive relationships permeate your company

a. In dealing with all relevant persons

(1) Employees (subordinates, peers, superiors, and all others among whom interactions occur)

(2) Customers and the public

(3) Unions

(4) Suppliers

(5) Other organizations

b. In every appropriate way and situation

(1) To what extent are measurements used throughout your organization for self-guidance in the total organization (or any subdivision thereof) and not for punitive purposes or control by the superior?

(2) To what extent, within the limits of financial resources, does your organization (and each superior) make available to each work group the equipment, material, and resources required to do its job?

(3) To what extent does your organization (and your superior) have contagious enthusiasm regarding the importance and significance of the organization's mission?

(4) To what extent does your organization (and your superior) try to understand your problems and do something about them?

(5) How interested is your organization (and your superior) in helping you with your personal and family problems?

(6) How free do you feel to approach your superior and to communicate with him? Is he friendly and easily approached?

(7) How well does he listen to you?

(8) To what extent are members of your organization interested in listening to you?

(*a*) Are they (and your superior) interested in knowing about your problems?

(*b*) Are they (and your superior) interested in suggestions?

(*c*) Do they (and your superior) ask your opinion when a problem comes up which involves your work?

(*d*) Do they (and your superior) value your ideas, seek them, and endeavor to use them?

(9) Is your organization (and your superior) eager to provide you with information important to you?

(*a*) To what extent does your organization (and your superior) try to keep you informed about matters related to your job?

(*b*) How fully does your organization (and your superior) share information with you about the company, its financial condition, earnings, etc., or do they keep such information to themselves?

(*c*) If there is information which you need or desire and your superior does not possess, does he try to obtain it for you?

(10) To what extent does confidence and trust permeate your organization?

(*a*) To what extent does your organization (and your superior) give you the opportunity to learn by doing, including the freedom to make mistakes and to learn from them?

(*b*) If you make a mistake, to what extent is it treated as an opportunity for you to learn, or is it handled punitively?

(*c*) To what extent are you free to set your own pace, or are your activities circumscribed by controls which reflect little confidence and trust in you?

(*d*) To what extent are you under unreasonable hierarchical pressure to produce?

(*e*) To what extent are you under general supervision rather than close, detailed supervision?

(*f*) To what extent is your superior employee-centered rather than process-centered?

(*g*) To what extent do you feel that your organization (and your superior) is sincere in dealing with you rather than being manipulative?

(*h*) To what extent does it (he) display confidence in your integrity?

(11) To what extent are you treated as a human being rather than just another person to get the work out?

(12) To what extent does your organization (and your superior) convey to you a feeling of confidence that you can do your job successfully?

(*a*) Does your superior's behavior convey to you that he has complete confidence in your capacity?

(*b*) Does your superior expect the "impossible" and fully believe you can and will do it?

(*c*) Does he give you candid, sincere criticism and suggestions for improvement but with an orientation that you have greater potential than you have yet realized?

(*d*) To what extent do you feel your organization (and your superior) will back you and support you on any matter?

(13) How much help do you get from your organization (and your superior) in doing your work?
  (*a*) How much is it (he) interested in training you and helping you learn better ways of doing your work?
  (*b*) How much does your superior help you solve your problems constructively—not tell you the answers, but help you think through your problems?

(14) To what extent is your organization (and your superior) interested in helping you get the training which will assist you in being promoted?

(15) How receptive is your organization (and your superior) to being influenced by you?
  (*a*) Will it (he) give serious consideration to matters you present?
  (*b*) Is it (he) inflexible, or will your proposals be weighed in a reasonable manner?

(16) To what extent does your organization (and your superior) hold group meetings to make decisions and solve work-related problems? Are such meetings worthwhile?
  (*a*) Does your organization (and your superior) help each group, including yours, develop skill in reaching sound solutions?
  (*b*) Does your organization (and your superior) help each group, including yours, develop its skill in effective interaction and in becoming a well-knit team rather than developing hostile subfactions?
  (*c*) Does your organization (and your superior) use the ideas and solutions which emerge, and does it (he) also help each group to apply its solutions?

(17) To what extent does your organization (and your superior) strive to see that you receive equitable compensation for your work? Is it (he) interested in helping you to achieve and maintain a good income?

2. Extent to which your organization (and your superior) has high standards; extent to which high standards are held with regard to

a. The company as a total institution and its general reputation (e.g., being a highly respected firm)
b. Performance levels (e.g., high productivity goals)
c. Quality of product and services
d. Scrap and waste
e. Customer service
f. Goods from suppliers
g. Quality of equipment and technology
h. Quality of equipment, plant, etc.
i. Quality of personnel (selection)
j. Quality of personnel development (training)
k. Level of "cooperative working relationships" (Cooperative working relationships are defined as the high level of confidence and trust, loyalties, and favorable and cooperative attitudes which are characteristic of highly effective groups and highly effective interaction-influence systems.)
l. Creativity, innovativeness (e.g., seeks constantly through R&D to improve products, processes, marketing, etc.)

3. Extent to which the organization uses multiple overlapping group structure.
   a. The group rather than the individual is the building block.
   b. The superior usually serves as vertical linking pin.
   c. Lateral coordination is facilitated through appropriate cross-function linking groups.
4. Extent to which group decision making and group methods of supervision are used by your organization (and your superior)
   a. Extent to which your organization (and your superior) uses group decision making in such cycles of activity as the following: setting organizational objectives; establishing departmental and subunit goals; deciding upon equipment, technology, methods, job organization, etc.; acting on selection and promotion, including peer participation in selection and use of peer and subordinate along with superior reactions in decisions on promotion; evaluating progress toward objectives and goals, and revising goals, procedures, etc. for a new cycle; deciding upon the compensation and reward system and the principles and procedures used in reviewing its operation and the fairness of the system
   b. Extent to which your organization (and your superior) uses "situational requirements" in dealing with such prob-

lems as setting objectives, deciding upon pricing and compensation policies, etc.

c. Extent to which authority and responsibility are vested in each individual but operationally vested in the relevant work group or delegated to it; extent to which accountability is still maintained by leader, even though each member is also accountable, thereby increasing total accountability and total amount of felt responsibility

5. Extent to which economic needs are used effectively to motivate behavior which facilitates the organization's efforts to achieve its objectives; extent to which the compensation system and its various processes are created, maintained, and operated in such a manner (e.g., via group decision making) that the members of the organization
   a. Feel that they are being compensated equitably
   b. See themselves as being rewarded for behavior which helps the organization achieve its goals in relation to the value of their contribution
6. Extent to which your organization measures at appropriate intervals those causal, intervening, and end-result variables which will enable the organization (or any subdivision thereof) to guide decision making and behavior in most efficient manner; extent to which your organization (and your superior) makes relevant measurements available to each unit or subunit for self-guidance and does not use them for punitive purposes
7. Extent to which your organization applies elementary principles of organization
   a. Extent to which each member of your organization has a reasonably clear, unambiguous, and functionally appropriate role in the organization and concept of it
   b. Extent to which each person has a correct understanding of the roles of those other persons with whom his own role requires him to interact
   c. Extent to which each person is well trained for his role and tasks
   d. Extent to which work and jobs are organized well, planning done well, etc.
8. Extent to which your organization seeks to be technologically well equipped and constantly seeks to improve via research and development and emphasis on innovation
9. Extent to which your organization expects each manager or superior to behave in ways consistent with the organization's

philosophy and values and encourages and facilitates productive problem solving to achieve this objective, including providing such resources as the relevant measurements to assist such problem-solving activities

10. Extent to which there is sufficient stability in personnel assignments and investment in organization building to create highly effective cooperative working relationships, even though rotation is used for training purposes
11. Extent to which your organization seeks to minimize the adverse effect of size by taking such steps as
    a. Creating many small units (e.g., plants) instead of a few large ones (within the limits of the technology and of low unit cost operation)
    b. Using multiple overlapping group structure, group decision making, and principle of supportive relationships

B. Extent to which the superiors of your organization are competent with regard to

1. Technical matters
    a. Technical and professional problems and technology, including research and development
    b. Processes
    c. Equipment
    d. Raw material
    e. Finished product
    f. Marketing
2. Administrative know-how in relation to
    a. Organization planning and structure
    b. Functionalization, etc.
    c. Fiscal management
3. Human interaction skills
    a. Interpersonal
    b. Group problem solving and decision making
        (1) Group building and maintenance
            (*a*) Leader and member roles
            (*b*) Creative and integrative problem solving, not win-lose orientation
        (2) Problem solving as cognitive process
        (3) Situational requirements taken into account
        (4) Use of assisted problem solving and searching question

C. The adequacy of the selection process. The level of aptitudes, qualifications, and intelligence among members of your organization

D. The adequacy of the training resources

E. The cultural and personality characteristics of members of your organization with regard to such variables as expectations of being involved in decisions dealing with one's work and the skills for doing so

F. The adequacy of capital and equipment

II. INTERVENING VARIABLES

A. Attitudinal, motivational, perceptual variables

1. The extent of member loyalty to your organization and identification with it and its objectives
2. The extent to which members of your organization at all hierarchical levels feel that the organization's objectives are consistent with their own needs and goals and that the achievement of the company's objectives will help them achieve their own
3. The extent to which the goals of units and of individuals are felt to be of a character to facilitate your organization's achievement of its objectives; the extent to which they actually facilitate the achievement of its objectives
4. The level of motivation and level of goals among members of your organization (for entire organization, for departments, and for each member of each unit, including peers and superior) with regard to such activities as
   a. Performance, including both quality and quantity of work done
   b. Elimination of waste and reduction of costs
   c. Improving the products
   d. Improving service to customers
   e. Improving technological processes
   f. Improving the organization, its procedures, the training and skill of personnel, etc.
5. The extent to which members of your organization feel that the atmosphere of the organization is supportive and helps each individual achieve and maintain his sense of personal worth and importance
6. The level of expectations of members of your organization with regard to such variables as
   a. Income and trends in income
   b. Stability of employment
   c. Promotion, training, and development opportunities
   d. Fringe benefits
   e. Working conditions

f. Interesting and psychologically rewarding work

g. Being involved in decisions related to their work and conditions of employment

h. All other aspects of their jobs and work

7. The level of satisfaction of members of your organization with regard to the variables listed under 6 above and such other variables as

    a. The company itself, their department, and their work group

    b. The treatment they receive including, e.g., recognition for good work

    c. All aspects of the management system of the company

8. The cognitive understanding of members of your organization, e.g., the extent to which each member of the organization is correctly informed about the content of his job, his job role, etc. (See also communication.)

9. The character of the interaction-influence system and the level of cooperative working relationships

    a. The extent to which cooperative attitudes exist

    (1) The degree of confidence and trust among peers, among the different hierarchical levels, and among the different organizational units

    (2) The extent to which attitudes toward superiors, peers, subordinates, and other relevant persons in organization are favorable

    (*a*) The level of peer-group loyalty (attitudes of subordinate members of work group toward each other)

    (*b*) The level of total-group loyalty (attitudes of all members of work group toward each other, i.e., peer-group loyalty, attitude toward superior, and attitude and behavior of superior toward subordinates)

    (3) The level of cooperative attitudes within each unit of your organization, among units, and among various parts of the organization, such as, line and staff, divisions, departments, and headquarters

    b. The perceived and actual efficiency and adequacy of the communication process upward, downward, laterally

    (1) The extent to which each member (or unit) feels he has the information he needs to do his job well

    (2) The extent to which each superior (your) and each of his subordinates have the same understanding as

to responsibilities, authority, roles, goals, and deadlines

(3) The extent to which each (your) superior is correctly informed as to the expectations, reactions, and perceptions of each of his subordinates and conversely

(4) The extent to which each (your) superior is correctly informed of the obstacles, problems, and failures each of his subordinates is encountering in his work; the assistance each subordinate finds helpful or of little value; and the assistance each wishes he could get

(5) The extent to which members of your organization at all hierarchical levels are motivated to communicate fully and accurately all the important information to all persons for whom the information is relevant and valuable and to omit the irrelevant in order to avoid overloading the communications system

(6) The extent to which each member feels that the organization, his superiors, peers, and subordinates earnestly endeavor

- (*a*) To communicate to him information of value to him
- (*b*) To listen to him, to seek his ideas, views, experiences

(7) Extent to which there is motivation to accept downward communication, not distort it, and to react favorably to it

(8) Upward communication

- (*a*) Extent to which upward communication via line organization is perceived as adequate
- (*b*) Extent to which upward communication via line organization is perceived as accurate
- (*c*) Extent to which subordinates feel responsible for initiating and maintaining accurate upward communication, e.g., extent to which members are motivated to call to the attention of the relevant persons information requiring action and to persist in doing so until the necessary action is taken
- (*d*) Extent to which there are forces leading to accurate or distorted information and nature of these forces
- (*e*) Extent to which there is a felt need for supple-

mentary upward communication systems (e.g., suggestion systems, etc.) (The greater is this need, the poorer is the communication system.)

(9) Extent to which lateral communication is perceived as adequate and accurate

(10) Psychological closeness of superiors to subordinates

(*a*) How close does each feel he is to the other in understanding and mutual trust? How close does he seek to be?

(*b*) How well does each (your) superior know and understand the problems faced by his subordinates and conversely?

(*c*) To what extent are perceptions by superiors and subordinates of attitudes, roles, and problems of others accurate?

(11) The extent to which each person feels that the formal organization provides him with all the channels for communication and interaction which he feels he needs

c. The perceptual and motivational consequences of the decision-making process

(1) How do members of the organization feel about the decision-making process?

(*a*) To what extent do they feel that decisions are made at the right level and by the right people? Are persons involved in decisions related to their work?

(*b*) To what extent do members feel that their ideas, information, knowledge of processes, and experiences are being used?

(*c*) To what extent do members feel that important problems are recognized and dealt with promptly and well?

(*d*) To what extent do they feel that the decision-making process makes full use of all of the relevant information available within or to the organization?

(*e*) To what extent do they feel that the decisions adequately take into account the important situational requirements?

(*f*) To what extent do the members feel that the decision-making process of the organization is such that they can exert sufficient influence on the decisions to enable them to feel that their working situation is satisfactorily predictable, dependable, and controllable with regard to objectives, goals, evaluation and reward processes, and organizational performance and success?

(2) To what extent are the decision makers fully and correctly aware of problems, particularly those problems at lower levels in the organization?

(3) To what extent does the decision-making process encourage efficient and accurate communication?

(*a*) Upward

(*b*) Downward

(*c*) Laterally

(4) To what extent are the decisions of your organization made at the best level and in the best way with regard to the motivational consequences?

(*a*) Does the decision-making process help to create the necessary motivations in those persons who have to carry out the decision?

(*b*) What forces are created to accept, resist, or reject goals?

(*c*) Is every hierarchical level motivated to strive for high performance?

(*d*) What is the magnitude of the motivational forces created in persons to carry out the decision or defeat its intent and block its execution?

d. The perceptual and motivational consequences of the influence, control, and coordination processes in each unit and throughout the organization

(1) The amount of influence that different members of your organization and the different hierarchical levels feel they exercise, and the amount of influence others see them actually exercising, e.g., the extent to which superiors feel they can influence the goals, methods, and activities of their units and departments and the extent to which their subordinates see them as being able to do so; and, conversely, the extent to which subordinates feel they can influence such goals, etc., and the extent to which their superiors see them as being able to do so

(*a*) As seen by superiors

(*b*) As seen by peers

(*c*) As seen by subordinates

(2) The extent to which members of your organization at all hierarchical levels are motivated to try to discover the intent of a communication and to react to its true intent, instead of reacting to the letter of the communication and ignoring or actively defeating its intent

(3) The extent to which members of your organization at all hierarchical levels are motivated to carry out to the best of their ability the objectives of the organization and the goals of their department, instead of blocking action and sabotaging these objectives and goals in every way they dare to

(4) The extent to which members of your organization feel responsible for seeing that the organization as a whole, each work group, and each person achieve the established objectives and goals; the extent to which they are motivated to implement this felt responsibility

10. The extent to which economic needs are effectively used to create motivational forces focused on helping your organization achieve its objectives

   a. The extent to which the compensation system rewards and motivates behavior oriented toward achieving organizational objectives and does not reward or motivate behavior which is not so oriented

   b. The extent to which the compensation system is seen as equitable; the extent to which each person feels his pay is too low, about right, or on the high side

   (1) In comparison with others in the organization
   (2) In comparison with jobs elsewhere
   (3) In an absolute sense

   c. The extent to which the members of the organization feel that the decision-making procedure used by the organization in deciding upon compensation is fair and equitable.

11. The extent to which the motivational forces arising from the noneconomic motives are consistent with and reinforce those created by the economic needs; the extent to which all the different motivational forces are in harmony and are focused on cooperative efforts seeking to achieve the organization's objectives

12. The extent to which members of your organization feel under "unreasonable pressure" to produce (and react unfavorably

to it); the extent to which members feel that pressure to produce is self-imposed instead of imposed by others

13. The extent to which members of the organization (or of its units) seek to press for high productivity or to restrict production—both individually and by work groups; the extent to which members in your organization have favorable attitudes toward high producers and encourage, rather than discourage, them to produce at a high level
14. The extent to which there are good versus poor labor relations and the extent to which attitudes exist which provide an atmosphere in which differences can be resolved in a constructive problem-solving manner versus attitudes inducing bitter, irreconcilable conflict
15. Level of mental health
    a. Level of hostile, resentful attitudes
    b. The amount of stress and anxiety felt by members of the organization and the sources of stress; extent to which members feel they have the organizational means to reduce stress and deal constructively with the causes of stress
    c. Levels of emotional maturity, self-esteem, and self-confidence
16. The effect of any anxiety upon health, well-being, and the capacity to function effectively as revealed by high rates of sickness, absence, accidents, and similar symptoms
    a. Evidence from psychological tests and reports
    b. Evidence from physiological tests and health examinations and reports
17. Level of shareholder confidence and loyalty
18. Level of customer confidence and loyalty
19. Level of supplier confidence and loyalty

B. Intervening behavioral variables

1. The extent to which there is wide participation in decision making versus highly centralized decision making
2. The extent to which members of your organization apply principle of supportive relationships to subordinates, peers, superiors, customers, etc.
3. The extent to which members of your organization coach, counsel, and train their peers, share new knowledge on how best to do job, and in other ways help to perform leadership roles
4. The extent to which members of your organization constantly seek and actually carry out ways to improve methods, tech-

nology, and products, and to eliminate waste and unnecessary work; extent to which they are well trained to do so

5. The extent to which members in your organization have high performance standards and goals and through group norms encourage peers and others to share equally high standards ("High standards" refers to the entire list under Causal I A2.)
6. The extent to which the review and control functions are concentrated at the top of your organization or performed as coordinated and reciprocally responsible behavior by work groups throughout the organization and at all levels
7. The extent to which a highly effective interaction-influence system is used and is being strengthened
   a. The operational character of the organizational structure: what it is in actual fact as compared with what it is supposed to be, e.g., who reports to whom about what, the the number of superiors and subordinates each person has, the extent to which the structure consists of overlapping groups, the amount of multiple overlapping, the adequacy of linking pins and the strength of linkage provided by each linking pin, and the extent to which the informal organization and the formal organization are the same
   b. Extent to which this system employs group rather than man-to-man interaction
   c. Extent to which this system sets and modifies its own objectives, goals, and procedures
      (1) Extent to which these objectives are a creative integration of the needs, desires, and aspirations of the members of the organization and of all persons functionally related to the organization or served by it, such as
         (*a*) Shareholders
         (*b*) Customers
         (*c*) Suppliers
      (2) Extent to which the goals of each department, unit, and subunit of the organization reflect a constructive integration of the needs and desires of its members, the goals of other departments, and the objectives of the entire organization; the extent to which the members of the department or unit are involved in the decision-making processes used in establishing the department's goals
      (3) Extent to which departments and other parts of the organization evaluate progress toward their objectives

and goals at appropriate intervals and make appropriate modifications in the objectives of the entire organization and the goals of departments and units; extent to which this is done also with regard to the strategies, methods, and technologies to be used for the achievement of these objectives and goals

d. Extent to which this interaction-influence system evaluates, builds, and maintains its multiple overlapping group structure and cooperative working relationships and thereby maintains a highly effective interaction-influence system

e. Extent to which the organization through the group-decision procedures of its interaction-influence system establishes, maintains, evaluates, and operates in an equitable manner (as seen by members of the organization and by persons served by the organization) its compensation, pricing, and dividend processes and policies; extent to which these processes and policies are reviewed and evaluated at appropriate intervals and adjusted to maintain their equitable character

f. The character of the decision-making process of the interaction-influence system

(1) Which individuals and which groups at which levels make what decisions?

(2) What facts are used in making these decisions, and how accurate and adequate are these facts?

(3) To what extent is the technical and professional knowledge existing in the organization or available to it used in decision making?

(4) To what extent do members of the organization skillfully use group problem-solving and decision-making processes both cognitively to solve problems and for group building and group maintenance?

(*a*) Extent to which they seek to use integrative, constructive problem solving rather than a win-lose approach

(*b*) Extent to which differences and conflicts are accepted as necessary and desirable and are worked through to constructive innovative solutions

(*c*) Extent to which the abilities, knowledge, and experience of each individual member are used fully; the extent to which each member gives advice, counsel, and support to other members while recognizing individual accountability and specialization

(*d*) The extent to which each member accepts responsibility for keeping discussions relevant and for the integrity of the team operation

(*e*) The extent to which individual differences and individuality are desired, used, and respected

(*f*) The extent to which diversity in outlook and differences of point of view are welcomed and used in an innovative and constructive manner in decision making

g. Extent to which all the members in your organization perform communication processes well

(1) Extent to which they communicate to others (peers, superior, subordinates) in a candid, frank, and sincere manner because of an atmosphere of confidence, trust, and support—rather than being cautious and guarded in their communication

(2) Extent to which they listen attentively and earnestly and without suspicion to information from others (i.e., from peers, subordinates, and superiors)

(3) Extent to which they try to (and do) communicate rapidly and efficiently to others all relevant information by emphasizing the important information and filtering out the trivia; extent to which knowledge and action on essential matters are assured by repeating important information and even relaying it when necessary through alternate channels

8. Level of cooperative behavior among the members of your organization oriented toward helping the organization achieve its objectives

9. Extent to which such variables as the following are at a level optimum for the organization and its members
   a. Turnover rates
   b. Absence rates
   c. Manpower development rates
   d. Growth rate of the firm

10. Extent to which accident and sickness rates are at a minimum

III. END-RESULT VARIABLES (This list is illustrative only and is incomplete.)

A. Performance variables
   1. Level of productivity
   2. Level of quality of product and service

   3. Level of scrap loss and waste
   4. Level of share of market
- *B*. Financial variables
   1. Level of costs
   2. Level of sales and income
   3. Level of profits
   4. Level of compensation
   5. Level of financial reserves
   6. Current value of investment in plant, equipment, inventories, R&D, markets, etc.
   7. Current value of investment in human organization
   8. Current value of investment in customer loyalty

BIBLIOGRAPHY

Ames, B. C. Payoff from product management. *Harvard Business Rev.*, 1963, **41**(6), 141–152.

Argyris, C. Human problems with budgets. *Harvard Business Rev.*, 1953, **31**(1), 97–110.

Argyris, C. *Integrating the individual and the organization.* New York: Wiley, 1964.

Argyris, C. *Interpersonal competence and organizational effectiveness.* Homewood, Ill.: Irwin, 1962.

Argyris, C. *Organization and innovation.* Homewood, Ill.: Irwin, 1965.

Argyris, C. *Personality and organization.* New York: Harper & Row, 1957.

Argyris, C. Understanding human behavior in organizations: one viewpoint. In M. Haire (Ed.), *Modern organization theory.* New York: Wiley, 1959.

Argyris, C. Interpersonal barriers to decision making. *Harvard Business Rev.*, 1966, **44**(2), 84–97.

Bennis, W. G. *Changing organizations.* New York: McGraw-Hill, 1966.

Blake, R. R., & Mouton, J. S. *The managerial grid.* Houston, Tex.: Gulf, 1964.

Blau, P., & Scott, W. *Formal organizations.* San Francisco: Chandler Publishing Co., 1962.

Bowers, D. G. (Ed.) *Applying modern management principles to sales organizations.* Ann Arbor, Mich.: Foundation for Research on Human Behavior, 1963.

Bowers, D. G. Organizational control in an insurance company. *Sociometry,* 1964, **27**(2), 230–244.

Bowers, D. G., & Seashore, S. E. Peer leadership within work groups. Paper read at International Congress of Applied Psychology, Ljubljana, Yugoslavia, August, 1964.

Bowers, D. G., & Seashore, S. E. Predicting organizational effectiveness with a four-factor theory of leadership. *Administrative Sci. Quart.*, 1966, **11**(2), 238–263.

Bradford, L. P., Gibb, J. R., & Benne, K. D. (Eds.) *T-group theory and laboratory method: innovation in re-education.* New York: Wiley, 1963.

Brayfield, A. H., & Crockett, W. H. Employee attitudes and employee performance. *Psychol. Bull.*, 1955, **52**, 396–424.

Burns, T., & Stalker, G. M. *The management of innovation.* London: Tavistock Publications, 1961.

Cartwright, D., & Zander, A. (Eds.) *Group dynamics: research and theory.* (2d ed.) New York: Harper & Row, 1960.

Coch, L., & French, J. R. P., Jr. Overcoming resistance to change. *Human Relat.*, 1948, **1**(4), 512–532.

Cooley, C. H. *Social organization.* New York: Scribner, 1909.

Croome, Honor. *Human problems of innovation.* London: Dept. of Scientific & Industrial Research, 1959.

Dalton, M. *Men who manage.* New York: Wiley, 1959.

Davenport, R. Enterprise for everyman. *Fortune,* 1950, **41**(1), 55–59.

Dunnington, R. A. Research for organization theory and management action, introduction and conclusion. In G. G. Somers (Ed.), *Proceedings of the 16th annual meeting* (Boston, Dec. 27–28, 1963). Madison, Wis.: Industrial Relations Research Ass., 1963. Pp. 150–154, 176–179.

Emery, F. E., & Trist, E. L. Socio-technical systems. In *Management sciences models and techniques.* Vol. 2. London: Pergamon Press, 1960.

Farris, G. F. A causal analysis of scientific performance. Unpublished doctoral dissertation, Univer. of Michigan, 1966.

Fleishman, E. A., & Harris, E. F. Patterns of leadership behavior related to employee grievances and turnover. *Personnel Psychol.,* 1962, **15,** 45–53.

French, J. R. P., Jr., Ross, I. C., Kirby, S., Nelson, J. R., & Smyth, P. Employee participation in a program of industrial change. *Personnel,* November–December, 1958, 16–29.

Gellerman, S. W. *Motivation and productivity.* New York: Amer. Mgmt. Ass., 1963.

General Systems Yearbook, published by the Society for the Advancement of General Systems Theory.

Guest, R. H. *Organizational change.* Homewood, Ill.: Irwin, 1962.

Harris, E. F. Measuring industrial leadership and its implications for training supervisors. Unpublished doctoral dissertation, Ohio State Univer., 1952.

Hermanson, R. H. *Accounting for human assets.* East Lansing, Mich.: Michigan State Univer., Bureau of Business and Economic Research, 1964.

Herzberg, F., Mausner, B., Peterson, R. O., & Capwell, Dora F. *Job attitudes: review of research and opinion.* Pittsburgh: Psychological Services of Pittsburgh, 1957.

Heslin, J. A., Jr. A field test of the Likert theory of management in an ADP environment. Unpublished master's thesis, The American Univer., 1966.

Hood, R. C. Concern for cost: a participative approach. Amer. Mgmt Ass., *Manufacturing Ser.,* No. 221, 1956, 33–40.

Kahn, R. L. Human relations on the shop floor. In E. M. Hugh-Jones (Ed.), *Human relations and modern management.* Amsterdam: North Holland Publishing Co., 1958. Pp. 43–74.

Kahn, R. L., Wolfe, D. M., Quinn, R. P., Snoek, J. D., & Rosenthal, R. A. *Organizational stress: studies in role conflict and ambiguity.* New York: Wiley, 1964.

Katz, D., & Kahn, R. L. Some recent findings in human relations research. In E. Swanson, T. Newcomb, & E. Hartley (Eds.), *Readings in social psychology.* New York: Holt, 1952. Pp. 650–665.

Katz, D., & Kahn, R. L. *The social psychology of organizations.* New York: Wiley, 1966.

Katz, D., Maccoby, N., & Morse, Nancy. *Productivity, supervision and morale in an office situation.* Ann Arbor, Mich.: Institute for Social Research, 1950.

Kepner, C. H., & Tregoe, B. B. *The rational manager.* New York: McGraw-Hill, 1965.

Klein, S. M. Two systems of management: a comparison that produced organizational change. In G. G. Somers (Ed.), *Proceedings of the 16th annual meeting* (Boston, Dec. 27–28, 1963). Madison, Wis.: Industrial Relations Research Ass., 1963. Pp. 166–175.

Lesieur, F. G. *The Scanlon plan.* New York: Wiley, 1959.

Lewin, K. *Resolving social conflict.* (Gertrud Lewin, Ed.) New York: Harper & Row, 1948.

Lewin, K. *Field theory in social science.* (D. Cartwright, Ed.) New York: Harper & Row, 1951.

Likert, R. A technique for the measurement of attitudes. *Arch. Psychol., N.Y.,* 1932, **140,** 1–55.

Likert, R. A method for measuring the sales influence of a radio program. *J. appl. Psychol.,* 1936, **20**(2), 175–182.

Likert, R. Developing patterns of management. I. Amer. Mgmt Ass., *Gen. Mgmt Ser.,* No. 178, 1955, 32–51.

Likert, R. Motivational approach to management development. *Harvard Business Rev.,* 1959, **37**(4), 75–82.

Likert, R. *New patterns of management.* New York: McGraw-Hill, 1961.

Likert, R. New patterns of sales management. In M. R. Warshaw (Ed.), *Changing perspectives in marketing management.* Ann Arbor, Mich.: Univer. of Michigan, Bureau of Business Research, 1962.

Likert, R. Some new patterns in management. In R. M. Young (Ed.), *New horizons in management.* Proceedings of the 9th Annual Los Angeles County Management Conference. Los Angeles: Los Angeles County Civil Service Commission, 1964.

Likert, R., & Seashore, S. E. Making cost control work. *Harvard Business Rev.,* 1963, **41**(6), 96–108.

Likert, R., & Willits, J. M. *Morale and agency management.* Hartford, Conn.: Life Insurance Agency Management Ass., 1940. 4 vols.

Litterer, J. A. *Analysis of organizations.* New York: Wiley, 1965.

McAnly, L. C. Maytag's program of expense reduction. Amer. Mgmt Ass., *Manufacturing ser.,* No. 221, 1956, 24–32.

McGregor, D. *The human side of enterprise.* New York: McGraw-Hill, 1960.

McGregor, D. *Leadership and motivation.* Cambridge, Mass.: M.I.T., 1966.

Maier, N. R. F. *Problem-solving discussions and conferences.* New York: McGraw-Hill, 1963.

Maier, N. R. F., & Hayes, J. J. *Creative management.* New York: Wiley, 1962.

Mann, F. C. Studying and creating change: a means to understanding social organization. In *Research in industrial human relations.* Madison, Wis.: Industrial Relations Research Ass., 1957. Pp. 146–167.

Mann, F. C., & Baumgartel, H. J. *The supervisor's concern with costs in an electric power company.* Ann Arbor, Mich.: Institute for Social Research, 1953.

Mann, F. C., Indik, B. P., & Vroom, V. H. *The productivity of work groups.* Ann Arbor, Mich.: Institute for Social Research, 1963.

Mann, F. C., & Neff, F. W. *Managing major change in organizations.* Ann Arbor, Mich.: Foundation for Research on Human Behavior, 1961.

March, J. G., & Simon, H. A. *Organizations.* New York: Wiley, 1958.

Marrow, A. J. Behind the executive mask. Amer. Mgmt Ass., *Mgmt Rep.,* No. 79, 1964. (a)

Marrow, A. J. Risks and uncertainties in action research. *J. soc. Issues,* 1964, **20**(3), 5–20. (b)

Marrow, A. J., Bowers, D. G., & Seashore, S. E. (Eds.) *Strategies of organizational change.* New York: Harper & Row, 1967.

Mathewson, S. B. *Restriction of output among unorganized workers.* New York: Viking, 1931.

Meltzer, L. Comparing relationships of individual and average variables to individual response. *Amer. soc. Rev.*, 1963, **28**, 117–123.

Meyer, H. H., Kay, E., & French, J. R. P., Jr. Split roles in performance appraisal. *Harvard Business Rev.*, 1965, **43**(1), 123–129.

Miles, R. E. The affluent organization. *Harvard Business Rev.*, 1966, **44**(3), 106–114.

Miller, D. C., & Form, W. H. *Industrial society: the sociology of work organizations.* (2d ed.) New York: Harper & Row, 1964.

Miller, J. G. Toward a general theory for the behavioral sciences. *Amer. Psychologist*, 1955, **10**, 513–531.

Morse, Nancy, & Reimer, E. The experimental change of a major organizational variable. *J. abnorm. soc. Psychol.*, 1956, **52**, 120–129.

Parker, T. C. Relationships among measures of supervisory behavior, group behavior, and situational characteristics. *Personnel Psychol.*, 1963, **16**, 319–334.

Patchen, M. *Supervisory methods, group standards, and performance at the Dobeckmun Company.* Ann Arbor, Mich.: Institute for Social Research, 1960.

Paton, W. A. *Accounting theory.* Chicago: Accounting Studies Press, Ltd., 1962.

Pelz, D. C., & Andrews, F. M. Scientists in organizations: productive climates for research and development. New York: Wiley, 1966.

Pigors, P., & Myers, C. A. *Personnel administration.* (5th ed.) New York: McGraw-Hill, 1964.

Rice, A. K. *Learning for leadership.* London: Tavistock Publications, 1965.

Roethlisberger, F. J., & Dickson, W. J. *Management and the worker.* Cambridge, Mass.: Harvard Univer., 1939.

Ronken, H. O., & Lawrence, P. R. *Administering changes.* Boston: Harvard Graduate Sch. of Business Administration, 1952.

Scanlon, J. N. Profit sharing under collective bargaining: three case studies. *Industr. & Labor Relat. Rev.*, 1948, **2**(1), 58–75.

Schein, E. H., & Bennis, W. C. *Personal and organizational change through group methods.* New York: Wiley, 1965.

Schleh, E. C. *Management by results.* New York: McGraw-Hill, 1961.

Seashore, S. E. Studies in three sales organizations. In D. G. Bowers (Ed.), *Applying modern management principles to sales organizations.* Ann Arbor, Mich.: Foundation for Research on Human Behavior, 1963. Pp. 23–40.

Seashore, S. E. Field experiments with formal organizations. *Human Organization*, 1964, **23**, 164–170.

Seashore, S. E., & Bowers, D. G. *Changing the structure and functioning of an organization.* Ann Arbor, Mich.: Institute for Social Research, 1963.

Shultz, G. P. Worker participation on production problems. Amer. Mgmt Ass., *Personnel*, 1951, **28**(3), 201–211.

Sirota, D. A study of work measurement. In G. G. Somers (Ed.), *Proceedings of the 16th annual meeting* (Boston, Dec. 27–28, 1963). Madison, Wis.: Industrial Relations Research Ass., 1963. Pp. 155–165.

Sloan, A. P., Jr. *My years with General Motors.* Garden City, N.Y.: Doubleday, 1964.

Stieglitz, H. *Organizational planning.* New York: National Industrial Conference Board, 1962.

Tannenbaum, A. S. The concept of organizational control. *J. soc. Issues,* 1956, **12**(2), 50–60.

Tannenbaum, A. S. The application of survey techniques to the study of organizational structure and functioning. *Publ. Opinion Quart.*, 1957, **21**(3), 439–442.

Tannenbaum, A. S. *Social psychology of the work organization.* Belmont, Calif.: Wadsworth Publishing Co., 1966.

Tannenbaum, A. S., & Bachman, J. G. Structural versus individual effects. *Amer. J. Sociol.*, 1964, **69**, 585–595.

Tannenbaum, A. S., & Smith, C. G. The effects of member influence in an organization: phenomenology versus organizational structure. *J. abnorm. soc. Psychol.*, 1964, **69**, 401–410.

Thurstone, L. L. Attitudes can be measured. *Amer. J. Sociol.*, 1928, **33**, 529–554.

Thurstone, L. L. Theory of attitude measurement. *Psychol. Rev.*, 1929, **36**, 222–241.

Thurstone, L. L., & Chave, E. J. *The measurement of attitude.* Chicago: Univer. of Chicago, 1929.

Trist, E. L., Higgin, G. W., Murray, H., & Pollock, A. B. *Organizational choice.* London: Tavistock Publications, 1963.

White, K. K. *Understanding the company organization chart.* New York: Amer. Mgmt Ass., 1963.

White, R., & Lippitt, R. *Autocracy and democracy: an experimental inquiry.* New York: Harper & Row, 1960.

Whyte, W. F. (Ed.) *Money and motivation.* New York: Harper & Row, 1955.

Whyte, W. F. *Men at work.* Homewood, Ill.: Irwin, 1961.

Wolff, H. The great GM mystery. *Harvard Business Rev.*, 1964, **42**(5), 164–176, 192–202.

Wyatt, D. *Performance appraisal and review.* Ann Arbor, Mich.: Foundation for Research on Human Behavior, 1958.

Yuchtman, E. A study of organizational effectiveness. Unpublished doctoral dissertation, Univer. of Michigan, 1966.

Zander, A. F. (Ed.) *Performance appraisals.* Ann Arbor, Mich.: Foundation for Research on Human Behavior, 1963.

NAME INDEX

SUBJECT INDEX